DATE DUE

OC3 1 '00		
FE 12 '04		

DEMCO 38-296

Criminal Justice Statistics

Criminal Justice Statistics

A Practical Approach

Arthur J. Lurigio

Department of Criminal Justice
Loyola University–Chicago

Magnus J. Seng

Department of Criminal Justice
Loyola University–Chicago

M. L. Dantzker

Department of Political Science
Georgia Southern University–Statesboro

James M. Sinacore

Department of Family Medicine
University of Illinois–Chicago

With special assistance from

Bruce Johnson

Statistical Product and Service Solutions, Inc. (SPSS, Inc.)

Butterworth-Heinemann

Boston   Oxford   Johannesburg   Melbourne   New Delhi   Singapore

Library of Congress Cataloging-in-Publication Data

Criminal justice statistics : a practical approach / Arthur J. Lurigio
 ... [et. al.].
   p.   cm.
  Includes index.
  ISBN 0-7506-9672-9 (alk. paper)
   1. Social sciences—Statistical methods.   2. Criminal justice,
Administration of.   3. Criminal statistics.   I. Lurigio, Arthur J.

  HA35.C68   1997
  364′.01′5195—dc20   96-15887
                                                                    CIP

British Library Cataloguing-in-Publication Data
A catalogue record for this book is available from the British Library.

The publisher offers special discounts on bulk orders of this book.
For information, please contact:
Manager of Special Sales
Butterworth-Heinemann
313 Washington Street
Newton, MA 02158-1626
Tel: 617-928-2500
Fax: 617-928-2620

For information on all Criminal Justice and Security publications available, contact our World Wide Web home page at:
http://www.bh.com

10 9 8 7 6 5 4 3 2 1

Printed in the United States of America

Contents

Preface

Despite the popular myths, writing a textbook is far from being easy. This is particularly true when more than one person attempts such a project, especially if the topic is something like statistics. Throughout our collegiate experiences, as students and as teachers, we have all heard moans and groans about taking a statistics course. However, as we have all learned and hope to influence others' learning, statistics is not the ogre of academe but actually is quite friendly and useful. Nowhere does this seem more true than in the field of criminal justice.

Crime rates, arrests, numbers of inmates, percentage of successful prosecutions, number of persons on probation, and lengths of sentences, for example, are common statistics. All criminal justice consumers and practitioners must be aware of these statistics and must recognize their meaning. This seems especially true for students whose goals may lead them into the criminal justice field.

More and more universities, particularly those that offer degrees in a discipline related to criminal justice, seem to be recognizing the importance of students becoming familiar with statistics and how they work. These institutions have begun requiring that students take a statistics course. Because this requirement is relatively new, there have been few attempts to provide a statistics textbook for criminal justice students. *Criminal Justice Statistics: A Practical Approach* is our attempt to begin filling the void.

Acknowledgments

This is a co-authored text; it should be recognized that no one person takes more credit than another. It was a group effort in which all four authors worked equally hard to produce a product that we believe will assist students to learn and accept statistics for what they really are: numbers that simply represent some occurrence, item, group, function, or happenstance.

In completing this book we have some thanks to offer. First, we thank our acquisitions editor, Laurel DeWolf, for her support and belief in the project; Catherine Judge Allen, copy editor for her diligence and efforts in "the cleaning and final shaping of the text"; Barbara Hart, University of Texas–Tyler, and Joan Crowley, New Mexico State University, for their inspiration and reviewing efforts; our colleagues for their support; our families for their strength, patience, and love, which undoubtedly helped provide us with the courage to continue and complete this text; and each other for all the work and effort each put into fulfilling what originally was nothing more than a whim and a challenge. Finally, a special debt of gratitude is owed Bruce Johnson, M.A., who prepared the text and graphics on SPSS software and its application. We are very grateful for his invaluable contribution to this text.

We trust that you will find this text, as we have, to be easily understood yet challenging and that learning statistics can be enjoyable and provide useful knowledge. We wish you the greatest success in your education and future endeavors.

Arthur J. Lurigio
M. L. Dantzker
Magnus J. Seng
James M. Sinacore

Introduction

For many years, psychology, sociology, political science, and other social science undergraduate students have been required to take courses in research methods and statistics, which are relatively new requirements for many criminal justice students. In response to the increasingly broad scope of criminal justice undergraduate education, many criminal justice programs have now begun to require students to take research classes. These classes are offered either in one semester in which both methods and statistics are taught or in two semesters in which one semester is devoted to methods and the other is devoted to statistics. In either case, textbooks are needed to provide a clear and simple understanding of what is often perceived as "a very scary topic." Statistics, however, does not have to be viewed as scary; neither do statistics books.

We believe that there is a critical demand for a statistics book that not only meets the needs of criminal justice students but also does so without being too frightening. Such a book should provide a clear yet simple approach to understanding statistics and their application to the criminal justice field. With this in mind, we offer you *Criminal Justice Statistics: A Practical Approach*. The goals of this text are as follows:

1. To fill a void in statistics books currently available in the field of criminal justice
2. To desensitize criminal justice students to statistics
3. To show students that they can "do" statistics and to help them to understand how statistics are used and why they are important tools for researchers and practitioners
4. To present statistical examples from the discipline to illustrate how statistics are useful to criminal justice practitioners

Overview of the Text

This text was specifically designed for undergraduate criminal justice students, who may not see graduate study as a high priority.*

Rather than going to graduate school it is likely you already are or will be employed in some capacity in the criminal justice field in which it is unlikely that you will conduct large scale research efforts or be involved in the design of such endeavors. You may, however, be required to produce statistical reports, especially if you are employed at an administrative or supervisory level. Furthermore, you are probably a frequent consumer of statistical reports on crime and system operations, which are used by criminal justice practitioners in all phases of the

---

*Both the breadth and depth of the material covered in this text, however, are equal to or greater than material presented in undergraduate statistics texts in disciplines in which many students pursue graduate study.

system (police, courts, and corrections). Therefore, you must comprehend statistics to use such material effectively.

This text focuses on basic statistical problems criminal justice practitioners are likely to encounter. It presents statistics as a set of tools or procedures for addressing specific data analysis problems rather than as a formal, abstract subject. Examples of such problems might be the need for police administrators to compare performance among divisions, for court administrators to analyze caseload distributions, or for corrections administrators to predict prison populations. All the statistical techniques addressed in this text are presented in the context of practical problems. This method is used to allow you to learn the practical application of statistical methods. An added focus of the text relates to our goal of presenting statistics in a nonthreatening manner.

It has been our experience that students invariably approach a statistics course with anxiety. This reaction occurs despite the frequent and impassioned efforts by advisors and teachers to convince them that proficiency in mathematics is not a prerequisite for an introductory statistics class. Our goals are to have students leave the course with the sense that they can "do this stuff"; to prove that statistical techniques are really a set of tools used to deal with specific problems and that such techniques do not have to be complex to be useful; and to demonstrate that even the more complex techniques, such as correlation and regression, are not that overwhelming. We are convinced that our textbook will greatly help in accomplishing these goals.

A final note concerns what this book is not. *Criminal Justice Statistics: A Practical Approach* is not a research methods book; yet it could be used together with a text for a methods course. We have limited our focus to statistics for two reasons: it relates to students who are not likely to be researchers and we find it very difficult to teach both methods and statistics in the same course—one or both suffer. Either way, separate textbooks are often required. Therefore, as stated in the footnote, the content and depth of discussion of statistical techniques presented in this text are more than sufficient for undergraduate students. Hence, this book would be a useful companion to a methods text or can stand on its own as a statistics text.

Book Contents

The purpose of this text is to make learning statistics easy, understandable, and applicable to the field of criminal justice. Our coverage of the material is in two parts. Part One, Description and Comparison, includes chapters 1 through 5. Part Two, Explanation, includes chapters 6 through 11. The introduction to the computer section at the end of chapter 1 sets the stage for the software we encourage you to use with the text.

Each chapter begins with a vignette that offers a realistic situation in which you could easily find yourself at some point in your criminal justice career. In addition, each chapter provides exercises for the techniques being taught. We show you how to do the exercises by hand and with a computer using *SPSS 6.1 for Windows*, student version. These exercises are an essential aid in helping you become familiar with the techniques and in proving that you can compute, interpret, and use statistics in a painless manner.

The content of the chapters presents the basic statistical concepts and techniques encountered by criminal justice practitioners in the context of day-to-day work. Topics include definition of statistics and discussion of basic terms (chapter 1); an examination of various techniques for managing and making sense of data (chapter 2); measures of central tendency (chapter 3); measures of variability (chapter 4); comparative statistics for crime and systems analyses (chapter 5); the relationship between nominal variables and how to measure and test these relationships (chapter 6); the relationship between interval variables: correlation (chapter 7); prediction (chapter 8); multiple correlation and regression (chapter 9); comparing scores by means of t tests (chapter 10); and an introduction to analysis of variance (chapter 11).

In closing, we want to emphasize that our approach is simple. We want to stress the application of statistics to the criminal justice field in a way that you will find interesting and easy to comprehend. We believe our use of the vignettes, which describe scenarios in which you could easily place yourself, opens the door to understanding the practical importance of statistics. The data used in the exercises involve some aspect of the criminal justice system that is relevant to prospective criminal justice practitioners. In all, we believe you will find this text easy and enjoyable, at least as enjoyable as you can find statistics, and will discover that statistics is not as scary as once imagined.

Part One
Description and Comparison

1. The Language of Statistics

The Summer Internship

Summertime, and it is the first day of your internship with the city planning office. Because you are majoring in criminal justice and criminology, you've been assigned to the city's criminal justice planner. Although you are extremely excited about the opportunities that lie ahead, you are also somewhat worried. When you interviewed for the job, you were advised that you might have to do some statistical analyses. Unfortunately, you have never taken a statistics course. Therefore, you agreed that if you were offered the position, you would take the criminal justice statistics course offered during the summer, at night. You were offered the job.

Your first day at work involves becoming acclimated to the people, surroundings, and the duties of the job. It looks relatively easy and no one has said a word about the statistics course. By day's end you are feeling rather good about the summer and your job.

The next day, soon after you have reported to work, your supervisor calls you into her office. She begins explaining that the city manager-mayor is growing more concerned over a couple of criminal justice-related issues in the city and wants this office to investigate them. Apparently there are some problems with the police department. In recent months there appears to have been escalating discontent. Several experienced officers have transferred to other police agencies, the local union has been criticizing the police administration, citizen complaints over how police officers are handling calls for service are at an all-time high, and the morale of many officers seems low. The city manager-mayor wants to know why.

Your supervisor tells you that it will be your task to find some answers—your deadline is the end of the summer. Furthermore, you are advised strongly that statistically based reports are preferred. Your stomach begins to churn.

Gathering the information should not be a problem. You had some experience doing research and even took a research methods course. However, the statistical aspect may be a problem. Although you understand that computerized statistical packages are available that can compute all the analyses you will need, you will have to learn to interpret the results, be able to explain why a certain statistical analysis was used, and what it means. Therefore, it becomes apparent you will have to take that statistics course.

That night you register for your first statistics course. While purchasing your book you meet other students who are taking the course. One of them has just finished talking to the instructor. So you decide to see the instructor to discuss your job and its expectations. You also admit you are a little concerned and a little apprehensive about the course. The instructor assures you that statistics are not as scary as many students perceive and that you are not alone when it comes to fears about statistics. Furthermore, you're advised that the course will take you through a methodical, yet friendly, process that will introduce you to all the information you will need to understand why we use statistics, how we use statistics, when we use certain statistics, and what they mean—all concerning the field of criminal justice. Despite the reassurances you again voice your concern, especially because you are not very good with math. The instructor advises you that you need not worry, especially about the math because, mathematically, statistics are much easier than students tend to imagine them. You leave the instructor's office a little less apprehensive.

The next day at work you begin the process of collecting your data. The next two weeks go by quickly. Tonight is the first night of class. You enter the classroom, find a seat, and take a deep breath. The instructor begins by informing the class that the focus for tonight will be on the fundamental terms or basic language of statistics. Although, the instructor admits, many of you should already be familiar with these terms from your methods courses, going over them again allows everyone to be on the same wavelength and to make sure there is a common understanding. Let's get started!

Statistics

Most students are confused about the meaning of *statistics*. The term has a variety of meanings. To some, statistics simply means fragments of data or information. To others it encompasses the theories and procedures used for understanding data (Hinkle, Wiersma, & Jurs 1982). Statistics consists of a variety of tools for criminal justice practitioners, administrators, researchers, and anyone else who collects and uses information. In short, statistics provides techniques for understanding and interpreting data.

Statistics may also be defined as collections of facts expressed as numbers. For example, in 1990, 341,387 full-time law enforcement officers were working in the United States; this is a statistic. So is the fact that 7,830 bank robberies occurred in the same year (*Crime in the U.S.* 1990) and that four million offenders were under some form of correctional supervision (*Sourcebook of Criminal Justice Statistics* 1992). The list of statistical facts about the criminal justice system in any given year is virtually endless. More trivial kinds of information also may be regarded as statistics. One coauthor of this text is 58 years of age and the average age of all four authors is 41.5 years. These are statistics. The three dollars in your bank account is a statistic. Your age, your shoe size, and your height are all statistics. Indeed, any fact that can be expressed as a number, whether it is important or not, is a statistic.

Although the definitions presented so far are accurate and informative, for now, the most practical definition of statistics is that it is a set of problem-solving procedures. This definition will drive the remainder of this text.

Practical Application of Statistics

Criminal justice practitioners deal with a host of problems that statistics can help to solve. For example, how does one describe crime in a city, or the composition of a police department, or the overcrowding problem in a county jail, or the case processing rate of a criminal court? If you were to attempt to address any of these

questions, you would find yourself quite naturally using basic statistical procedures. You would count, classify, compare, and organize your information in a
way that would allow you to describe your findings to others. By doing so, you
would be using statistics.

Other problems that arise in criminal justice go beyond simple description and
into areas such as prediction and evaluation. For example, if a police department
were to add 60 officers to its force, what would be the predicted impact on crime
rates, staff morale, or gasoline consumption? How many new probation officer
positions would be required in the next five years to keep up with the current
growth in caseloads? If sentences to prison continue at their present rate, for how
many new prison beds must the state plan? Is probation more effective than
prison? Which community-based corrections programs work better than others?
How successful is community-oriented policing or judicial training or the public
defender's office? Answering these types of questions involves various statistical techniques that are discussed throughout this text.

Defining statistics as a set of problem-solving procedures should help to dimin-
ish some apprehension many people feel about the subject. Many of these people
believe that statistics is mathematics and that they are not good at math. However, a knowledge of addition, subtraction, multiplication, and division suffices
in most statistical situations.

Only two basic skills are required to "do" statistics. The first is to identify the
procedure that is most appropriate for addressing a particular problem. The second is to interpret the information produced by a particular analysis. These skills
are taught in this text and are the basis for our definition of statistics. Before one
can proceed, however, it is necessary to have a basic understanding of the related
terminology.

Types of Statistics: Descriptive and Inferential

Anyone who collects and analyzes data must decide whether the data are describing something or inferring something. Statistics whose function it is to describe what
data looks like are referred to as *descriptive statistics*. Statistics from which an
inference can be made are known as *inferential statistics*.

It is the job of descriptive statistics to display what the data look like, "where
their center is, how broadly they spread, and how they are related in terms of one
aspect to another aspect of the same data" (Leedy 1985, p. 175). For example, in
the opening vignette the intern is seeking answers to several police-related problems such as why morale is low. So the intern decides to study job satisfaction. A
questionnaire that measures the officers' perceived level of satisfaction with various aspects of the police organization is distributed and collected. When the data
are analyzed, descriptive statistics might include how many officers completed
the questionnaires, the age, racial/ethnic composition, sex, and rank of those who
completed questionnaires, the overall average score for each organizational division, and the percentage of officers extremely satisfied with a given aspect of the
job as opposed to the percentage extremely dissatisfied.

These descriptive statistics provide the intern with data relevant to the local
police agency. What if, however, the intern wanted to apply the results of the data
analysis to all police officers? This is when inferential statistics are necessary.
Inferential statistics allow us to take "small samples of a population and from
those samples make inferences as to the statistical characteristics of the population in general" (Leedy 1985, p. 176). In other words, instead of describing the

data that relates to the police agency the intern is studying, the intern now might make inferences about the population of police officers from the sample studied. For example, in the data collected the intern finds that level of education is related to level of job satisfaction. The officers with a college degree were more satisfied with the organization than were officers with only a high school education. The intern might infer that the typical police officer with a college degree would be more satisfied than the typical police officer without a college degree.

In short, descriptive statistics describe what the data look like. Inferential statistics allow us to infer and make estimates and predictions.

Basic Concepts

Descriptive and inferential statistics are two divisions of statistics and are terms with which you should be familiar. However, before we discuss any specific statistical problems or procedures, we define and explain other basic concepts and statistical vocabulary. These include terms such as *data*, *variable*, *levels of measurement*, and *measurement scales*.

Data and Variables

The word *data* is the plural of *datum*, which is defined as an individual piece of information. However, we typically use the plural form *data* because we rarely deal with only a single or isolated fact. Data may be defined as the units of information we collect and analyze. For example, the Federal Bureau of Investigation (FBI) collects the number and types of criminal offenses that occur every month.

A *variable* is defined as a characteristic or attribute that is not the same for all the persons, objects, or events being studied. For example, the racial or ethnic composition of students in an introductory criminal justice course would be a variable. In an applied sense, criminal justice is concerned with an almost endless list of variables that includes persons, objects, or events. Persons can include criminals, inmates, correctional officers, judges, attorneys, police officers, and court clerks. Objects can include police cars, felony cases, jails, prisons, judges' chambers, guns, and bodies. Events can include crimes, sentences, incarcerations, victimizations, and executions.

In criminal justice research, we do not study any of these persons, objects, or events in a general or abstract way. Instead, we focus on specific characteristics or attributes. If we studied a group of offenders, for example, we might record age, race, sex, and number of convictions. In a general study of criminal offenders, most are not the same age, have not committed the same offense, and have not used a weapon.[1] Similarly, most police officers differ in their job satisfaction, and most felony cases are not disposed of in equal lengths of time.

These different characteristics are called variables because their values are not the same for each member of the group. Because the characteristics or attributes of persons, objects, or events are not the same for all members of a group under study, that is, they *vary*, they are called *variables*.

Once we decide what we want to study, we do not examine all possible variables but select only those we regard as most relevant to our study. We go through a formal or informal process of asking, "What do I want to know about these particular persons, objects, or events?" The answer to that question usually results in a list of possible variables for study. Investigators studying the backgrounds of probation officers might be interested in their age, sex, race, and years of education. Those who study the condition of police cars might focus on their age, mileage, make, and accident record. Researchers studying the characteristics of judges might examine their age, race, sex, political affiliation, jurisdiction, and number of dispositions.

Exercise 1–1 Identification of Variables

Identify five possible variables for each of the following studies. Compare your list with the list provided in the answer section at the end of the chapter.

1. Jail populations in the United States
2. Women state police officers
3. Homicides in your state

Variable Types

Variables can be classified in different ways. One way is to consider the values that a variable can assume. Some variables can be recorded only with a restricted number of values, whereas others can be recorded with an infinite number. The former are called discrete variables and the latter continuous variables. *Discrete variables* can have only a finite number of values that arise from counting. The number of prisoners in a jail is an example of a discrete variable. For example, a jail can have 134 prisoners or it can have 135 prisoners, but it cannot have 134.5 prisoners. The number of prisoners can be recorded only as a whole number without a fraction. Therefore, number of prisoners is a discrete variable.

A *continuous variable* can assume an infinite number of values. An example of a continuous variable is the time it takes an emergency operator to dispatch an ambulance in answer to a call for help. The time can be measured as 20 seconds, 20.3 seconds, or 20.32 seconds. Another example of a continuous variable is the ages of all the prisoners in a jail.

Levels of Variables and Their Scales

Variables can be discrete or continuous, but they also can be classified according to how they are measured. The simplest type of variable is the *nominal variable*, which merely categorizes or classifies. The second level of variable is the *ordinal level*. This variable allows for the measurement of degree of difference. An *interval variable* is one in which the same unit of measurement is applied throughout the range of values. A *ratio variable* has an absolute zero point.

Nominal

Some variables are measured in a way that allows us only to say that one thing is different from or similar to another. Some patrol cars are Fords whereas others are Chevrolets. Fords are a different make but are not more or less of a make than any other. Nominal variables (sometimes referred to as qualitative variables) have no level of measurement. We cannot conclude that one thing has more or less of the variable (i.e., the Ford is neither greater than or less than the Chevrolet). In fact, all we can do with such variables is assign *names* to the different categories that comprise the variables. For example, gender is a qualitative variable expressed as male or female. Although we can classify a group of police officers according to gender, we cannot say that one officer has more gender than another. Each is either male or female. Because all we can do is classify these types of variables into categories, they are called nominal or categorical variables. Such variables are measured at the nominal level.

Numbers or values assigned to nominal variables constitute a *nominal scale*. These scales are useful when data are being tabulated or grouped into categories. Referring to our gender example, we can designate number 1 for males and number 2 for females. These numbers from a nominal scale have no mathematical properties. As such, number 2 does not suggest more gender than 1. These numbers are simply a code for a category name and are completely arbitrary. We can even switch or modify the nominal codes for male and female and not alter the information about gender.

Because the values of nominal scales are names, they cannot be meaningfully added, subtracted, multiplied, or divided. For example, it makes no sense to compute an average gender. The numbers of a nominal scale can only be counted. Thus if we have a sample of 120 police officers, we can determine that there are 91 men and 29 women. These counts can be converted to percentages so that we can say that the force consists of 76% men and 24% women. A variety of nominal variables or scales are used in criminal justice research. Some of the more common ones are crimes, incarceration sites, levels of incarceration, types of sentences, and methods of patrol.

Ordinal

Some variables are measured in a way that allows us to make statements or comparisons of amounts. For example, a patrol car with 17,000 miles has more miles than one with 16,000 miles. Such variables are called *quantitative*. Important distinctions can be made among these variables. With some quantitative variables, we can say that one person (or object or event) has more of the variable than another, but we cannot indicate how much more. For example, assume that a large sample of police officers was surveyed about their job satisfaction. Some were found to be highly satisfied, some moderately satisfied, and others slightly satisfied. This measurement allows us to conclude that some officers are more satisfied than others. We know from these findings that those who are moderately satisfied are more content than those who are slightly satisfied. We also know that the moderately satisfied group is less satisfied than the highly satisfied group and that the highly satisfied group is more content than anyone else. We can rank these groups of police officers in order of job satisfaction from highly satisfied to slightly satisfied or from slightly satisfied to highly satisfied. Because this variable has an underlying *order* to it, it is called an ordinal variable.

One important limitation of ordinal variables is that we cannot say how much more or less satisfied one officer is compared with another. We know that an officer who is highly satisfied is more satisfied than another who is only moderately satisfied, but we cannot say how much more. All we can do is rank respondents in terms of more or less. Such variables are said to be measured at the *ordinal level*, and numbers assigned to these variables constitute an *ordinal scale*.

The distinguishing feature of ordinal scales is order. Thus we can ask the police officers in our survey to circle a number that best reflects their overall job satisfaction: 1 for slight, 2 for moderate, and 3 for high. We can then rank the officers on their job satisfaction by using these numbers, because we know that 3 is greater than 2, and 2 is greater than 1.

Although the values of an ordinal scale can be ranked, we should not overlook the fact that the values themselves are usually quite arbitrary. For example, we can assign the values 10, 20, and 30 to stand for slight, moderate, and high satisfaction. We can just as easily assign the values 8, 15, and 62.

Although ordinal variables can be assigned values, a more common usage is to list several variables and ask respondents to rank order the variables. For example, rank from 1 to 5 (most serious to least serious) the following crimes: burglary, robbery, theft, embezzlement, and fraud. Another example is rank from least needed (7) to most needed (1) ways to fight rising crime rates: more police officers, stricter laws, stiffer penalties, citizen watch groups, more lawyers, additional courts, and new jails.

Interval

Although a quantitative variable, the ordinal variable has limited uses. A variable with greater measurement potential because there is an equal distance between any two measures is the *interval variable*. Fahrenheit and Celsius temperatures are examples of this type of variable. For example, if the temperature in one cell wing is 80° F and the temperature in another cell wing is 75° F, the difference is 5°. Similarly, if the cell wing temperatures rose to 100° F and 95° F, the difference is also 5°. In each case, the difference reflects the same amount of temperature change. This is because the units of the thermometer are spaced at equal intervals. Therefore, the amount of heat it takes to raise the temperature from 60° F to 61° F is the same unit amount of heat it takes to raise it from 150° F to 151° F.

Variables that measure people's attitudes are another illustration of interval variables. For example, in a study of attitudes toward criminal defendants, we can ask judges to rate the extent to which they agree or disagree with the statement: "Many criminal defendants are knowledgeable about court procedures." The judges then can select one of five numbers that designate their response: 1 for strongly agree, 2 for agree, 3 for neither agree nor disagree, 4 for disagree, and 5 for strongly disagree. Although the numbers are somewhat arbitrary (unlike temperature values), they are designed to reflect equivalent changes in attitude across consecutive units of the scale. In other words, the amount of attitude change in going from strongly agree to agree is the same as going from disagree to strongly disagree.

Variables that have equal intervals are measured at the *interval level*, and the numbers assigned to those variables constitute an *interval scale*. Interval level variables possess a relative rather than an absolute zero point. For example, 0° F does not mean the absence of heat, it is merely a relative point on the temperature scale; that is, meaningful temperatures do exist below 0° F.

The consequence of a relative zero point is that measurements cannot be converted into ratios. For example, 120° F is warmer than 40° F; the former is 80° higher than the latter. However, we are unable to say that the former is three times warmer than the latter because the value of zero is not the absolute beginning point of the scale. In criminal justice studies, interval variables or scales are often linked to attitudinal or perceptual questions such as:

1. How safe do you feel walking alone at night in your neighborhood?

Extremely Unsafe	Somewhat Unsafe	Neither	Somewhat Safe	Extremely Safe
1	3	5	7	9

2. Alleged nonviolent criminal offenders should not be held in jail before trial.

Strongly Disagree	Somewhat Disagree	Neutral	Somewhat Agree	Extremely Agree
1	2	3	4	5

Ratio

Some interval level variables have equal measurement intervals, and they have a true zero point. Such variables are measured at the *ratio level*, and numbers assigned to these variables constitute a *ratio scale*. Age is an example of a variable measured at the ratio level. No measurements are possible below zero. Thus if we know that the average ages of inmates in prisons X and Y are 54.3 years and 39.7 years respectively, we can say that the average age of prisoners in prison X is 1.37 times that of prison Y. A police officer who is 55 years of age not only is 30 years older than an officer who is 25 but also is 2.2 times older than the junior officer. It is because time has an absolute zero point that we can make ratios such as these.

Exercise 1–2   Recognizing Types of Variables

For the following data sets, identify the variables as nominal, ordinal, interval, or ratio. Also identify three values of each.

Inmate Data

Case No.	Age	Race	Education (Grade)	Previous Commitments	Offense	Years of Sentence	IQ
1	22	B	5	0	Rape	6	90
2	26	B	6	0	Rape	14	110
3	59	W	14	3	Robbery	25	135
4	27	B	12	2	Robbery	13	125
5	25	H	10	0	Burglary	3	130

Self-reported Drug Use Among College Students

Case No.	Gender	Age	Ethnicity	Year in College	Smoke Marijuana	No. of Times per Week
1	M	18	Cau	Fresh	Yes	Over 10
2	F	20	Cau	Junior	Yes	1–5
3	F	19	Afro-Am	Soph	Yes	6–10
4	M	19	His	Soph	Yes	Over 10
5	M	21	Afro-Am	Senior	Yes	1–5
6	F	20	His	Junior	Yes	6–10

Assaults Against Police Officers (Any State, U.S.A.)

Assignment	Circumstance	Weapon Used	Injury Status	Days Off
Patrol	Traffic stop	Handgun	Serious	45
Tact.	Drug raid	Shotgun	Slight	5
CID	Homicide inv.	Handgun	Serious	30
Patrol	Domestic dist.	Knife	None	0
Patrol	Traffic stop	Knife	Moderate	11

CID, Criminal Investigations Division.

Hierarchy of Measurement Scales

Criminal justice researchers can describe persons, objects, or events by using variables measured at any of the levels: nominal, ordinal, interval, and ratio. For example, criminal offenders can be studied by gender, seriousness of offense, attitude toward the law, or number of prior convictions. Gender is a nominal variable, seriousness of offense is ordinal, attitude toward the law is interval, and number of prior convictions is ratio. Jails (an object) can be measured according to location (city, county, north, south, east, west), level of violence, or average daily population. Bank robberies, which are events, can be measured according to the type of institution robbed, degree of threat involved, or dollar amount stolen.

Nominal, ordinal, interval, and ratio scales can be placed in a hierarchy. Table 1.1 lists each of the scales with its distinguishing feature. The scales are ordered from top to bottom with respect to increasing sophistication. The properties of a scale are its distinguishing feature and all the features of the preceding scales. For example, a ratio scale has a true zero point, equal intervals, order, and categories.

The hierarchy of measurement scales shows that one can always express a variable in terms of a lower scale but not in terms of a higher one. For example, we can express the measurements of an interval scale in terms of an ordinal or nominal scale but not in terms of a ratio scale.

Variables that are originally measured at the ordinal level can also be expressed at the nominal level. For example, public opinions about the death penalty can be measured on an ordinal scale where 1=strongly supports the death penalty, 2=moderately supports the death penalty, and 3=does not support the death penalty. In addition, we can classify people's opinions on a nominal scale where 1=supports the death penalty and 2=does not support the death penalty.

Variables measured at the nominal level can be expressed only at the nominal level. For example, the race of prisoners in a state penitentiary might be classified as 1=Caucasian, 2=African American, 3=Hispanic, and 4=other. This nominal scale can only be expressed as another nominal scale such as 1=Caucasian and 2=not Caucasian.

Let us now consider an example of real data to help understand measurement scale hierarchy better. Table 1.2 presents information from the *Sourcebook of Criminal Justice Statistics* (1992). The table contains the projected 1995 prison populations for eleven midwestern states.

The variable being displayed is projected occupancy and is expressed as a frequency or headcount. As it stands, the variable is measured on a ratio scale. That is, it has an absolute zero point and the differences in the measure are equal. It is possible, however, also to measure this variable on an ordinal scale. For example, one may be interested in studying projected occupancy as "levels" rather than as individual headcounts. Here we can designate 1=high (25,000 or more occupants), 2=medium (24,999–10,000 occupants), and 3=low (fewer than 10,000 occupants).

Table 1.1   The Four Scales of Measurement with Their Distinguishing Features

Scale	Distinguishing Feature
Nominal	Names or categories
Ordinal	Order
Interval	Equal intervals
Ratio	True zero point

Table 1.2   Projected 1995 Prison Populations for 11 Midwestern States

State	Projection
Illinois	42,109
Indiana	19,238
Iowa	6,000
Kansas	6,269
Minnesota	4,003
Missouri	15,031
Nebraska	3,535
North Dakota	581
Ohio	37,301
South Dakota	1,787
Wisconsin	11,841

Source: *Sourcebook of Criminal Justice Statistics,* 1992

We can also measure projected inmate occupancy on a nominal scale. For example, we might want to know if the present capacity of prisons in these states is adequate for the projected prison populations. In this case, we are interested in deciding yes or no and could define 1=yes and 2=no. Table 1.3 presents the values of the ordinal and nominal scales in relation to the original information about projected inmate occupancy.

Exercise 1–3   Converting Scales

Using the data sets provided in Exercise 1–2, convert the ratio scales from each data set into nominal and ordinal scales. For age, construct one set of nominal and ordinal scales that can be applied to both data sets in which age is a variable. Compare your scales to ours.

Table 1.3   Data from Table 1.2 Expressed in Terms of Ratio, Ordinal, and Nominal Scales

State	Projection (Ratio)	Level (Ordinal)	Capacity (Nominal)
Illinois	42,109	1	2
Indiana	19,238	2	2
Iowa	6,000	3	2
Kansas	6,269	3	1
Minnesota	4,003	3	1
Missouri	15,031	2	1
Nebraska	3,535	3	2
North Dakota	581	3	1
Ohio	37,301	1	2
South Dakota	1,787	3	2
Wisconsin	11,841	2	2

Source: *Sourcebook of Criminal Justice Statistics,* 1992

Population, Element, Census, and Sample

Population, element, census, and *sample* are four terms found in nearly all statistics textbooks. Yet students are often confused about the meaning of these terms. A *population* is the total set of persons, objects, or events that we wish to study. For example, all the students at a university, all the ships in the United States Navy, all the felony cases in the United States filed in 1993, and all crimes reported in the uniform crime reports in a given year are different populations. Although populations are typically thought to be very large groups, size is irrelevant in defining a population. Populations can be quite small. For example, if we were interested in knowing something about the psychological history of mass murderers, it would be difficult to find a large number of such persons in the United States or even the world. The collection of mass murderers would be the population, even if it included no more than 10 or 20 individuals.

An *element* is a single person, object, or event in a population of interest. Thus one student would be an element of the population of all students at a university. Similarly, the USS *Constitution* would be an element of the population of all United States naval ships. In contrast, a *sample* is a group of elements from a population of interest. If we studied only 30 percent of the students at a university, we would be studying a sample from the population of students. If we studied only 1,000 United States naval ships, we would be studying a sample from the population of ships. Studying only some felony cases filed in 1993 instead of all the felony cases from that year would involve a sample.

Finally, a *census* is a study of all the elements in a population. Every ten years, the United States Census Bureau counts all the people in the country. This is called the decennial census. Studying all the students at a university or all the ships in the United States Navy also would be a census.

Exercise 1–4   *Which Is it? Population, Element, Sample, or Census?*

_____ All correctional officers in the United States
_____ Felony courts in a county
_____ One district attorney
_____ 100 federal prisons
_____ One maximum prison
_____ Number and characteristics of public defenders in 1990
_____ Police departments with fewer than 250 sworn personnel
_____ Women prison inmates
_____ Characteristics of all parolees 1990–1993
_____ 500 deputy sheriffs

Note: Because of its nature, each item can be viewed as being in more than one of the four categories. These items were chosen to afford students the opportunity to see the breadth of the terms so often used in criminal justice.

Summary

This chapter discusses several basic concepts that are important in gaining a basic understanding of statistics and the subjects addressed in subsequent chapters.

Statistics is defined as a set of problem-solving procedures. Key terms such as *variable*, *measurement levels*, *measurement scales*, *population*, *element*, *census*, *sample*, and *descriptive* and *inferential statistics* are defined and discussed. Although these terms may not be familiar to you now, they will be used frequently throughout this text and their meaning will become clear as you use them in different problems and exercises. Chapter 2 addresses the problem of how to organize data. It deals with variables, measurement scales, and descriptive statistics.

Answers to Exercises

Exercise Answer 1–1   Identification of Variables

1. Jail populations in the United States

   Population size, sex, age, ethnicity, type of offense, type of incarceration (e.g., presentence or postsentence), type of facility (e.g., city, county, or state), programs offered, average length of incarceration, state.

2. Women state police officers

   Age, education, years of service, marital status, number of children, division, rank, shift, geographic assignment, career goal.

3. Homicides in the United States

   Total by state, age of victim, sex of victim, race of victim, age of offender, sex of offender, race of offender, method (e.g., firearm, physical, knife), circumstances (e.g., family dispute, drug deal, other felony), contributing factors (e.g., alcohol, drugs, jealousy, greed).

Exercise Answer 1–2   Recognizing Types of Variables

1. Inmate data

   Age—Ratio, Race—Nominal, Education—Interval, Previous commitments to prison—Ratio, Offense—Nominal, Years of sentence—Ratio, IQ—Interval.

2. Self-reported drug use among college students

   Sex—Nominal, Age—Ratio, Ethnicity—Nominal, Year in College—Ordinal, Smoke marijuana—Nominal, Number of times per week—Ratio.

3. Assaults against police officers

   Assignment—Nominal, Circumstance—Nominal, Weapon used—Nominal, Injury status—Ordinal, Days off—Ratio.

Exercise Answer 1–3   Converting Scales

Age

   Nominal (Cannot be done)
   Ordinal—1 = Younger than 18, 2 = 19–21, 3 = 22–25, 4 = Older than 25

Previous commitments to prison

   Nominal (Cannot be done)
   Ordinal—1 = Fewer than 5, 2 = 6–10, 3 = 11–15, 4 = More than 15

Years of sentence

  Nominal (Cannot be done)
  Ordinal—1 = Fewer than 2, 2 = 3–5, 3 = More than 5

Exercise Answer 1–4   Which Is It?
Correctional officers—Population; Felony courts—Population or sample; One district attorney—Element; 100 federal prisons—Sample; One maximum prison—Element; Number and characteristics of public defenders in 1990— Census; Police departments with fewer than 250 sworn personnel—Population or sample; Women prison inmates—Population; Characteristics of all parolees 1990–1993—Census; 500 deputy sheriffs—Sample

---

Introduction to the Computer

In the past 40 years or so, social science research has become more complicated. It involves large data sets and poses empirical questions that demand powerful and in-depth statistical analyses. Resourceful researchers turned to the computer as a tool for confronting these challenges. At first, the use of computers was beyond the capabilities of most social scientists, because these researchers knew little about computer languages or they had limited access to mainframe computers. This changed with the advent of software (i.e., program packages) that contains the computer language or instructions required for a variety of statistical techniques. These packages were later adapted for use on personal computers (PCs). *Statistical Product and Service Solutions* (SPSS) is one of the oldest and most widely used statistical programs in the social sciences.

SPSS was first developed in the late 1960s by Norman Nie, Tex Hull, and Dale Bent, three graduate students at Stanford University. They developed the software themselves to assist in performing statistical analyses for their social science research. The product was initially introduced for use on large mainframe computers. In 1984, SPSS developed the first statistical product for use with PCs. Before that, statistical analyses were performed mostly with large mainframe computer systems in large corporations, academic computing centers, and government offices. In 1992, SPSS introduced the first major statistical software package for Microsoft *Windows*. *SPSS 6.1 for Windows*, Student Version, is the third generation of the SPSS product line operating in the *Windows* environment.

We will use *SPSS 6.1 for Windows*, Student Version, to solve most of the exercises in this book. *SPSS 6.1 for Windows* runs on an IBM or compatible PC. It requires at least 4 MB of random access memory and at least 21 MB of hard disk space. You must also be running Microsoft *Windows 3.1* or Microsoft *Windows 95* for this software to work properly. If you are using *Windows 95*, make sure that you have the 6.1.3 release of *SPSS for Windows*, Student Version.

SPSS 6.1 for Windows, Student Version, is somewhat limited, but it is still a powerful version of the original *SPSS for Windows*. The student version contains all of the data analysis tools you need for the exercises here. However, it can handle only 50 columns and 1,500 rows of data. If your data analysis must grow beyond these limits, consider using the original version of *SPSS for Windows*, which can accommodate unlimited columns and rows and contains many advanced statistical techniques and data handling procedures.

Detailed instructions for using the student version are found in the manual that accompanies the *SPSS 6.1 for Windows*, Student Version, software. Your instructor may have packaged both the software and the manual with this textbook. Follow the instructions in chapter 2 of the SPSS manual to install your software. If you have only 4MB of memory in your system, be sure to follow the special instructions in the chapter.

If you have problems installing or running the software, talk to your instructor or local computer support staff first. SPSS provides telephone technical assistance to instructors who use the student version. Instructors who have not received technical support can obtain more information by calling Prentice Hall Customer Service at (800) 922-0579. More information on service and support is located in the preface of the student version manual.

When the software installation is complete, you will see the SPSS program group on the front of your screen (Figure 1.1).

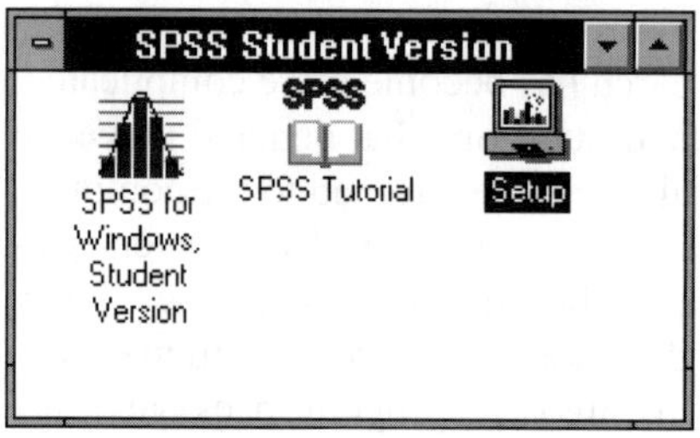

Figure 1.1

Turn to chapter 3 of the software manual. Work through the steps to familiarize yourself with how the system works. This chapter takes you step by step through a sample analysis session. You are introduced to the basic structure and operation of dialog boxes in *SPSS for Windows*. The manual also introduces you to the names of the various parts of the program used throughout the manual and in our solution guides at the conclusion of each chapter of this book. Chapter 4 of the manual shows you how to access the online help system.

The three basic steps in using SPSS software are entering, defining, and analyzing your data. SPSS and other statistical programs follow a specific format for entering and defining data. The *units of analysis* that you are studying (e.g., offenders, police departments, prison systems) are entered as rows. The characteristics of those units, which are called *variables*, are entered as columns. Each row contains all the information about a specific unit. It is important to keep all that information in a single row so that you can compare the rows and better understand the combinations of characteristics that make units differ from one another.

A sample data set that shows offender information on five variables (age, race, sex, prior arrests, and crime) is shown in Figure 1.2.

In *SPSS 6.1 for Windows* you enter your data directly into the Data Editor. Review chapter 5 of the SPSS manual for more information on how to enter and save your data. Doubleclick on the SPSS Tutorial icon in the SPSS program group for additional assistance with entering and saving your data.

For more information on obtaining the full version of *SPSS for Windows*, contact your professor or campus bookstore. If they cannot give you information, contact the SPSS sales line directly at (800) 543-2185. For more information on

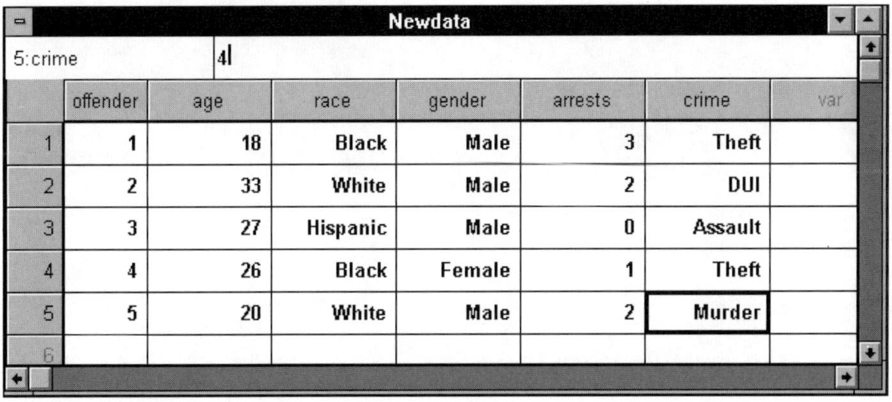

	offender	age	race	gender	arrests	crime	var
Newdata							
5:crime	4|						
1	1	18	Black	Male	3	Theft	
2	2	33	White	Male	2	DUI	
3	3	27	Hispanic	Male	0	Assault	
4	4	26	Black	Female	1	Theft	
5	5	20	White	Male	2	Murder	
6							

Figure 1.2

the SPSS product line or on statistics in general, you might want to visit the SPSS home page on the Internet. Point your browser at **http://www.spss.com** to see the latest information on SPSS products or to obtain links to statistical information all over the Internet.

Note

1. One may wish to study a group of offenders, all of whom are men. In this case, gender is a constant and not a variable.

References

Crime in the U.S. 1990. Washington, DC: Federal Bureau of Investigation.

Hinkle, D.E., Wiersma, W., and Jurs, S.G. 1982. *Basic Behavioral Statistics.* Boston: Houghton Mifflin.

Leedy, P.D. 1985. *Practical Research.* 3d ed. New York: Macmillan.

Sourcebook of Criminal Justice Statistics, 1992. Washington, DC: United States Department of Justice.

2. Organizing and Describing Data Frequency Distributions and Graphic Techniques

The Prison Report

Working in a correctional facility has pretty much been as you imagined it would be from what you learned in your corrections courses. One day, you are in a reverie that is broken by another officer, who informs you that the lieutenant wants you in the office "on the double." You feel uneasy. After all, you have been a state prison correctional officer for only three months. During this time you've discovered that the only time anyone is ordered to the lieutenant's office is when the person has screwed up.

With some apprehension you knock on the lieutenant's door, enter, and, to your surprise, are warmly welcomed. After offering you a seat and complimenting you on the job you've done thus far, the reason for your presence is revealed. The lieutenant informs you that the warden has requested a comprehensive report describing the inmate population.

The lieutenant explains that inmate files contain a large array of variables, such as age, date of commitment, offense, security classification, educational level, ethnic origin, and gang affiliation. The warden wants all the data organized into a report that can be presented to the governor. "Your résumé states that you took a statistics course as part of your criminal justice degree. Therefore, you are in charge of this project. I want to see a draft in a couple of days," the warden says.

As you leave the office you realize it's panic time. Where do you begin? It has been several years since you took that statistics course. What should you do? How do you start? Then you recall: your statistics professor always said, "When in doubt, review your stat text." So that's what you do, starting with the chapter on organizing data.

Organizing and Describing Data

One of the problems we face when collecting data is that data do not come neatly organized. We use the term *raw data* to denote this fact. As such, our first task is to organize raw data so that we (as well as others) can understand the information the data convey. One technique for organizing raw data is to construct a *frequency distribution*. This is a table that simply shows how often the scores or measurements occur in a sample.

We discuss four types of frequency distributions in this chapter: absolute frequency distributions, relative frequency distributions, cumulative frequency distributions, and cumulative relative frequency distributions. Although you may feel that the names of these distributions imply sophisticated procedures, they are all quite easy to construct. We also discuss ways of presenting frequency information visually. Such displays are useful because they are efficient at conveying the information in data. We discuss pie charts, bar graphs, histograms, and polygons.

We discuss central tendency, variability, skewness, and kurtosis. These four properties allow us to characterize frequency distributions and help us to differentiate one distribution from another. We conclude the chapter with a discussion of a basic statistical phenomenon called the *normal distribution* or normal curve. We describe how this is a special type of frequency distribution.

We wish to make a final note about the techniques presented in this chapter in terms of two maxims that we believe will help readers who are experiencing statistics anxiety. These maxims are: (1) Just because a statistical technique is simple does not mean it is not useful, and (2) just because a statistical technique is useful does not mean it has to be complex.

Types of Frequency Distributions
Absolute Frequency Distributions

Statistical analyses begin with raw data. For example, assume that it is your task to analyze the type of crime recorded in a sample of 20 offense reports. (Recall from chapter 1 that a sample is a group of elements from a population. In this example not all offense reports are being examined, only a sample of 20.) Initially, the data might look like this: theft, robbery, auto theft, burglary, burglary, auto theft, robbery, assault, theft, burglary, burglary, auto theft, robbery, assault, theft, theft, burglary, theft, theft, auto theft. You would quite naturally organize these raw data by counting the different types of crime and then document your results in a clear and useful way. In doing this, you would be constructing an absolute frequency distribution, that is, a table that shows how frequently each crime type occurs in the sample of 20 reports. Table 2.1 is an example of an absolute frequency distribution for the foregoing raw data.

This is a simple display that is useful for organizing and summarizing raw data. Frequency distributions help us to understand and present our results in a way that is much more efficient than working with raw data.

In a succinct way, Table 2.1 tells us that five categories of crime were observed in the sample: theft, auto theft, burglary, robbery, and assault. Theft had the high-

Table 2.1 Absolute Frequency Distribution of Crime Types from Twenty Hypothetical Offense Reports

Type of Crime	Absolute Frequency
Theft	6
Robbery	3
Auto theft	4
Burglary	5
Assault	2
	$N = 20$

est frequency (it was observed six times in the sample) whereas assault had the lowest frequency (it was observed only two times).

The letter N at the bottom of Table 2.1 is a standard abbreviation for the number of observations in a sample. In this case, $N = 20$ because there is a total of 20 offense reports, each of which contains a single crime type. The sum of the frequencies for each of the crime types must equal N. We would have to look for and correct a mistake if the sum of the frequencies did not total N.

Relative Frequency Distributions

An absolute frequency distribution is the basis for constructing a relative frequency distribution. The latter is simply the percentage equivalent of the former. A relative frequency is formed by dividing an absolute frequency by N and multiplying by 100 percent. Thus the relative frequency of theft crimes in Table 2.1 is $6/20 \times 100\% = 0.30 \times 100\% = 30\%$. This indicates that theft accounts for 30 percent of the crimes that were documented on the offense reports. Table 2.2 displays relative frequencies for all the crime types.

A relative frequency is so named because it allows one to discuss a frequency distribution without being bound to a particular or absolute number of observations. For example, assume that a village mayor has commissioned a poll of a sample of 500 community residents about the purchase of new squad cars for the police department. The results indicate that 98 respondents are favorable toward the purchase but 402 are against it. No doubt, the mayor would be interested in these absolute frequencies, but converting them to relative frequencies is more useful. The absolute frequencies could be converted to relative frequencies by dividing the former by 500 (which is N) and multiplying by 100 percent. This would show that about 20 percent of the respondents ($98/500 \times 100\%$) are favorable toward the purchase and about 80 percent ($402/500 \times 100\%$) are against it. Assuming that the polled sample is randomly selected, the mayor could infer that only about 20 percent of the entire community would favor purchasing new squad cars at this time. As such, the mayor might decide to postpone the purchase for a while. Exactly how one can infer that what is true of a sample is also true for the population from which it came is discussed in chapter 10.

Cumulative Frequency Distributions

Both absolute and relative frequency distributions provide information about individual observations. For example, Table 2.2 shows that five (25 percent) of the crimes reported on the offense reports were classified as burglary. Similarly,

Table 2.2   Absolute and Relative Frequency Distributions of Crime Types from Twenty Hypothetical Offense Reports

Type of Crime	Absolute Frequency	Relative Frequency (%)
Theft	6	30
Robbery	3	15
Auto theft	4	20
Burglary	5	25
Assault	2	10
	$N = 20$	100

three (15 percent) were classified as robbery. Each absolute and relative frequency denotes a single crime type.

There are times, however, when researchers want to talk about a collection or group of observations. For example, someone might be interested in the occurrence of the different theft crimes in the offense reports. In Table 2.2 the frequencies for theft and auto theft could be added, showing that 6 + 4 or 10 crime types were in the theft category.

A special procedure is used to group observations of an entire frequency distribution. This is called a *cumulative frequency distribution* and is constructed by means of systematic addition of all the frequencies in an absolute frequency distribution. Table 2.3 shows how this is done.

Starting at the top of the table,[1] one forms the first cumulative frequency by simply copying the absolute frequency for theft, which is 6. The second cumulative frequency is formed by adding the first cumulative frequency to the absolute frequency for robbery, 6 + 3, which is 9. The third cumulative frequency is the sum of the second cumulative frequency and the absolute frequency for auto theft, 9 + 4, or 13. This process continues until all the absolute frequencies have been added together.

Cumulative frequencies are interpreted with "grouping" in mind. Thus the cumulative frequency of auto theft means that there were 13 offense reports that had theft, robbery, or auto theft listed. It is easy to see that the last cumulative frequency takes into consideration all the observations in the sample and thus must be equal to N.

Relative Cumulative Frequency Distributions

To talk about cumulative frequencies in relative terms, one can construct a cumulative relative frequency distribution. If a relative frequency distribution is available, a cumulative relative frequency distribution can be developed in the same way as the cumulative frequency distribution. Table 2.4 provides an example.

Starting at the top of the table, one records the first cumulative relative frequency by simply copying the relative frequency for theft, which is 30 percent. The second cumulative relative frequency is formed by adding the first cumulative relative frequency to the relative frequency for robbery, 30% + 15%, which equals 45 percent. The third cumulative relative frequency is the sum of the second cumulative relative frequency and the relative frequency for auto theft, 45% + 20%, which is 65 percent. This process is continued until all the relative frequencies have been added together.

Table 2.3   Absolute, Relative, and Cumulative Frequency Distributions of Crime Types from Twenty Hypothetical Offense Reports

Type of Crime	Absolute Frequency	Relative Frequency (%)	Cumulative Frequency
Theft	6	30	6
Robbery	3	15	9
Auto theft	4	20	13
Burglary	5	25	18
Assault	2	10	20
	$N = 20$	100	

Table 2.4   Absolute, Relative, Cumulative, and Cumulative Relative Frequency Distributions of Crime Types from Twenty Hypothetical Offense Reports

Type of Crime	Absolute Frequency	Relative Frequency (%)	Cumulative Frequency	Cumulative Relative Frequency (%)
Theft	6	30	6	30
Robbery	3	15	9	45
Auto theft	4	20	13	65
Burglary	5	25	18	90
Assault	2	10	20	100
	$N = 20$	100		

Like cumulative frequencies, cumulative relative frequencies are interpreted with "grouping" in mind. Thus the cumulative relative frequency at auto theft means that 65 percent of the offense reports had theft, robbery, or auto theft listed. The last cumulative relative frequency takes into account all the observations in the sample and therefore must equal 100 percent.

Exercise 2–1   Frequency Distributions

While preparing your report for the warden, to the inmate data you decide to add information about the prison staff. Using the following raw data on educational status of prison staff members divided among the ten divisions within the prison, develop a table that shows the absolute, relative, cumulative, and cumulative relative frequencies. *N* equals 512. Begin by determining how many of the 512 staff members have high school degrees, associate's degrees, and so on.

	Staff Member Education			
Division	High School Only	Associate's Degree	Bachelor's Degree	Master's Degree
1	15	10	5	2
2	10	5	3	0
3	12	6	4	1
4	27	13	8	3
5	35	20	12	4
6	19	12	6	2
7	45	18	15	5
8	39	20	15	10
9	22	21	19	18
10	6	9	10	6

Interval Frequency Distributions

Up to this point, our examples of frequency distributions have required us to find the occurrence of a small number of values. The data for Tables 2.1 to 2.4 had only five crime types to consider. There are times, however, when one's data contain a large number or range of values. In such cases, frequency distributions of individual data values typically yield a long table with many low frequencies.

When this happens, the frequency distribution is not useful because it is not much more informative than the raw data. As an example, consider the hypothetical data in Table 2.5.

In its current condition, this distribution does not reveal much except that drivers were of different ages. To gain a better understanding of the information provided in these data we need to modify the way in which we construct the frequency distribution.[2] A useful modification would be to record age in terms of a segment or class interval and then to identify the number of observations that fall within each of those intervals. This is called an *interval frequency* and is shown in Table 2.6. Note how age is now grouped into class intervals. The first class interval represents people who are between the ages of 15 and 19 years (inclusive). The second interval stands for those who are between 20 and 24 years, and so on. The use of age intervals has shortened the table and presents information in a more interpretable manner. For example, we can see from the absolute frequencies in Table 2.6 that many of the drivers are 24 years or younger. The cumulative frequencies show us that 25 or 50 percent of the drivers fall into that age range. This tells the reader that half of the sample is composed of young adults and adolescents, and at least 20 percent are underage drinkers. Presenting the data in this manner is much more useful, but it does require that we group the data into intervals.

Steps in Constructing Interval Frequency Distributions

Constructing an interval frequency distribution is not difficult, but it requires that one use a few basic principles. The following principles guide the design of good interval frequency distributions, that is, distributions free from problems such as overlapping class intervals (Grimm 1993; McCall 1990).

1. Be sure the class intervals encompass all the data values. In the conviction for driving while intoxicated (DWI) example, the lowest age is 18 years and the highest is 59 years. As can be seen, the class intervals in Table 2.6 are designed so that these two ages can be included in the lowest and highest intervals.

2. Decide if you want to select the class interval size or the number of intervals. To construct an interval frequency distribution one must either determine

Table 2.5   Ages of Fifty Hypothetical Persons Convicted of Driving While Intoxicated

Age (years)	Absolute Frequency	Age (years)	Absolute Frequency
18	5	29	1
19	5	31	3
20	2	33	2
21	7	35	4
22	4	37	2
23	1	38	1
24	1	40	2
25	1	42	1
26	2	46	1
27	2	52	1
28	1	59	1
			$N = 50$

Table 2.6   Interval Frequency Distribution of Ages for Fifty Hypothetical Persons Convicted of Driving While Intoxicated

Age Interval (years)	Absolute Frequency	Relative Frequency (%)	Cumulative Frequency	Cumulative Relative Frequency (%)
15–19	10	20	10	20
20–24	15	30	25	50
25–29	7	14	32	64
30–34	5	10	37	74
35–39	7	14	44	88
40–44	3	6	47	94
45–49	1	2	48	96
50–54	1	2	49	98
55–59	1	2	50	100
	$N = 50$	100		

Table generated from the data in Table 2.5.

the class interval size or the number of intervals that the frequency table contains. Once one of these has been selected, the other is automatically determined.

3. Select the class interval size. The class interval size refers to the width or span of the interval. The frequency distribution in Table 2.6 is constructed with a class interval size of five. This means that each interval spans a width of five numbers. For example, the interval 15–19 encompasses the numbers: 15, 16, 17, 18, and 19. Some people believe the class interval size is the difference between the upper and lower values of the interval. This is not true. The difference between values gives one less than the interval size (i.e., 19 minus 15 is 4, not 5). Selecting five as the class interval size has appeal because many of us tend to characterize our numerical thinking in terms of fives and tens.[3] It is intuitively easier for us to work with age intervals of 5 or 10 rather than, say, 4 or 9 years.

Once class interval size is selected, the number of intervals is automatically determined. Table 2.6 shows that we needed nine intervals to encompass the lowest and highest ages in our data because we chose a class interval size of five. If we had chosen an interval size of 10, Table 2.6 would contain five intervals.

4. Select the number of intervals. We said in point 2 that one selects either the class interval or the number of intervals. Selecting the number of intervals is more complicated than selecting the class interval. In general, it is preferable that the number of intervals not exceed 15.[4] This is because a long list of class intervals with low frequencies communicates just as poorly as a long list of individual data values, as in Table 2.5. Choosing the number of class intervals means that the interval size must be approximated. This can be done with an equation used to compute the interval size estimate (ISE).

$$\text{ISE} = \frac{\text{Highest data value} + \text{Lowest data value}}{\text{Number of desired intervals}}$$

For example, let's take the information in Table 2.5 and cast it in an interval frequency distribution in which we want 10 class intervals.[5] Given that the youngest and oldest ages are 18 and 59 years, we can estimate the class interval size in the following way.

$$\text{ISE} = \frac{59 - 18}{10} = 4.1$$

If we want 10 intervals to encompass data values that range from 18 to 59 years, a class interval size of 4.1 is necessary. However, a class interval size of 4.1 does not make sense because ages are recorded as whole numbers. Therefore, the ISE must be rounded to the nearest whole integer, which in this case is four.

Table 2.7 shows the interval frequency distribution for the hypothetical age data with a class interval size of four (only the absolute frequencies are shown). However, simple inspection reveals that there are 11 class intervals, not 10. This is not a mistake, but a consequence of rounding the ISE. There would have been 10 intervals if we had chosen a class interval size of 4.1.

Table 2.7 shows that there is a frequency of zero for the interval 48–51. By convention, we try to avoid this. The solution is to reduce the number of desired class intervals from 10 to nine and see if that corrects the problem. Keep in mind, however, that a reduction of class intervals automatically means an increase in the interval size. This is seen in the computation of the ISE for nine class intervals.

$$\text{ISE} = \frac{59 - 18}{9} = 4.56$$

Rounding 4.56 to the nearest whole integer renders an interval size of five, which produces the frequency distribution of Table 2.6.

5. Be sure that the lower value of the class intervals is evenly divisible by the interval size. The reason for this principle is not self-evident, but some readers probably have noticed it operating in our illustrations. Although the lowest age in

Table 2.7 Interval Frequency Distribution of Ages for Fifty Hypothetical Persons Convicted of Driving While Intoxicated

Age Interval (years)	Absolute Frequency	
16–19	10	
20–23	14	
24–27	6	
28–31	5	
32–35	6	
36–39	3	
40–43	3	
44–47	1	
48–51	0	
52–55	1	
56–59	1	$N = 50$

Note: Class interval size is four on the basis of the stated preference for ten intervals. How many intervals are there in this table? Why?

our hypothetical example is 18 years, the first class interval is 15–19 years in Table 2.6 and 16–19 years in Table 2.7. Why not begin both intervals with 18?

Basically, the first class interval of both distributions could begin with the lowest score, but we follow a convention that tells us to be more sophisticated. The convention simply holds that the lower value of each class interval should be evenly divisible by the interval size. If we follow this convention, 18 cannot be the lower value of the first class interval if the interval size is either four or five because 18 is not evenly divisible by four or five.

If the interval size is five, the first class interval should begin with a value that is evenly divisible by five and contains the value of 18. To find this interval, we begin with 18 and count backward until we find a number that is evenly divisible by five. We stop counting when we reach 15. Therefore, the first class interval becomes 15–19 years.

If the interval size is four, the same technique is followed. Starting with 18, we count backward until we reach a number that is evenly divisible by four. That number is 16. Thus the first class interval is 16–19 years.

It is not absolutely necessary to follow this convention, but it ensures that one is working with an interval frequency distribution that technically begins at zero. To help understand this, consider the distribution in Table 2.6. If one were to compute the class intervals that come before 15–19, he or she would eventually reach the interval 0–4.[6] If the first class interval of Table 2.6 were 18–22 years, one could not find a prior class interval that begins with zero. The best he or she could do is to reach the interval −2 to +2, which contains zero but begins with a meaningless value for age.

6. Be flexible. See what communicates best. The reason we use interval frequency distributions is to help us understand our data better and to help others understand it. There is no one best way to display data in an interval frequency distribution. Therefore one needs to work with class intervals until a satisfactory presentation is found.

Exercise 2–2   Interval Frequency Distributions

Assume that the following frequency distribution comes from a survey of inmates conducted by a graduate student about the number of times the inmates had smoked marijuana during their incarceration. The distribution shows the number of inmates by number of years in prison at the time of the survey. Improve the way in which this information is displayed by constructing a year level interval size of three. Then construct an absolute and a relative frequency distribution. Do this using a year level interval size of five. Which of the two interval sizes seems to be best for displaying these data?

No. of Years in Prison	No. of Inmates Reporting Marijuana Use	No. of Years in Prison	No. of Inmates Reporting Marijuana Use
5	10	11	45
6	14	12	52
7	20	13	60
8	20	14	69
9	27	15	75
10	30	16	82

Graphic Techniques

Although tables of frequency distributions are useful, graphic displays often help us understand the information that is carried by our data, especially when we have a large number of observations. The term *graphic techniques* is used herein to describe various ways of drawing pictures or diagrams of frequency distributions. We discuss four graphic techniques that are often used in presenting data. These are pie charts, bar graphs, histograms, and polygons. You are probably familiar with these techniques because they are often used in newspapers, magazines, and reports. Recent issues of the *Uniform Crime Reports*, for example, make extensive use of graphic techniques.

Pie Charts

A useful method for displaying frequency data is to construct a pie chart. This type of chart shows frequencies as portions of a circle that look like pieces of a pie. These charts are best suited for nominal and ordinal variables, although interval and ratio variables also may be used. Pie charts communicate the same information as frequency distributions but in a manner that is more readily grasped. Compare the data in Table 2.8 with the same data displayed in a pie chart in Figure 2.1. The pie chart presents the same information as the relative frequency distribution in Table 2.8 but provides a visualization of the data that aids our interpretation. Both Figure 2.1 and Table 2.8 indicate that larceny-theft accounts for over half of the index crimes, yet the pie chart is better at giving us an appreciation of how that category of crime dominates the others.

Pie charts are drawn by a variety of computer programs, but they are quite easy to construct by hand with a compass, protractor, and straight edge. The size of the slices of a pie chart is determined by a relative frequency distribution. Each crime is represented by a slice, the size of which is determined by the relative frequency of the crime. Each relative frequency (i.e., percentage) is multiplied by $360°$ (the total number of degrees in a circle). This gives the number of degrees within the pie to be allocated for each slice. For example, Table 2.8 shows that aggravated assault makes up 7.29 percent of the index crimes. The slice of the pie chart in Figure 2.1 for that crime is therefore equal to $7.29\% \times 360°$, which is $0.0729 \times 360° = 26.24°$. Likewise, the slice of the pie for burglary is $21.24\% \times 360°$, which is $0.2124 \times 360° = 76.46°$.

Table 2.8   Index Crime in the United States, 1990

Crime Category	Absolute Frequency	Relative Frequency (%)
Murder	23,438	0.16
Forcible rape	102,555	0.71
Robbery	639,271	4.42
Aggravated assault	1,054,863	7.29
Burglary	3,073,909	21.24
Larceny-theft	7,945,670	54.89
Motor vehicle theft	1,635,907	11.30
	$N = 14,475,613$	100.01

Source: *Uniform Crime Reports*, 1990

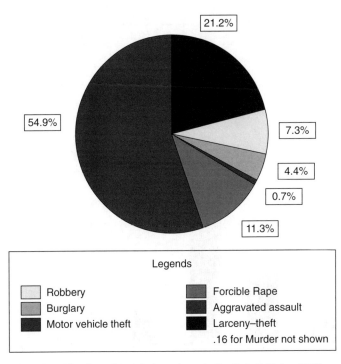

Figure 2.1   Pie chart shows index crimes in the United States, 1990.

Bar Graphs

Another method for displaying frequencies in pictorial form is to draw a bar graph. Bar graphs are constructed with two perpendicular axes. The horizontal axis is used to denote the values of a variable; the vertical axis is used to plot frequencies. Like pie charts, bar graphs are generated from a frequency distribution and are best suited for nominal and ordinal variables.

Figure 2.2 is a bar graph of the index crime data that are displayed in Table 2.8. The different crime types are listed on the horizontal axis and the frequency of each type is plotted as a vertical bar. The height of a bar is in direct relation to the magnitude of a frequency. Thus, taller bars indicate larger frequencies and shorter bars indicate smaller frequencies. Figure 2.2 is constructed with relative frequencies, but absolute frequencies can be used.

Bar graphs convey the same information as pie charts. As can be seen, both Figure 2.1 and Figure 2.2 show that larceny-theft is the most common index crime. Moreover, both illustrations indicate that larceny-theft, burglary, and motor vehicle theft constitute the three main categories of crime. The use of one graphic technique over the other is primarily a matter of taste and preference of presentation.

Histograms

A histogram is a special type of bar graph that is used to display the frequency distribution of a continuous variable. As such, histograms are used for interval and ratio variables. In chapter 1 we discussed how continuous variables are those that can assume an infinite number of values. By convention we indicate the continuous nature of a variable by drawing the bars of a histogram adjacent to each other.

Figure 2.3 is a frequency histogram of the time in office for a hypothetical group of county sheriffs. The figure is drawn from the relative frequency distribution presented in Table 2.9. As it can be seen, the histogram looks like a bar

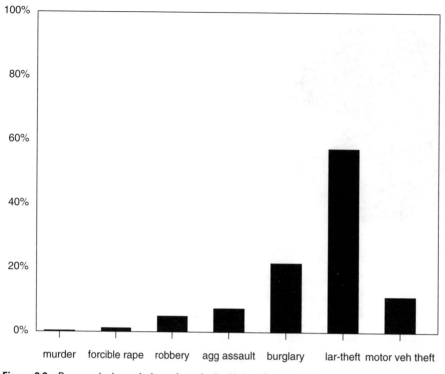

Figure 2.2   Bar graph shows index crimes in the United States, 1990.

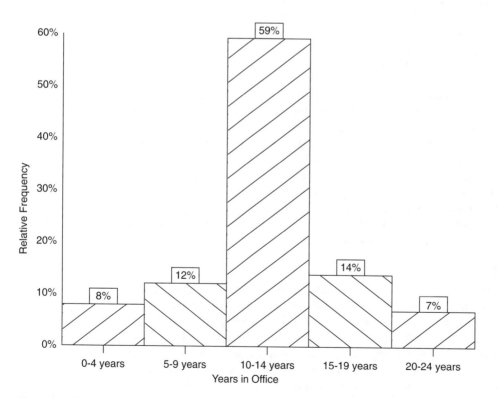

Figure 2.3   Histogram

Table 2.9 Length of Time in Office for a Hypothetical Group of County Sheriffs

Time Interval (years)	Relative Frequency (%)
0–4	8
5–9	12
10–14	59
15–19	14
20–24	7

graph, except for the touching bars. The figure clearly shows (as does the table) that the time frame for the tenure of the county sheriffs ranges from zero[7] to 24 years and that most were in office between 10 and 14 years.

A histogram was chosen to display the frequencies in Table 2.9 because time is a continuous variable. Someone could be in office for 2 years, 2.5 years, or 2.5691846243 years. Even though it would not be practical to measure tenure beyond one or two decimal places, time has a continuous nature. As such, we acknowledge this by joining the bars of the histogram. This is in contrast to the design of a bar graph, in which the free-standing bars indicate the frequency of discrete quantities.

Polygons

A polygon is a type of graph used to display the frequency distribution of a continuous variable. Polygons are similar to histograms, but they are constructed differently. Instead of drawing a bar to denote the frequency of a score or score interval, polygons use a dot. The dots are then connected with straight lines to reveal the shape of the distribution. Frequency polygons are so named because they look like multisided geometric forms.

Figure 2.4 is a polygon of the relative frequency distribution of the data in Table 2.9. One can see that a dot has been placed directly over each score interval to denote the interval frequency. In addition, two extra dots have been placed on the horizontal axis—one before the first interval and one after the last interval. This allows us to bring the tails of the polygon down to the horizontal axis. Although it is not necessary, we do this by convention so that the graph does not appear to be floating above the horizontal axis.

Polygons communicate the same information as histograms. It can be seen that the polygon in Figure 2.4 leads us to the same impressions as the histogram in Figure 2.3. Figure 2.5 shows how the two graphs can be superimposed. This being the case, the use of one graphic technique over the other is essentially a matter of taste and preference of presentation.

Exercise 2–3 Graphing Frequencies

1. Draw a pie chart and a bar graph using the relative frequencies from Exercise 2–1.
2. Draw a histogram and a polygon using the relative frequencies from the interval distribution in Exercise 2–2 that has an interval size of three.

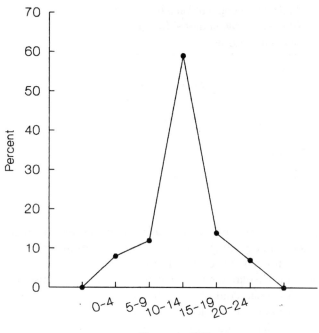

Figure 2.4   Polygon

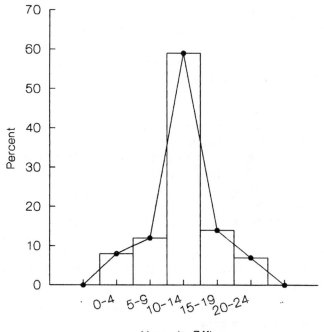

Figure 2.5   Superimposition of graphs.

Properties of Frequency Distributions

Frequency distributions have properties just like other numerical expressions. These properties help one differentiate one frequency distribution from another. The four main properties are: central tendency, variability, skewness, and kurtosis. These may appear to be foreboding names, but they are not difficult to understand and are very useful once they are learned. We present the conceptual basis of these properties at this point. Measures of central tendency and variability are discussed in chapters 3 and 4.

Central Tendency

The concept of central tendency has direct connection with peoples' common experience. For example, if we measured the age of a sample of undergraduate criminal justice students we would expect that the ages would be about 20 years. We could assume that some would be older than 20 and that others would be younger, but the ages, overall, would hover around 20.

Frequency distributions can be differentiated from each other by the way they differ in central tendency. For example, Figure 2.6 presents the frequency distributions of entrance examination scores for two groups of hypothetical police academy applicants: those who have taken the examination before and those who have not.[8] The two graphs differ in central tendency. The applicants who had taken the examination before (graph on the right) had higher test scores than those who did not. The figure shows how the scores of the former are centered at about 70, whereas the scores of the latter are centered at about 50.

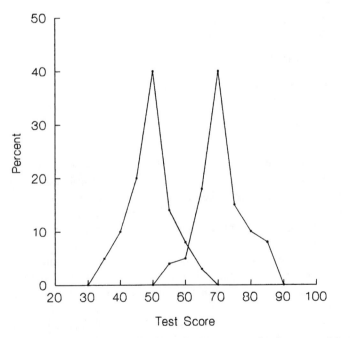

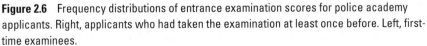

Figure 2.6 Frequency distributions of entrance examination scores for police academy applicants. Right, applicants who had taken the examination at least once before. Left, first-time examinees.

Variability

Variability refers to the degree to which values in a sample or group are different from each other. Variability is the extent to which scores differ from central tendency. Variability is sometimes referred to as *spread*.

Figure 2.7 shows two frequency distributions of police academy entrance examination scores that have similar central tendency but different variability. The dashed line represents applicants who took the examination in 1993; the solid line represents those who took the examination in 1992. Both distributions are centered at about 65, but the 1993 group has less variability or spread than the 1992 group. Scores range from 50 to 80 for the former and from 40 to 90 for the latter.

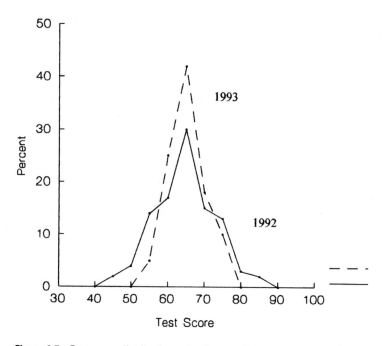

Figure 2.7 Frequency distributions of police academy entrance examination scores that have similar central tendency but different variability.

Skewness

Skewness refers to the symmetry of a frequency distribution. Distributions that are not perfectly symmetric, similar in shape on both sides or halves of the distribution, have some degree of skewness. There are times when we have one or more values that are very different from most of the others in a sample. Such scores are called *outliers*.

Figure 2.8 shows a frequency distribution that skews to the right, or is positively skewed. This means that there are one or more high outliers in the sample. As a result, the upper or right-hand tail of the distribution is dragged upward, producing a graph that is unbalanced. For the police academy entrance examination scores, Figure 2.8 indicates that one examinee (or perhaps a few) did much better than most of the others.

Figure 2.9 shows a frequency distribution that skews to the left, or is negatively skewed. This means that there are one or more low outliers in the sample. As a result, the lower or left-hand tail of the distribution is dragged downward, producing a graph that is clearly unbalanced. Figure 2.9 indicates that one examinee (or perhaps a few) had a score much lower than most of the others.

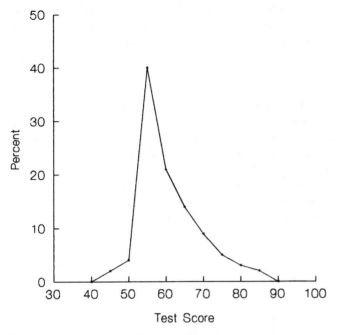

Figure 2.8 Frequency distribution that skews to the right.

Skewness is useful in alerting us to the presence of outliers in a population or sample because we might want to study such cases more closely or we may wish to examine the distribution without the outlier cases. This is common in criminal justice especially, because many of the variables we study have extreme values or outliers. For example, whereas the average time from arrest to case disposition in a particular jurisdiction may be seven months, a small

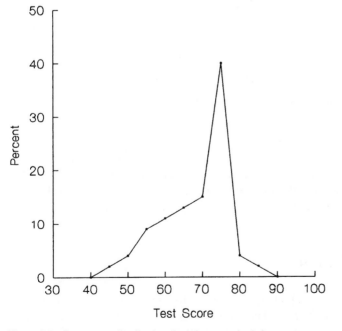

Figure 2.9 Frequency distribution that skews to the left.

percentage of cases far exceed this time frame. Whereas most prison inmates may have a few assault reports, a small percentage have a large number. Similarly, distributions of number of prior arrests, prior commitments to prison, length of sentence, number of felony cases heard, and similar factors are likely to be skewed.

Kurtosis

Kurtosis refers to the curvedness or the peakedness of a distribution. Figure 2.10 shows two distributions of academy entrance examination scores that are similar in central tendency and variability. Most of the scores in both distributions hover around 65 and are spread or vary between 40 and 90. However, they differ in kurtosis. The distribution for the group depicted with the solid line is said to be *leptokurtic*. The prefix *lepto* is a Greek word that means *thin*. Leptokurtic distributions are those that are thinly curved. These distributions characteristically have low frequencies except for one point at which there is a high frequency. This produces a thin spike in the distribution.

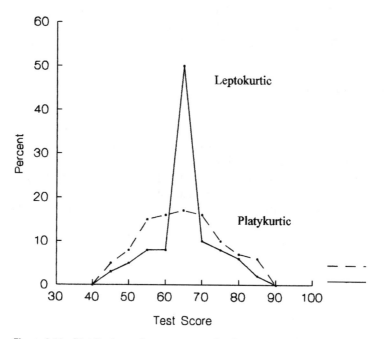

Figure 2.10   Distributions of entrance examination scores that are similar in central tendency and variability.

The distribution for the group depicted with the dashed line is said to be *platykurtic*. The prefix *platy* is from a Greek word that means *flat*. Platykurtic distributions are those that are flatly curved. These distributions have relatively equal frequencies for the data values in a sample. This produces a frequency distribution that looks flat.

Normal Distribution

We want to finish this chapter by briefly discussing a statistical phenomenon called the *normal distribution*.[9] The normal distribution depicted in Figure 2.11 is theoretical in nature and is sometimes called the *normal curve* or the *bell curve*.

The shape of the normal distribution is defined by a mathematical equation. In essence, a normal curve shows us what a frequency distribution would look like under perfect conditions. Perfect conditions mean an infinite number of measurements made at infinitesimally small divisions of a continuous variable. Because infinity is unattainable, normal distribution is theoretical.

Figure 2.11 shows that normal distribution, like all distributions, has central tendency and variability.[10] However, there is no skewness because the distribution is completely symmetric. The degree of kurtosis is such that the graph is perfectly peaked. It is neither too thin nor too flat.

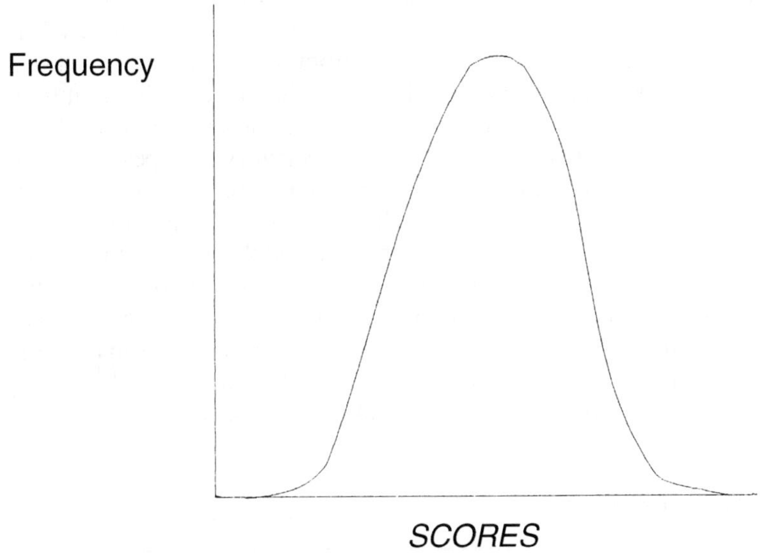

Frequency

SCORES

Figure 2.11   Normal distribution.

Because normal distribution is a mathematical concept, it is not something that one finds with a sample of data. At times, however, one's data approximate normal distribution. For example, the polygons of Figures 2.4, 2.6, and 2.7 have a normal-like (i.e., bell-shaped) appearance. It is not difficult for us to imagine that these polygons with their rough, multifaceted features would ultimately take on the smooth, curved appearance of the normal curve in Figure 2.11 as one approached the perfect conditions mentioned earlier.

The properties and utility of the normal curve are discussed in chapters 8 and 10. For now, it is enough to be aware of normal distribution and to appreciate how it is a model against which we can compare the distributions of our research data. Whether or not a distribution is normal or bell-shaped does not make it better or worse. It is simply a statement of fact.

Summary

Frequency distributions provide researchers with a fundamental way of organizing and describing data. In essence, a frequency distribution shows how often the values in a sample occur. Absolute, relative, cumulative, and cumulative relative frequency distributions are different methods for summarizing frequency information.

From time to time, one may have a large number or range of values to analyze. Depending on the sample size, a frequency distribution of individual data values might not be any more informative than the raw data. When this happens, one can choose *intervals* and produce a frequency distribution of those intervals. Four basic steps in constructing interval frequency distributions are discussed in this chapter.

Graphic displays are useful for displaying frequency information. *Pie charts* and *bar graphs* are best suited for nominal and ordinal data. Frequency *histograms* and *polygons* are best suited for interval and ratio variables.

Frequency distributions have properties like those of other numerical expressions. The four main properties are central tendency, variability, skewness, and kurtosis. *Central tendency* refers to the idea that values in a distribution hover around a central point. *Variability* is the extent to which scores differ among themselves and is defined as the degree to which scores differ from central tendency. *Skewness* refers to the symmetry of a frequency distribution. Values that are different from most of the others in a sample are called *outliers* and can cause a frequency distribution to be highly skewed to the right or to the left. *Kurtosis* is the peakedness or curvedness of a frequency distribution. Distributions that are abnormally thin are called leptokurtic, and those that are abnormally flat are called platykurtic.

The *normal distribution* or curve is mathematical and theoretical, not empirical. This means that we cannot generate a normal curve by way of experiment. Rather, we construct frequency distributions of our data to see if they approximate a normal distribution. In the following chapters, we discuss some of the properties and utility of this most important statistical phenomenon, beginning with chapter 3, in which we discuss measures of central tendency.

Answers to Exercises

Exercise Answer 2–1   Frequency Distributions

Educational Status	Absolute Frequency	Relative Frequency (%)	Cumulative Frequency	Cumulative Relative Frequency (%)
High school	230	45	230	45
Associate's degree	134	26	364	71
Bachelor's degree	97	19	461	90
Master's degree	51	10	512	100
	$N = 512$	100		

Exercise Answer 2–2   Interval Frequency Distributions

No. of Years in Prison	Frequency	Relative Frequency (%)
Using an Interval of 3:		
3–5	10	2
6–8	54	11
9–11	102	20
12–14	181	36
15–17	157	31
	$N = 504$	100

Using an Interval of 5:

5–9	91	18
10–14	256	51
15–19	157	31
	$N = 504$	100

The distribution with an interval size of three is somewhat better because the other distribution is too compact. In other words, too much information is forced into too few intervals when the interval size is five.

Exercise Answer 2–3   Graphing Frequencies

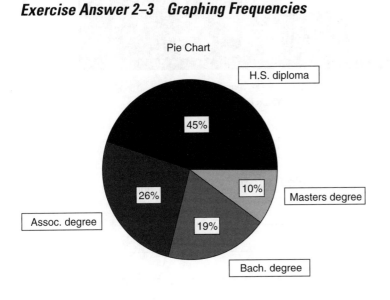

Pie Chart

H.S. diploma
45%
Masters degree 10%
Assoc. degree 26%
Bach. degree 19%

Figure 2.12

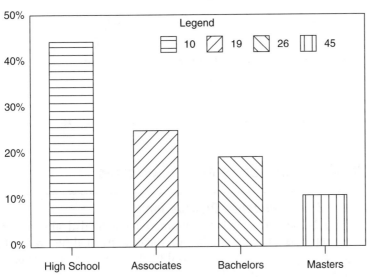

Bar Graph

Legend: 10 19 26 45

High School   Associates   Bachelors   Masters

Figure 2.13

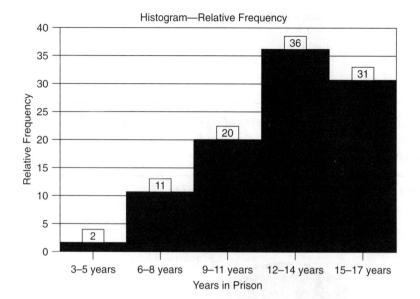

Figure 2.14

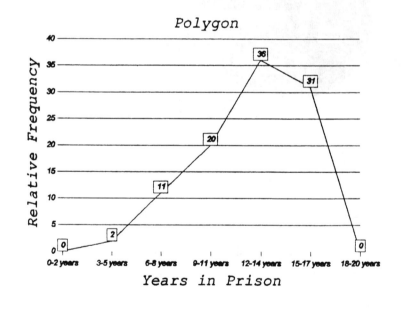

Figure 2.15

Computer Applications for Selected Exercises

Exercise Answer 2–1   Frequency Distributions

The data in Exercise 2–1 are presented as a summary table. Statistical software programs usually require data measured at the person or individual survey level. The data in this exercise are already summarized by division. The original data may have looked like those in Table 2.1A.

Computer Applications Table 2.1A

Staff Number	Division	Degree
1	1	High School Only
2	2	Associate's Degree
3	1	High School Only
4	3	Bachelor's Degree
5	4	Master's Degree
6	4	Associate's Degree
7	3	High School Only
8	1	Associate's Degree
9	2	High School Only
10	2	Bachelor's Degree

The data for each staff member are along a row. The answers to each question are given in the columns. When the data are summarized by division, as are the data in this exercise, they look like those in Table 2.1B.

Computer Applications Table 2.1B

	Staff Member's Education			
Division	High School Only	Assoc. Degree	Bach. Degree	Master's Degree
1	2	1	0	0
2	1	1	1	0
3	1	0	1	0
4	0	1	0	1

To use already summarized information to produce a frequency distribution, you need to tell the statistical program that the data you are entering are already at a summary level.

Each piece of information in the body of the data table for Exercise 2–1 can be represented as a cell in a grid. The combination of division number and educational level acts as the X-Y coordinate pair for the cell. Set up the data so that each coordinate pair in the grid is represented in the Data Editor. Go through the table a second time and enter the number of people who have that educational level in each division. The educational level variable is called *degree*. It has values of 1 through 4, which are labeled in the dialog box (Figure 2.16).

A portion of the completed Data Editor is shown in Figure 2.17.

Tell *SPSS for Windows* that the data are already partly summarized by using the **Weight Cases** command. It is found in the Data menu (Figure 2.18).

Weight the data by the number of people with each educational level (Figure 2.19).

Click on OK to apply the cell weights to the analysis. When this is completed, a Weight On message appears at the bottom right of the screen (Figure 2.20). When you run the Frequencies procedure, *SPSS* knows that you are resummarizing data you received in summary form.

The Frequencies procedure is found in the Statistics menu under Summarize (Figure 2.21).

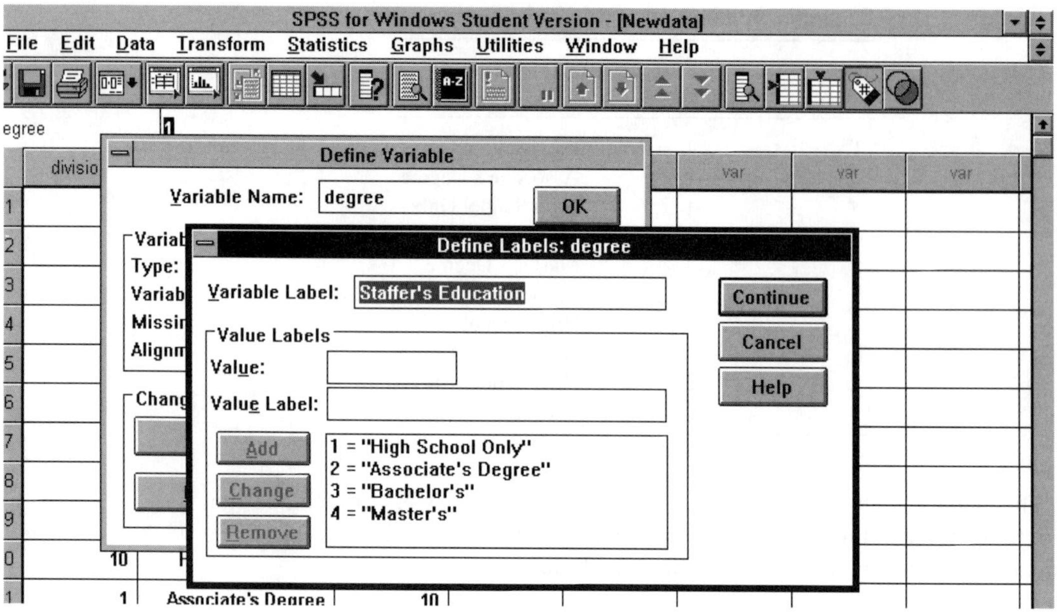

Figure 2.16

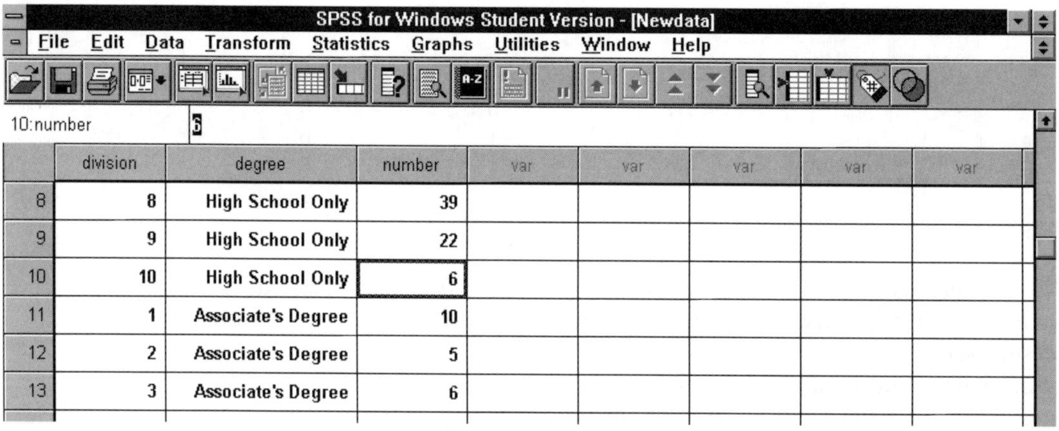

Figure 2.17

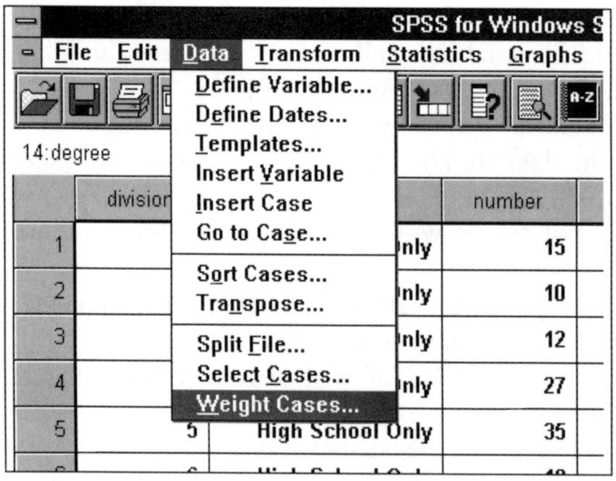

Figure 2.18

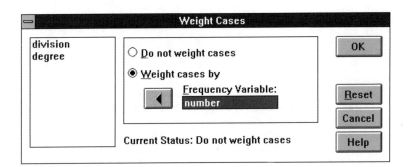

Figure 2.19

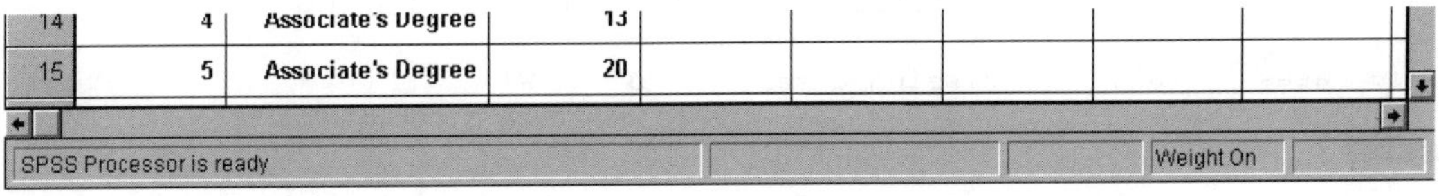

Figure 2.20

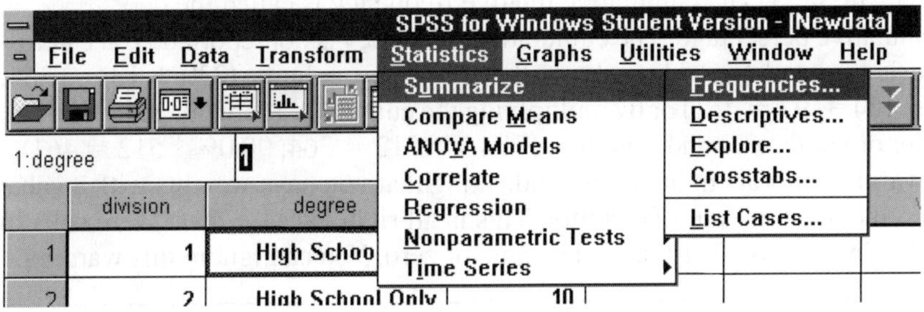

Figure 2.21

To run the Frequencies procedure, push the variable you want to summarize into the center box by highlighting it and then clicking on the large arrow in the middle of the box (Figure 2.22). When the analysis is ready, click on OK to see the results.

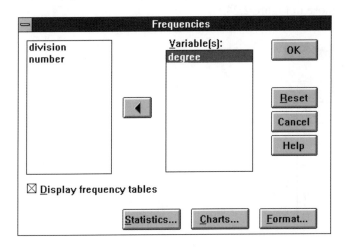

Figure 2.22

The results are shown in Figure 2.23.

```
DEGREE     Staffer's Education


                                              Valid    Cum
Value Label                 Value  Frequency  Percent  Percent  Percent

High School Only              1       230      44.9     44.9     44.9
Associate's Degree            2       134      26.2     26.2     71.1
Bachelor's                    3        97      18.9     18.9     90.0
Master's                      4        51      10.0     10.0    100.0
                                    -------  -------  -------
                    Total             512     100.0    100.0

Valid cases      512    Missing cases      0
```

Figure 2.23

SPSS uses slightly different terminology than our text does. The absolute frequency is called `Frequency` in the SPSS output. The relative frequency is called `Percent` in *SPSS*. The cumulative relative frequency is called the `Cum Percent`, or cumulative percentage. The cumulative frequency is not reported. You can calculate it by hand by adding down the frequency column (230 + 134 = 364; 230 + 134 + 97 = 461) or by multiplying the cumulative percentage by the total number of valid cases and rounding (71.1% * 512 = 364; 90.0% * 512 = 461).

A warning appears in the output indicating that you have weights with a value of zero included in your data editor. This is all right because there were cells in the table in Exercise 2–1 that had a value of zero. You can ignore this warning.

Exercise Answer 2–2   Interval Frequency Distributions

As in Exercise 2–1, the data are given to you in an already summarized form. The raw form would be data on each individual inmate. Again, tell *SPSS* that you are using partially summarized data by using the weight command. For this exercise, enter two columns of data in *SPSS*: one for the number of years in prison and one for the number of inmates reporting marijuana use. Because you are actually studying inmates, weight by the number of inmates to produce the analysis. The data should look like those in Figure 2.24.

	years	number
1:years	5	
1	5	10
2	6	14
3	7	20
4	8	20
5	9	27
6	10	30

Figure 2.24

Running frequencies on the years variable after weighting by the number of inmates reproduces the original data. First show the Frequencies dialog box (Figure 2.25).

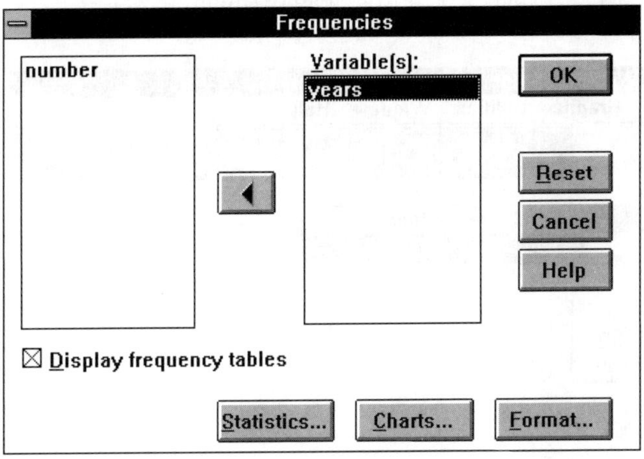

Figure 2.25

Use the output in Figure 2.26 to verify that your data entry was correct. Look at the values in the first two columns. The numbers in the Value column represent the number of years in prison. Value Labels is not used because when the natural form of the data is a number (as it is for years), it is usually redundant to label it. The number of inmates reporting marijuana use is in the Frequency column. Your output should match the data in the table for Exercise 2–2.

Now that you have the data, you can regroup it. Do that by creating a new column in the data set that contains codes that represent each group. Create a

YEARS

Value Label	Value	Frequency	Percent	Valid Percent	Cum Percent
	5	10	2.0	2.0	2.0
	6	14	2.8	2.8	4.8
	7	20	4.0	4.0	8.7
	8	20	4.0	4.0	12.7
	9	27	5.4	5.4	18.1
	10	30	6.0	6.0	24.0
	11	45	8.9	8.9	32.9
	12	52	10.3	10.3	43.3
	13	60	11.9	11.9	55.2
	14	69	13.7	13.7	68.8
	15	75	14.9	14.9	83.7
	16	82	16.3	16.3	100.0
		-------	-------	-------	
	Total	504	100.0	100.0	

Valid cases   504   Missing cases   0

Figure 2.26

grouping column for each grouping scheme. Then ask for a year summary using the new grouping variable.

Start with the first request: to group the inmates into 3-year intervals. Use the `Recode` function from the `Transform` menu to create the groups. For this example, use the recode `Into Different Variables` feature (Figure 2.27).

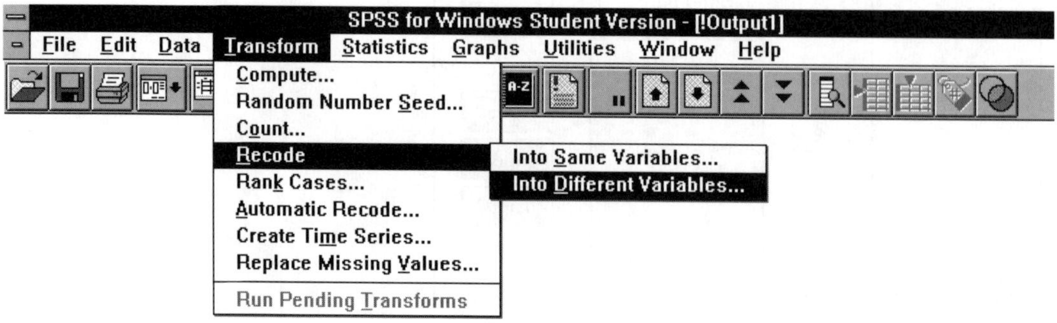

Figure 2.27

Use the large arrow in the center of the dialog box to move the raw form of the grouping variable into active position in the center of the box. Then assign a new name and label for the new grouping variable. When that is done, click on `Change` to assign the new information to the new variable (Figure 2.28).

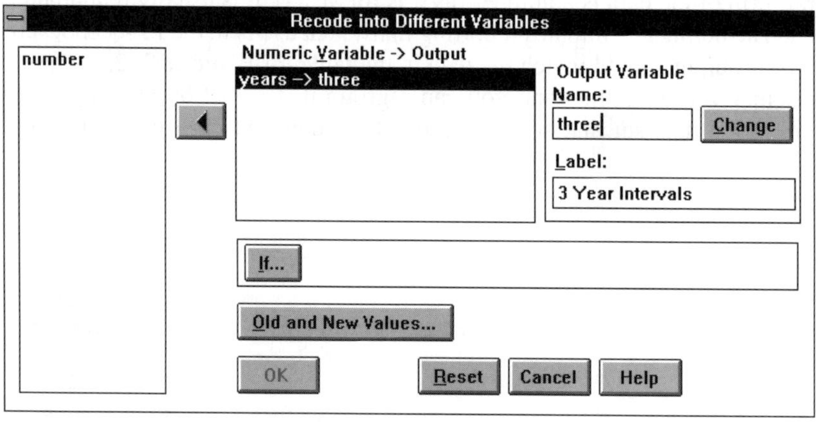

Figure 2.28

Now click on `Old Value` and `New Value` to create the new grouping or interval scheme (Figure 2.29).

The old values are represented on the left. The new values are represented on the right. For this exercise, use the `Range` feature on the left to create the 3-year groupings. Each range forms a category in our new grouping variable. Enter the category number in the `New Value` position on the right. Use the mouse to reposition the cursor in the box in the upper right. After you enter the new value, click on `Add` to add that specification to the list. Repeat the process for each interval. The dialog box in Figure 2.29 shows what the completed scheme should look like. Now click on `Continue` in this dialog and `OK` in the next one to load the new column into the Data Editor (Figure 2.30).

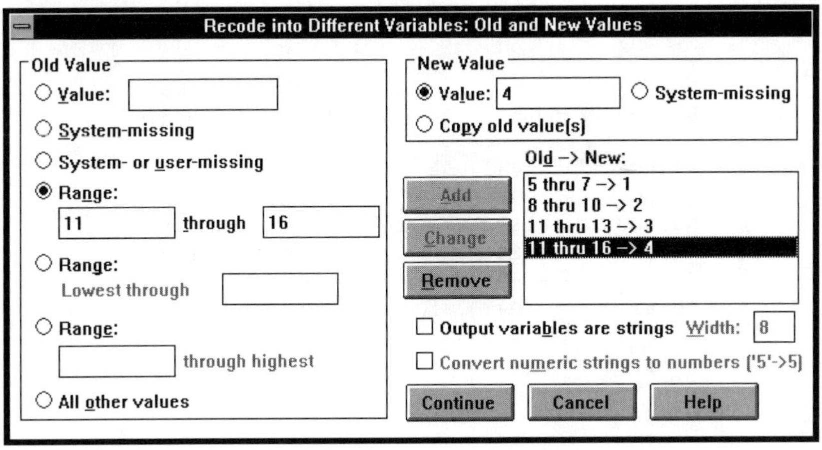

Figure 2.29

Your Data Editor should look like the one in Figure 2.30. You can label the year intervals by double-clicking on the column heading and filling in the information on the `Labels` sub-dialog box.

Now check the frequencies for the 3-year intervals. Go to the `Statistics` menu and choose `Summarize` and then `Frequencies`. This time, run the frequencies on the new grouping variable. The results are shown in Figure 2.31.

If your total number of valid cases is not 504, make sure that you used the Weight procedure before running the analysis. The example divides the data into 3-year groups without checking whether the result makes sense.

Repeat the recode process to make a new grouping variable for 5-year intervals. The data displayed in Figure 2.32 follow the form discussed in this book for

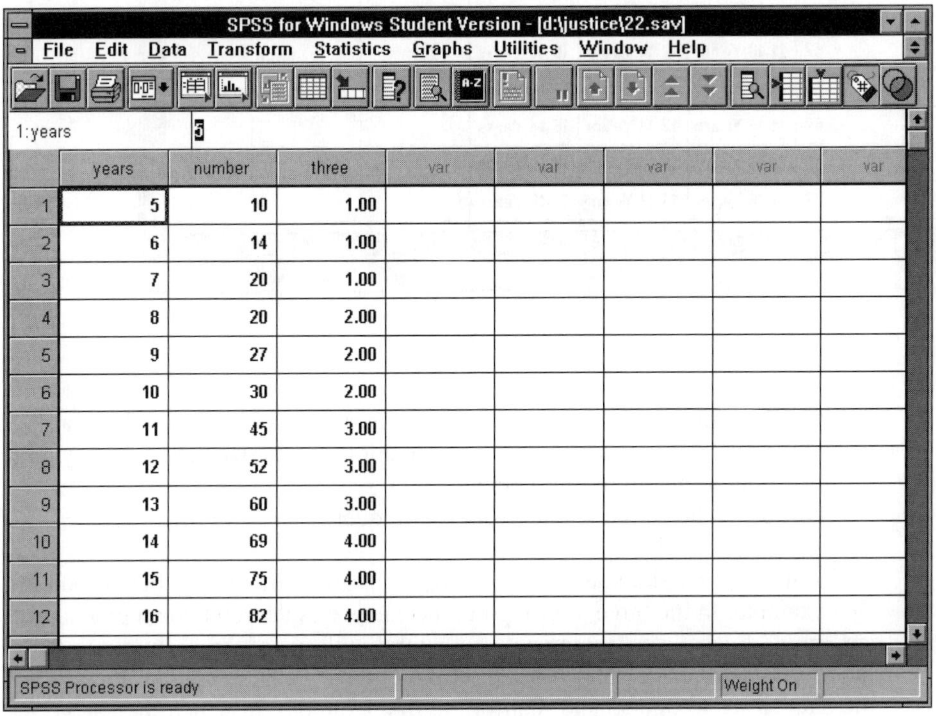

Figure 2.30

```
THREE     3-Year Intervals

                                                        Valid     Cum
Value Label           Value  Frequency  Percent   Percent   Percent

5-7 Years              1.00         44      8.7       8.7       8.7
8-10 Years             2.00         77     15.3      15.3      24.0
11-13 Years            3.00        157     31.2      31.2      55.2
14-16 Years            4.00        226     44.8      44.8     100.0
                                -------  -------   -------
                      Total        504    100.0     100.0

Valid cases     504     Missing cases      0
```

Figure 2.31

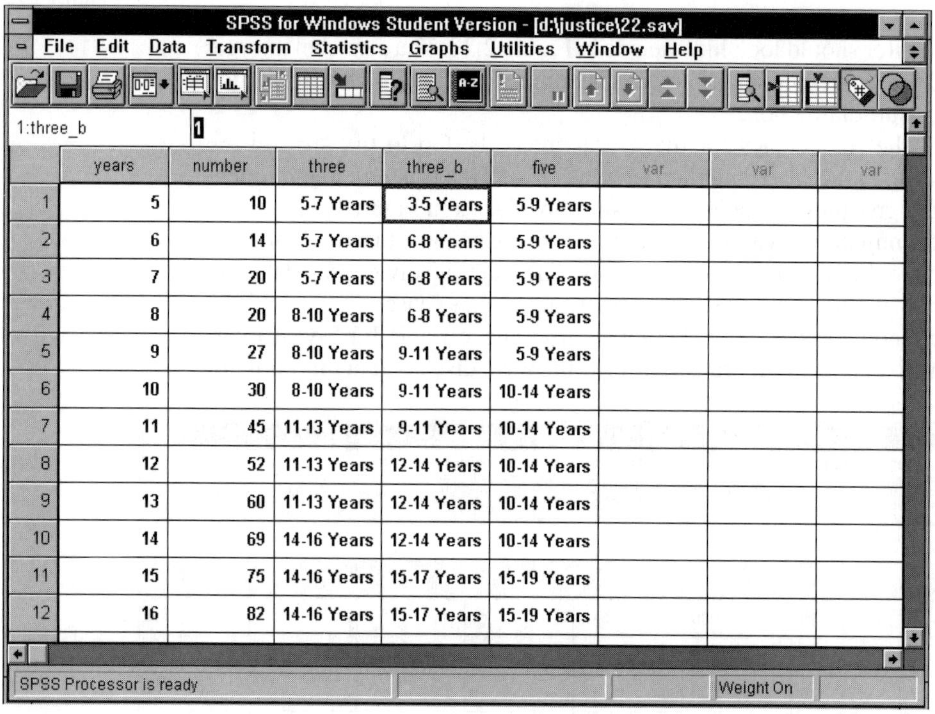

	years	number	three	three_b	five	var	var	var
1	5	10	5-7 Years	3-5 Years	5-9 Years			
2	6	14	5-7 Years	6-8 Years	5-9 Years			
3	7	20	5-7 Years	6-8 Years	5-9 Years			
4	8	20	8-10 Years	6-8 Years	5-9 Years			
5	9	27	8-10 Years	9-11 Years	5-9 Years			
6	10	30	8-10 Years	9-11 Years	10-14 Years			
7	11	45	11-13 Years	9-11 Years	10-14 Years			
8	12	52	11-13 Years	12-14 Years	10-14 Years			
9	13	60	11-13 Years	12-14 Years	10-14 Years			
10	14	69	14-16 Years	12-14 Years	10-14 Years			
11	15	75	14-16 Years	15-17 Years	15-19 Years			
12	16	82	14-16 Years	15-17 Years	15-19 Years			

Figure 2.32

dividing the groups (`three_b` and `five`). What rule was violated in the example using the variable called *three*? Is the information summarized more clearly with one of the other two grouping schemes?

Figure 2.33 shows the results from the frequencies run for the `three_b` and `five` variables.

The new 3-year summary using three_b to regroup the data is better than the first example. In the three_b grouping, the categories descend down to a natural zero point. Each 3-year increment is a natural multiple of three. In other words, the beginning of each interval is a multiple of three (3, 6, 9, 12, 15). This makes the data easier to understand than in the first example, in which the categories seemed to have arbitrary start points (5, 8, 11, 14).

THREE_B   Number of Inmates Using Marijuana

| | | | | Valid | Cum |
Value Label		Value	Frequency	Percent	Percent	Percent
3-5 Years	1.00	10	2.0	2.0	2.0
6-8 Years	2.00	54	10.7	10.7	12.7
9-11 Years	3.00	102	20.2	20.2	32.9
12-14 Years	4.00	181	35.9	35.9	68.8
15-17 Years	5.00	157	31.2	31.2	100.0
			-------	-------	-------
	Total	504	100.0	100.0	

Valid cases   504   Missing cases   0

- -

FIVE   Number of Inmates Using Marijuana

| | | | | Valid | Cum |
Value Label		Value	Frequency	Percent	Percent	Percent
5-9 Years	1.00	91	18.1	18.1	18.1
10-14 Years	2.00	256	50.8	50.8	68.8
15-19 Years	3.00	157	31.2	31.2	100.0
			-------	-------	-------
	Total	504	100.0	100.0	

Valid cases   504   Missing cases   0

Figure 2.33

The 5-year grouping has categories that start with multiples of 5. Which table is easier to understand? The 3-year breakdown or the 5-year breakdown? Which would you use? Why?

Notes

1. We did not have to begin at the top of Table 2.3 to construct the cumulative frequency distribution. We could have begun at the end of the table and added the frequencies going from bottom to top. In constructing a cumulative frequency table one needs to decide whether it is more meaningful to add frequencies top-down or bottom-up. In the case of nominal variables (such as crime type), it does not really matter which way one adds the absolute frequencies.

2. A useful rule in data analysis is that if the technique you are using does not describe a situation to your satisfaction, use another technique.

3. This is one of the reasons why the metric system of measurement is popular among scientists. The metric system is based on multiples of 10.

4. There is nothing mystical about the limit of 15 class intervals; it simply tends to be a good rule to follow. More than 15 intervals may be needed if many cases are spread over a wide range of data values.

5. There is nothing special about ten class intervals. We are simply giving in to our tendency to think in terms of fives and tens. We could have chosen any number of class intervals that we deemed appropriate.

6. The intervals that come before 15–19 are not necessary for our data but they exist technically.

7. The unit of time for the data in Table 2.9 is one year. Thus the zero in the interval 0–4 stands for sheriffs in office less than one year.

8. It should be noted that the frequency distributions in Figures 2.6 through 2.10 have individual scores plotted on the horizontal axis instead of score intervals. This is possible with large samples, as would be expected with academy applicants.

9. This distribution has been studied and used for more than two centuries and is fundamental to various aspects of contemporary data analysis. The French mathematician Abraham De Moivre (1738) is credited with the discovery of the normal distribution. His initial work was later expanded upon and popularized by three other mathematicians: Thomas Simpson (1755), Pierre Laplace (1810), and Carl Gauss (1809).

10. The term *normal distribution* does not stand for a single entity but for a general form of a frequency distribution that can have a variety of values for central tendency and variability.

References

De Moivre, A. 1738. *The Doctrine of Chances.* 2d ed. London: Woodfall.

Gauss, C. F. 1809. *Theoria motus corporum celestium.* Hamburg: Perthes et Besser. Translated by C. H. Davis. 1857. *Theory of motion of the heavenly bodies moving about the sun in conic sections.* Boston: Little, Brown.

Grimm, L. G. 1993. *Statistical Applications for the Behavioral Sciences.* New York: John Wiley & Sons.

Laplace, P. S. 1810. Memoire sur les approximations des formules qui sont fonctions de tres grands nombres et sur leur application aux probabilites. Memoires de l'Academie des sciences de Paris, 353–415, 559–565.

McCall, R. B. 1990. *Fundamental Statistics for Behavioral Sciences.* San Diego, CA: Harcourt, Brace, Jovanovich.

Simpson, T. 1755. A letter to the right honourable George Earl of Macclesfield, president of the Royal Society, on the advantage of taking the mean of a number of observations, in practical astronomy. *Philosophical Translations of the Royal Society of London* 49:82–93.

Crime in the U.S., 1990. Washington, DC: Federal Bureau of Investigation.

3. Measures of Central Tendency

Community-Oriented Policing: Does It Work?

It is becoming one of the hottest trends in policing—community-oriented policing (COP). Your city and police department have been testing COP for more than a year in six districts. Recently the mayor and city council have been discussing whether to provide funding for expansion of COP to the remaining districts.

During a class meeting of your police-community relations course the subject of COP and its effectiveness arises. Many of your classmates don't believe COP is effective, that it's a waste of money, and should not be expanded. You take issue with this stance because you've been living in one of the COP test districts since it began. You argue that COP has been effective in reducing crime. Although you feel strongly about your position and attempt to make a case, many of your classmates are not convinced and will not accept your observations and perceptions and want proof that COP has been effective. Your instructor agrees with the other students and suggests that you provide some statistical evidence that COP is working. In your aroused state you accept the challenge. As class is ending, however, you begin to wonder, just how am I going to support my position? What type of evidence can I supply?

Before leaving the classroom you approach the instructor and relate your concern. The instructor suggests you provide a statistical summation with measures of central tendency of reported crime for the year (by month) in your district and the other COP districts in comparison with the non-COP districts. You thank the instructor for the advice and leave the classroom. Yet as you leave the classroom you realize you have no idea what measures of central tendency are. Off to the library you go.

Measures of Central Tendency

Chapters 1 and 2 discuss a variety of techniques to organize raw data. Those chapters show that data do not usually appear neatly organized; the first task is to learn how to describe data in a coherent and orderly way. Problem-solving techniques include frequency distributions and graphs, which allow us to gain a much better sense of the data we collect. These procedures help us to better understand and interpret data.

Chapter 2 begins with a large set of numbers and reduces them to a smaller set of numbers. It starts with 20 offense reports and reduces them to a frequency distribution that contains only five numerical categories (see Table 2.1). It also takes a set of 50 ages and reduces them to nine numerical categories (see Table 2.6). We can reduce a group of numbers even further using as few as three or four numbers that fully describe the essential elements of an entire distribution. These descriptors or measures fall into two classes: *measures of central tendency*, which describe the common or summary values in a distribution, and *measures of variability*, which describe how values in a distribution differ from each other. Chapter 3 examines measures of central tendency. Chapter 4 describes measures of variability.

In addition to describing a distribution with only a few numbers, measures of central tendency also solve a practical problem that exists in many agencies: How do we describe a distribution to someone who does not have the data in front of him or her? For example, the chief of police calls you and wants to know the types of crimes that citizens are likely to report in a particular police district. Reading the numbers in a frequency distribution to summarize these crimes would be cumbersome and uninformative. However, reporting summary statistics (i.e., measures of central tendency) would communicate a great deal of information in a brief amount of time. Measures of central tendency are particularly useful in describing large distributions.

The most common measures of central tendency are the *mean, median,* and *mode*. We discuss each of these measures to learn what they are, how they are calculated, how they are interpreted, and most important, what each contributes to the task of describing a distribution. We pay most attention to the mean because it has important statistical properties in procedures discussed in later chapters.

The Mean

The mean, commonly known as the *average*, is an important and useful statistic. When we state that the average age of college freshman in the United States is 18.6 years, we are communicating that this number is representative or typical of all the ages in the distribution. Statisticians use the word *mean*, rather than the more familiar word *average*, to refer to the arithmetic mean as differentiated from other means such as the geometric mean or harmonic mean, which are also averages.

Calculation of the Mean

Most of us have calculated a mean at one time or another. If we asked you to calculate the average age of students in your statistics class, you would first add all the ages and divide by the number of students in the class. Stated another way, you would sum all the values of the variable and divide by the number of observations. If we designate the variable values (in this case, ages) with the letter x and indicate that you should add the values with a symbol call a summation sign, which looks like this Σ, we could describe the procedures to calculate the mean in the language of the following mathematical formula:

$$\overline{X} = \frac{\Sigma X}{N}$$

As you see in the equation, the mean is represented by a symbol called the *x bar*.

The following example is meant to help you understand this procedure more clearly. Table 3.1 presents data on the number of bank robberies in the western United States in 1990. The question is: What was the mean number of bank robberies per state in 1990?

We begin by summing the values of the variable (bank robberies) and then divide the sum by the number of observations. The values are expressed as numbers per state, and there are 13 states or observations. Expressed as a formula:

Table 3.1   Bank Robberies in Western States, 1990

State	No. of Bank Robberies
Alaska	11
Arizona	224
California	2,656
Colorado	69
Hawaii	17
Idaho	1
Montana	5
Nevada	68
New Mexico	63
Oregon	171
Utah	21
Washington	218
Wyoming	1

Source: FBI, *Bank Crime Statistics,* 1990

$$\overline{X} = \frac{\Sigma X}{N} = \frac{3,525}{13} = 271.2$$

The mean is the number of bank robberies that summarizes the observations across the 13 western states in 1990; its value is 271.2 per state. Calculation and interpretation of the mean are straightforward. The mean is one of the most frequently calculated and used statistics.

Measures of central tendency communicate important information about a distribution with only a few numbers. We must be sure that what we communicate, even if accurate, is not misleading. The fact that the mean number of bank robberies in these states in 1990 was 271.2 per state is accurate with respect to the calculation of the mean (i.e., the sum the values of the variable divided by the number of observations is 271.2). However, we must ask ourselves whether this number accurately describes this particular distribution. In other words, when we examine the distribution, does the mean number of bank robberies in these states really capture the overall nature of the observations in this distribution?

Exercise 3–1   *Calculating the Mean*

As part of the report supporting your stance for COP you have gathered lots of crime data about your district. Calculate the means for selected data sets.

Year	No.
Homicides, 1990–1994	
1990	18
1991	18
1992	25
1993	16
1994	11
Index Crimes, 1989–1994	
1989	672
1990	808
1991	629

1992	690
1993	880
1994	751

Arrest Rates (per 100,000), 1985–1994

1985	16.2
1986	12.1
1987	15.2
1988	14.6
1989	15.1
1990	15.6
1991	14.9
1992	16.4
1993	16.4
1994	12.1

The Median

Inspection of Table 3.1 reveals that a number of extreme values were included in the distribution. For example, California had 2,656 bank robberies, whereas Idaho and Wyoming had only one each. In fact, most of the values were not even close to the mean. To report only the mean value, although accurately calculated, is somewhat misleading. We need to use another measure of central tendency either in place of or in addition to the mean to help us get closer to a more complete representation of all the numbers. The median is such a measure.

We define the median as the middle value in an array of values. The word *median* actually means *middle*, such as the median strip of a highway. What the median is and its usefulness are best illustrated with an example.

To find the median of a distribution we must first place the values in an array. An *array* is a listing of values that have been ordered from lowest to highest. When we array the data in Table 3.1 from lowest to highest we get the following:

$$1, 1, 5, 11, 17, 21, \mathbf{63}, 68, 69, 171, 218, 224, 2656$$

There are 13 values in the data set. The median is the middle value in the array of values, in this example 63. (The number 63 is highlighted in the array to show that it is indeed the middle value. Six values lie below 63 and six above.) The median of this distribution is 63 bank robberies (i.e., half the states had fewer than 63 bank robberies and half had more than 63). The median presents an entirely different picture of this distribution than would have been obtained from use of only the mean to describe it. Because this distribution is so varied, it is best to report both the mean and the median. We also want to measure its variability, which is discussed in chapter 4.

Another example (Table 3.2) is presented to help us understand the meaning of the median and addresses the problem of how to calculate the median from an even number of values. These data are already arrayed from lowest to highest, so all we need to do to find the median is locate the middle value. However, because the distribution has an even number of observations (i.e., cities), no immediately obvious middle value exists. In this case, we must find the average of the two middle values. The two middle values are the fifth from the top, which is 2,381, and the fifth from the bottom, which is 2,992. The average of these two is $(2,381 + 2,992) \div 2 = 2,685.5$ or 2,686. The median of this distribution is 2,686

Table 3.2   Number of Police Officers in Selected U.S. Cities

City	No. of Officers
Memphis	1,264
San Diego	1,704
San Francisco	1,864
Phoenix	1,888
Dallas	2,381
Baltimore	2,992
Houston	4,323
Detroit	4,944
Philadelphia	6,519
Los Angeles	7,305

Source: *Source Book of Criminal Justice Stats,* 1990

police officers. Half the cities had fewer than 2,686 officers, and half had more than 2,686.

Exercise 3–2   Identifying Medians

Using the data sets from Exercise 3–1, array and identify the medians for each set.

The Mode

The mode is simply the most frequently occurring value in a distribution. Consider the following hypothetical distribution of grades on a police promotion examination:

$$98, 95, 94, 88, 88, 88, 88, 80, 81, 77, 72$$

The most frequently occurring grade, the mode, in this distribution is 88. The mode in Table 3.1 is 1. However, many distributions do not have a mode because none of the values are the same, that is, repeated. This is the case in Table 3.2. Some distributions may have more than one mode. For example, a distribution such as the following

$$4, 5, 6, 6, 6, 7, 8, 9, 10, 10, 10, 10$$

has two modes, 6 and 10. This is known as a bimodal distribution.

Exercise 3–3   Identifying Modes

What are the modes for the data sets in Exercise 3–1?

Characteristics of the Mean and Median

A number of characteristics of the mean and median are important in helping us to decide which measure to use in reporting the central tendency of a distribution. The first characteristic is that the mean is sensitive to extreme values, but the median is sensitive primarily to the number of values. This point is demonstrated in the following example.

The following are the current salaries of six criminal justice graduates:

$22,000, $21,000, $21,000, $23,000, $19,500, $22,400

To calculate the *mean* of this distribution we sum the values and then divide by the number of observations. The mean salary is $21,483. To calculate the *median*, we array the values and then identify the middle value in the array. The values from lowest to highest produce the following array:

19,500, 21,000, 21,000, 22,000, 22,400, 23,000

Because there are an even number of observations, the median is the average of the two middle values—21,000 and 22,000, which is 21,500. Half the students in this distribution earned a salary of more than $21,500 and half earned a salary of less than $21,500. The mean and median are virtually identical, so reporting either one accurately describes the distribution as a whole.

Now we add a seventh criminal justice graduate, who is earning a salary considerably higher than the rest of the group ($500,000). The mean salary in this distribution then becomes $89,843 and its median becomes $22,000. The addition of an extreme value has had a dramatic effect on the mean but has only slightly affected the median. If we replace the seventh salary in the distribution with that of a student who has not yet found a full-time job and made only $200 last year, the mean salary would drop to $18,443 but the median would remain the same.

The mean is affected by extreme values. When a distribution contains extreme values, the median is a better representative of most of the scores than the mean is. When reviewing data in which the mean and median differ sharply, be alert for extreme values.

A second characteristic of the mean is that it is the best guess we can make about any value in a distribution that does not contain any extreme scores. If we were told that the mean age of judges in this state was 49.3, then our best guess of Judge Walker's age would be 49.3. The reason for this is found in the definition of the mean. The mean is the sum of all the values in a distribution divided by the total number of observations. If we had to select one value, we would be better off selecting a summarizing value that takes into account all the scores in the distribution.

Note that we did not say that the mean is always a typical score, but that it is a quantity that usefully characterizes all the scores in a distribution. We define the mean as a *summarizing* quantity rather than a *typifying* value, because sometimes the mean is a number that is not included in an actual list of values, and sometimes it is very different from the other numbers in a distribution.

A third characteristic of the mean is that it is somewhat of a focal or balancing point in a distribution. When we subtract the mean from every score $(x - \bar{x})$, we calculate a deviation score (how far the score deviates from the mean). If we add all the deviation scores and are careful to retain all the pluses and minuses that result, we find for every distribution that the sum of the deviation scores always equals zero. For example, the mean of the set of scores 6, 8, and 10 is 8. The sum of the deviation scores is $(6 - 8) + (8 - 8) + (10 - 8)$ or $(-2) + (0) + (2) = 0$. Thus the sum of the deviation scores equals 0. This property of the mean becomes important in understanding statistical formulas presented in later chapters.

A final point about the mean is that it is represented by a different symbol depending on whether it is the mean of a sample or the mean of a population. The mean of a sample is usually designated x̄, and the mean of a population is designated μ, which is the lower case Greek letter mu.

Computing the Mean from Grouped Data

To compute the mean of a distribution we sum the values of the variable and then divide by the number of observations. This procedure can be confusing when we try to compute the mean from data in frequency distributions. Frequency distributions are commonly presented without a mean (or other measures of central tendency), which makes attempts to compare distributions difficult. It is useful to compute the mean of frequency distributions, but this calculation requires additional steps.

For example, examine the distribution in Table 3.3. What is the mean number of weekend homicides per city? What numbers do we add and divide? What is the divisor? To avoid errors in these types of problems, we proceed by answering this series of questions:

1. What is the variable? The variable we are studying is the number of weekend murders.

2. What are the values of the variable? The values of the variable are 0, 1, 2, 3, 4, and 5 weekend murders.

3. What are the observations? The observations are the number of cities—2, 17, 38, 21, 9, and 1. The next step is to interpret the pairs of numbers in the distribution (i.e., the joint numbers of values and observations). In this case, two cities had no weekend murders, 17 cities had one weekend murder, two cities had 38 weekend murders, and so forth.

4. How many weekend murders occurred? Two cities had no weekend murders $(2 \times 0 = 0)$; 17 cities had one $(1 \times 17 = 17)$; 38 cities had two $(38 \times 2 = 76)$; 21 cities had three $(21 \times 3 = 63)$; nine cities had four $(9 \times 4 = 36)$; and one city had five weekend murders $(1 \times 5 = 5)$. Therefore, the total number of weekend murders was $0 + 17 + 76 + 63 + 36 + 5 = 197$.

5. How many cities were in the study? In this case, $2 + 17 + 38 + 21 + 9 + 1$, which sums to 88. The mean number of weekend murders per city is the number of weekend murders divided by the number of cities, which is $197 \div 88 = 2.2$ weekend murders per city. This procedure can be expressed in the formula shown at the top of the next page:

Table 3.3 Number of Weekend Homicides in Major American Cities

No. of Weekend Homicides	No. of Cities
0	2
1	17
2	38
3	21
4	9
5	1

Source: Hypothetical data

$$\overline{X} = \frac{\Sigma(fx)}{\Sigma N}$$

The formula tells us to first multiply each value (x) by its frequency (f) then add the products and divide by the sum of the observations (N). The comparisons are summarized in Table 3.4.

Table 3.4   Computation of the Mean for the Data in Table 3.3

No. of Weekend Homocides	No. of Cities	Product fx
0	2	0
1	17	17
2	38	76
3	21	63
4	9	36
5	1	5
Sum	88	197

Exercise 3–4   *Means for Grouped Data*

Calculate the mean for each set of grouped data.

1. Auto thefts in selected police districts in your city for one month. (Your COP district* is among the groups with the lowest amount of thefts.)

No. of Auto Thefts	No. of Districts
15	6*
20	9
25	15
30	4
35	2

   *Your district.

2. Number of police officers on foot patrol in six selected patrol districts (including yours) and burglaries reported for one month.

No. of Foot Patrol Officers	No. of Burglaries
0	15
7	8
12	22
19	35
24	28
31*	13

   *Your district

Computing the Median from Grouped Data

In the distribution in Table 3.4, the 88 values are arrayed from 0 to 5. Their frequencies indicate that listing all the values results in a long list that contains two 0s, seventeen 1s, thirty-eight 2s, twenty-one 3s, nine 4s, and one 5. The middle value in this array of 88 values would fall between the 44th and 45th values in the list. The 44th and the 45th values are among the 2s because $2 + 17 = 19$ and $19 + 38 = 57$. Therefore, the median is two murders per weekend. To demonstrate that this method is valid we list the values and identify the 44th and 45th values. Such a list looks like the following:

0, 0, 1, 1, 1, 1, 1, 1, 1, 1, 1, 1, 1, 1, 1, 1, 1, 1, 1, 2, 2, 2, 2, 2, 2, 2, 2, 2, 2, 2,
2, 2, 2, 2, 2, 2, 2, 2, 2, 2, 2, 2, 2, 2, 2, 2, 2, 2, 2, 2, 2, 2, 2, 2, 2, 2, 2, 3, 3,
3, 3, 3, 3, 3, 3, 3, 3, 3, 3, 3, 3, 3, 3, 3, 3, 3, 3, 3, 4, 4, 4, 4, 4, 4, 4, 4, 4, 5

$$\bar{x} = \frac{197}{88} = 2.2 \text{ homicides}$$

The 44th and 45th values in the list are both 2s. In this example, the mean number of weekend murders and the median are fairly close in value. What is the modal number of murders in this distribution?

Exercise 3–5 Median and Mode for Grouped Data
Using the data sets in Exercise 3–4, identify the median and mode for each set.

Estimating the Mean of an Interval Frequency Distribution

Computing the mean from an interval frequency distribution can be tricky, but the techniques we just learned also can be used here. In chapter 2 we presented an interval distribution of the number of years county sheriffs were in office. Adding absolute frequencies results in Table 3.5. What is the mean number of years in office? We proceed by asking our series of questions:

1. What is the variable? In this case, number of years in office.

2. What are the values of the variable? In this case, we are not sure because all we have are intervals of five years each. We do not know how many of each year

Table 3.5 Length of Time in Office of County Sheriffs

Time Interval (years)	Frequency
0–4	22
5–9	33
10–14	162
15–19	38
20–24	19
	274

Source: Hypothetical data.

Table 3.6   Time in Office of County Sheriffs

Length of Time (years)	Midpoint (x)	Frequency (f)	Product (fx)
0–4	2	22	44
5–9	7	33	231
10–14	12	162	1,944
15–19	17	38	646
20–24	22	19	418
Sum		274	3,283

there are in each interval. For example, we know from Table 3.5 that 22 sheriffs have been in office from less than 1 year to 4 years, but we do not know the specific time for any one sheriff. In the previous example, we multiplied the value (x) by its frequency (f). In the present situation, x is an interval, not a specific number. We have 22 sheriffs, so we assume that some have been in office less than 1 year, some have been in office 1 year, some 2 years, some 3 years, and some 4 years. If we had to speculate on the number of years of service for any particular sheriff in this group of 22, what would be our best guess?

Our best guess is the average of the upper and lower limits of the interval. This average is called the *midpoint of the interval* and represents the value of the variable for the individuals within that interval. Therefore, the midpoint for the interval 0 to 4 is $(0 + 4) \div 2 = 2$. The midpoint for the interval 5 to 9 is $(5 + 9) \div 2 = 7$, and so on. Each of the midpoints for the intervals in this example is listed in Table 3.6.

3. What are the observations? In this case, sheriffs. Reading the first two columns of numbers in the first line, we see that 22 sheriffs had an estimate of 2 years in office. The second line reads that 33 sheriffs had an estimate of 7 years of service.

4. How many total years in office are there? Twenty-two sheriffs had an estimate of 2 years, 33 had 7 years, 162 had 12 years, 38 had 17 years, and 19 had 22 years, which totals to 3,283 years. That is, the sum of the fx's equals 3,283.

5. How many sheriffs did we have? In this case $22 + 33 + 162 + 38 + 19 = 274$. That is, N equals the sum of the f's, which equals 274. The mean number of years in office then is $3,283 \div 274 = 11.98$ or 12 years in office. This is an estimated mean because it is based on the midpoint of each interval rather than on an exact time for each individual.

Estimating the Median of an Interval Frequency Distribution

To estimate the median of the distribution in Table 3.6, we proceed as we did earlier in the example for grouped data. We begin by recognizing that there are 274 individuals, each with a corresponding midpoint to designate his or her time in office as a county sheriff. If these midpoints are arrayed from smallest to highest value, there would be twenty-two 2s, thirty-three 7s, one hundred sixty-two 12s, thirty-eight 17s, and nineteen 22s. Given that $274 \div 2 = 137$, the median or midpoint is between the 137th and the 138th values (because there are an even number of values). Using the information in Table 3.6, we can see that the 137th and 138th midpoints are both 12s. Therefore, the median is 12, which is very close to the estimated mean. What is the mode for the data in Table 3.6?

One problem with attempts to calculate the mean from grouped data is that we are really unable to do so for distributions with open-ended intervals. For example, let us consider a distribution of the ages of drivers convicted of driving while intoxicated (DWI) that begins and ends with the open-ended intervals "younger than 21" and "older than 40." Although we could guess the limits of some intervals (e.g., the lower end should not be less than 16 because of age limits on driver's licenses), without more precise data we cannot calculate a mean.

Comparing Mean, Median, and Mode

In a symmetric distribution, such as the bell or normal curve, the mean, median, and mode are all equal. A symmetric distribution has only one mode (i.e., it is unimodal) and has two identical halves. The highest point in the distribution, which is the location of the score with the highest frequency, is the mode. Its value is equal to that of the balancing point (the mean) and of the value of the score that divides the distribution exactly in half (the median). As a distribution starts to depart from its symmetric shape, that is, as it becomes skewed, the relative positions of the mean, median, and mode change.

The scores in skewed distributions are bunched at one end and trail out at the other, which is the tail of the distribution. The direction of the skew is the direction in which the tail is pointing. The mean, which depends on the magnitude of each score and uses all the information in the numbers, is sensitive to the extreme scores in the tail. A positively skewed distribution, referred to as a distribution that is skewed to the right, is bunched up at the lower scores and trails out to the higher scores.

What happens to the mean as a distribution becomes skewed to the right? Recall the foregoing example in which an extreme salary was added to the income distribution. The mean changed drastically, but the median was hardly affected. The value of the mean is pulled toward the tail while the values of the median and the mode mostly stay put. In fact, the mean, because it takes into account the actual values of all the scores, always follows the tail in a skewed distribution.

A negatively skewed distribution is bunched at the higher scores and trails out at the lower scores. It is skewed to the left, which is the direction that the tail is pointing. The mean is sensitive to these deviations in the tail and its value moves in that direction.

The relative positions of the measures of central tendency tell us the shape of a distribution. In a positively skewed distribution, the order (from left to right) is mode, median, and mean. The mean is numerically greater than the median, which is numerically greater than the mode. In a negatively skewed distribution, the order (from left to right) is mean, median, and mode. The mean is numerically less than the median, which is numerically less than the mode. Thus we can determine the shape of a distribution (symmetric, bimodal, skewed to the right, skewed to the left) when we know the relative positions of the mean, median, and mode (Figure 3.1).

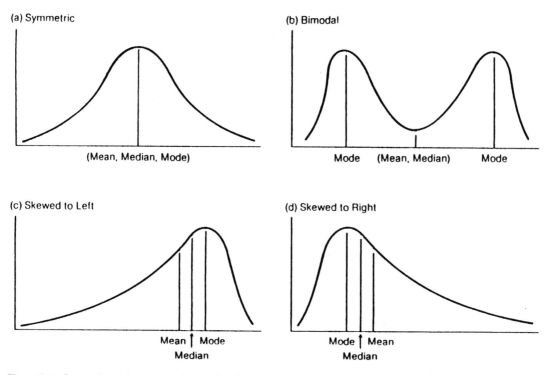

Figure 3.1   Comparison of mean, median, and mode.

When to Use Measures of Central Tendency: A Final Word

As a rule, when describing a distribution, it is always useful to report all three measures of central tendency. Together, they provide a clear and full picture of what a distribution looks like in terms of its shape. Nonetheless, if the situation calls for making a choice among the three, you should consider the nature of the distribution and the facts you want to communicate about it. If the distribution is markedly skewed, the mean presents a distorted view of the distribution (as in the salary example). In this case, the median represents the data more clearly and accurately than the mean does. The median also is used for open-ended distributions when it is not possible to calculate the mean.

With a symmetric distribution and with quantitative data (measured at the ratio or interval levels), the mean is always the measure of choice. It also is desirable to use the mean when further statistical tests or manipulations are to be performed on the data. Later chapters show that the mean is used for important analyses.

When a "quick-and-dirty" measure of central tendency is needed or when you require information about the most common case, the mode is appropriate. Furthermore, the mode is suitable for describing qualitative variables. In fact, the mode is the only measure of central tendency we can use when all we can do is count the number of observations in the categories of a nominal variable (e.g., sex, type of crime, classification level). The mode cannot be used if no score occurs more than once. If several scores occur with similarly high frequencies, then there is no one mode to use as a measure of central tendency.

Exercise 3–6   Mean, Median, Mode for Interval Data

Calculate the mean and median for the following data set. What is the mode?

Years of Police Service for All Police Officers Assigned to Your COP District.

No. of Years of Service	No. of Officers
0–3	40
4–7	37
8–11	52
12–15	29
16–19	13
20–23	30
24–27	8

Summary

This chapter discusses measures of central tendency, specifically the mean, the median, and the mode. These are the most widely used statistical measures, not only in criminal justice but also in most of the social sciences. They are relatively simple to calculate and communicate important information about a distribution. The *mean* is the average value in a distribution, the *median* is the middle value, and the *mode* is the most frequently occurring value. Because these measures are so useful, and because they are not always reported with frequency distributions, the chapter reviews the techniques used to calculate the mean and median from grouped data.

The chapter also identifies a number of characteristics of the mean, median, and mode that help one decide which of these measures to report. The *mean* is best when working with quantitative data in distributions that do not have extreme scores. The *median* is useful for describing the data in highly skewed or open-ended distributions. The *mode* is appropriate for working with qualitative data and for describing the most typical case in a distribution. To gain a full picture of a distribution, it is advisable to use all three measures. The fact that values in a distribution differ from the mean is the subject of chapter 4, which discusses variability.

After completing all the exercises, you should have the ability to provide statistical support for your support of COP. You should also be able to identify and calculate the measures of central tendency for other variables that could help support your stance.

Answers to Exercises

Exercise Answer 3–1   Calculating the Mean

1. Homicides, 1990–1994

   Mean = 17.6 homicides per year

2. Index crimes, 1989–1994

   Mean = 738.33 index crimes per year

3. Rate of arrests (per 100,000) 1985–1994

   Mean = 14.86 arrests per 100,000

Exercise Answer 3–2   Medians

1. Homicides

   11, 16, 18, 18, 25

   Median = 18

2. Index crimes

   629, 672, 690, 751, 808, 880

   Median = 720.5

3. Arrest rates

   12.1, 12.1, 14.6, 14.9, 15.1, 15.2, 15.6, 16.2, 16.4, 16.4

   Median = 15.15

Exercise Answer 3–3   Modes

1. Homicides

   11, 16, 18, 18, 25

   Mode = 18

2. Index crimes

   629, 672, 690, 751, 808, 880

   No mode

3. Arrest rates

   12.1, 12.1, 14.6, 14.9, 15.1, 15.2, 15.6, 16.2, 16.4, 16.4

   Bimodal, 12.1 and 16.4

Exercise 3–4   Means for Grouped Data

1. Auto thefts

   Mean = 23.19

2. Burglaries

   Mean = 17.02

Exercise Answer 3–5   Median and Mode for Grouped Data

1. Auto thefts

   Median = 25

   Mode = 25

2. Burglaries

   Median = 19

   Mode = 19

Exercise Answer 3–6 Mean, Median, and Mode for Interval Data

Mean = 2,225.5 ÷ 209 = 10.65

The median is the 105th value (because there are an odd number of values). This compares to the midpoint of 9.5.

The mode also is 9.5.

No. of Years of Service	Midpoint (x)	No. of Officers (f)	Product (fx)
0–3	1.5	40	60
4–7	5.5	37	203.5
8–11	9.5	52	494
12–15	13.5	29	391.5
16–19	17.5	13	227.5
20–23	21.5	30	645
24–27	25.5	8	204
Sum		209	2,225.5

Computer Applications for Selected Exercises

Exercise Answer 3–1 Calculating the Mean

For this exercise, you are summarizing crimes by years. You can put all the information into one data set arranged by year. Enter Year as the first column and then fill in the Data Editor where information is present. Where no information is recorded, do not type anything. A dot (·) appears in the Data Editor in cells where there is no or missing data. Figure 3.2 shows the completed data set for this exercise.

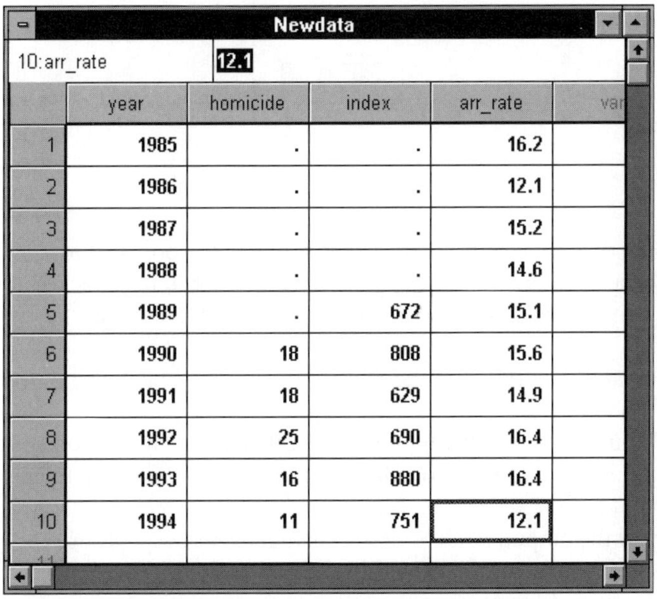

	year	homicide	index	arr_rate	var
1	1985	.	.	16.2	
2	1986	.	.	12.1	
3	1987	.	.	15.2	
4	1988	.	.	14.6	
5	1989	.	672	15.1	
6	1990	18	808	15.6	
7	1991	18	629	14.9	
8	1992	25	690	16.4	
9	1993	16	880	16.4	
10	1994	11	751	12.1	

10: arr_rate   12.1
Newdata

Figure 3.2

To calculate the mean, go to the Statistics menu, choose `Summarize`, and then choose `Descriptives` (Figure 3.3).

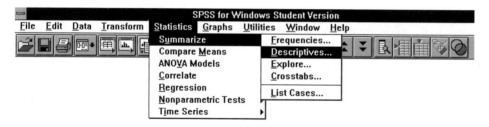

Figure 3.3

Move all three variables of interest into the `Variable(s):` area of the dialog box. Click on the first variable and while holding down the mouse button, drag to the last one. Let go of the mouse after the last variable is highlighted. Click on the large arrow in the center of the dialog box to move all three variables to the center (Figure 3.4).

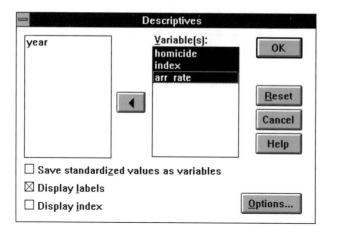

Figure 3.4

Click on `Options` in the lower right-hand corner. Click in the box next to `Mean`. There should now be an `X` in the box. You can leave the other items checked, or click once in each checked box to uncheck it. Figure 3.5 shows what the box should look like when you are ready.

Click on `Continue` and then on `OK` in the Descriptives dialog box. The output is shown in Figure 3.6.

The variable (column) name is shown on the far left. The mean is listed next, followed by the number of cases used to calculate that value. The variable label appears on the far right.

The line at the top of the output, `Number of valid observations (listwise)`, indicates how many cases (rows in the Data Editor) have valid information for all columns. In this case, five of the rows of the Data Editor have valid information for all of the variables.

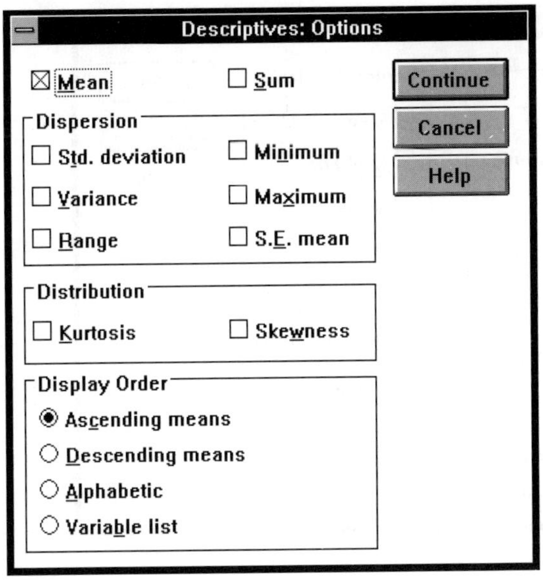

┌───┐
│ ─   **Descriptives: Options**   │
│   │
│ ☒ Mean   ☐ Sum   ┌──────────────┐   │
│   │ Continue   │   │
│ ┌Dispersion────────────┐ └──────────────┘   │
│ │ ☐ Std. deviation ☐ Minimum   ┌─────────┐ │
│ │   │ Cancel │ │
│ │ ☐ Variance   ☐ Maximum   └─────────┘ │
│ │   ┌─────────┐ │
│ │ ☐ Range   ☐ S.E. mean │ Help   │ │
│ └───────────────────────────────└─────────┘ │
│   │
│ ┌Distribution──────────────────┐   │
│ │ ☐ Kurtosis   ☐ Skewness │   │
│ └───────────────────────────────┘   │
│   │
│ ┌Display Order──────────────────┐   │
│ │ ⦿ Ascending means   │   │
│ │ ○ Descending means   │   │
│ │ ○ Alphabetic   │   │
│ │ ○ Variable list   │   │
│ └───────────────────────────────┘   │
└───┘

Figure 3.5

```
Number of valid observations (listwise) =        5.00

                       Valid
Variable      Mean       N   Label

ARR_RATE     14.86      10   Arrest Rates (per 100,000)
HOMICIDE     17.60       5   Homicides
INDEX       738.33       6   Index Crimes
```

Figure 3.6

Exercise Answer 3–2   Identifying Medians

It might be useful to actually write out the arrays by hand for this exercise. On your job, though, you would likely have a larger data set, and it would make sense to use the computer to find the median. Using the data set from Exercise 3–1, go to the Statistics menu and choose Summarize, then choose Frequencies. Move all three variables into the center variables area.

Click on Statistics at the bottom. In the upper right of this dialog box, there is an area for measures of Central Tendency (Figure 3.7). The statistics names in this area give you different ways of describing the middle of a distribution. You have already looked at the Mean. Leave it checked so you can compare this output with that from Exercise 3–1.

Click your mouse in the box next to Median. Make sure all other boxes are clear. Click on Continue.

You have one more thing to do before you choose OK. Click in the Display Frequency Tables check box in the lower left corner of the main Frequencies dialog box (Figure 3.8). It should be empty. This suppresses printing of the frequencies table and shows only the summary statistics requested.

Click on OK. The output is shown in Figure 3.9. Only the summary statistics are printed. The mean values are the same as the ones found in Exercise 3–1.

Each variable has a separate summary printed. The number of cases used to calculate the median is printed after Valid cases at the bottom of each section.

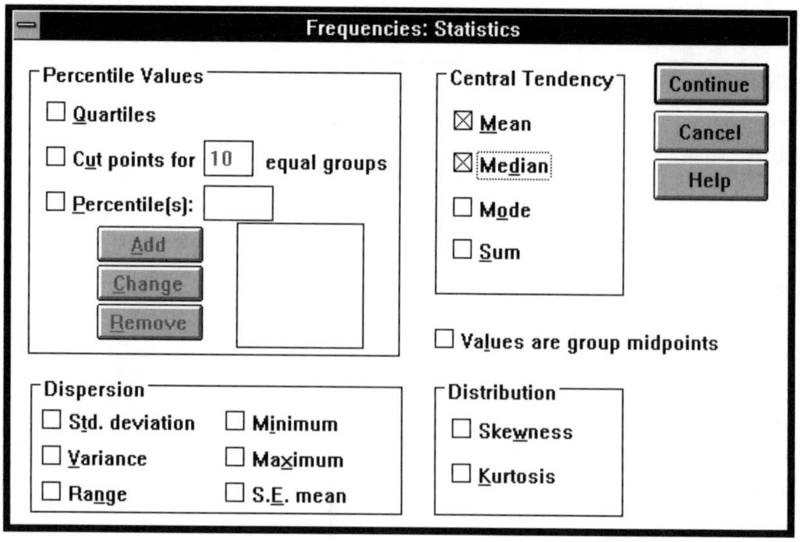

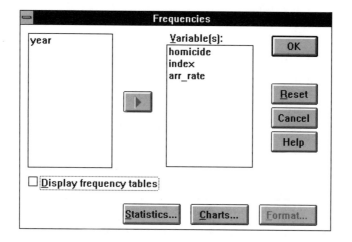

Figure 3.7

Figure 3.8

The missing cases in the homicide and index columns were not used in the calculation of the mean or the median.

Exercise Answer 3–3   Identifying Modes

Use the same procedures here as you did for Exercise 3–2. To retrieve the Frequencies dialog box, use `Dialog Recall` on the tool bar. This feature holds the location for the last 12 procedures you ran. The procedure selected most recently is at the top of the list (Figure 3.10). Click once on the button and once on the first item of the list to return to the Frequencies dialog box.

All the work you did in this session is still there. All you have to do is modify the selections in the Statistics sub-dialog box. Click on `Statistics` and add `Mode` to the list of selected summaries of `Central Tendency`. Your `Frequencies: Statistics` sub-dialog box should look like Figure 3.11.

Click on `Continue` here and `OK` in the main Frequencies dialog box.

Look at the output (Figure 3.12). The one for `HOMICIDE` is easy. The mode is 18. But for `INDEX` and `ARR_RATE` you are told that multiple modes exist. What does this mean?

```
HOMICIDE   Homicides

Mean          17.600      Median       18.000

Valid cases        5      Missing cases        5
- - - - - - - - - - - - - - - - - - - - - - - - - - - - - - - - - - - - -
INDEX      Index Crimes

Mean         738.333      Median      720.500

Valid cases        6      Missing cases        4
- - - - - - - - - - - - - - - - - - - - - - - - - - - - - - - - - - - - -
ARR_RATE   Arrest Rates (per 100,000)

Mean          14.860      Median       15.150

Valid cases       10      Missing cases        0
```

Figure 3.9

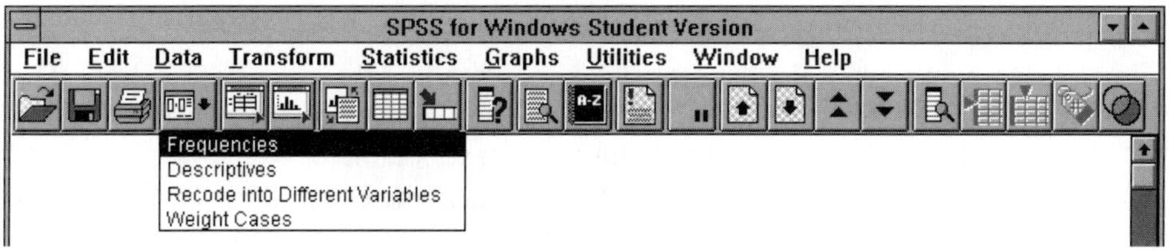

Figure 3.10

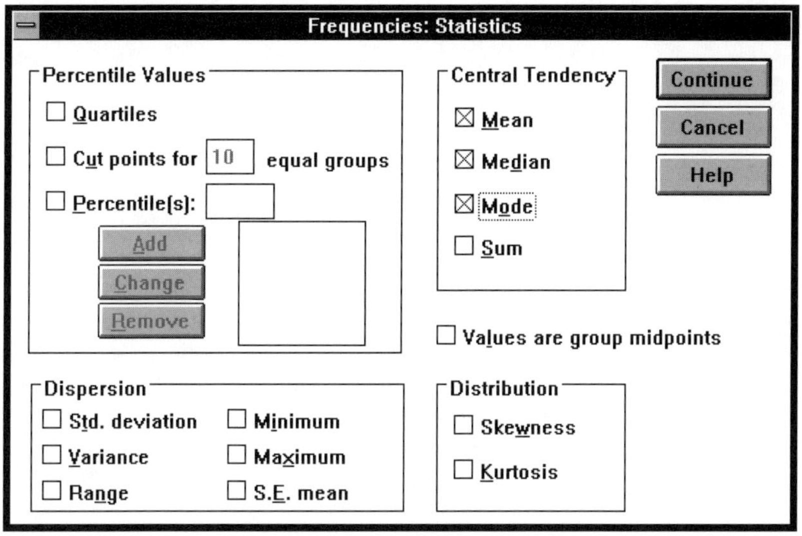

Figure 3.11

```
HOMICIDE   Homicides

Mean          17.600     Median      18.000     Mode        18.000

Valid cases      5       Missing cases       5

- - - - - - - - - - - - - - - - - - - - - - - - - - - - - - - - - -

INDEX      Index Crimes

Mean         738.333     Median     720.500     Mode       629.000

* Multiple modes exist.  The smallest value is shown.

Valid cases      6       Missing cases       4

- - - - - - - - - - - - - - - - - - - - - - - - - - - - - - - - - -

ARR_RATE   Arrest Rates (per 100,000)

Mean          14.860     Median      15.150     Mode        12.100

* Multiple modes exist.  The smallest value is shown.
```

Figure 3.12

When you look at the data for index, you see that the values are unique. The computer is telling you that all of the values are modes. Another way of saying this is that there is really no mode for the index variable.

The arrest rate variable is different. The data in the Data Editor show that 12.1 is a mode and so is 16.4. As the program states, only the mode with the smallest value is shown.

4. MEASURES OF VARIABILITY AND RELATED TOPICS

The Promotion Examination

In 1993, Dave, your close friend and a city police officer, took the department examination for promotion to detective and achieved a score of 87. Although he scored well, Dave was not promoted to detective. Soon after Dave took the examination, the department hired a consultant, who completely redesigned the examination. The new examination recently was administered to officers seeking advancement to detective. Discouraged over not being promoted after the last examination, Dave decided not to take the new examination. Dave's partner, Mike, however, took the test, scored 47, and was promoted. Dave was shocked!

"How can this be?" said Dave to Mike. "I had a higher test score, but you got a promotion!"

"Don't forget," said Mike, "the two tests were structured differently and our scores are not comparable. What's important is how you and I scored relative to other officers who took the test at the same time that we did."

"OK," said Dave. "When I took the test, the mean score was 42. That shows I scored 45 points above the average. When you took the test, the mean was 37. You scored only 10 points above the average. Doesn't this mean that, relatively speaking, I did better than you on the test? Shouldn't I have been promoted to detective?"

Mike said, "Maybe you're right, but I'm not sure. We need to figure out a way to think about this."

Knowing that you had just finished taking a statistics course, Dave comes to you with his and Mike's question. Initially, you are as stymied as Dave and Mike. After a few minutes of thought, you realize that the best way to explain to Dave and Mike why the different outcomes occurred is because of variability.

Variability

In chapter 3, we examined ways to describe the central tendency of a distribution. We found that the mean, median, and mode are measures of central tendency that provide an index of the general magnitude of scores in a distribution. We now discuss measurement of another important property of distributions called *variability*. Chapter 2 showed that variability is the degree to which scores in a group differ. Specifically, variability is defined as the extent to which scores differ from central tendency. This is an important statistical concept that was overlooked by the characters in the opening vignette.

Table 4.1   Number of New Probation Cases from January to June 1990 and 1991 in the Probation Department of Alex County

Month	1990	1991
January	20	20
February	26	15
March	19	30
April	21	6
May	22	56
June	20	10
Total	128	137
Mean	21.33	22.83

Note: These are hypothetical data.

An example of variability is provided in Table 4.1, which presents data on the number of new probation cases for the first six months of 1990 and 1991 in a suburban county. Probation supervisors need to keep track of such data for their case assignment decisions. Likewise, probation administrators use such data to assess staffing needs.

An initial look at Table 4.1 shows us that the total and mean number of new cases in both years are similar. Closer examination, however, reveals that the two distributions are different. The number of new probation cases during the months of 1990 are relatively similar. The values in this distribution are fairly close to one another and fairly close to the mean. This, however, is not the case for 1991. In that year, the number of new probation cases in each month differs substantially. Not only are the values in the 1991 distribution considerably different from each other, they are also quite different from the mean.

Variability is defined as the extent to which scores differ from central tendency. Scores that are close to their mean exhibit less variability than scores dispersed over a wider range. Given this, we can visualize how the distribution of new probation cases in 1991 has more variability then the distribution of cases in 1990. We can measure or quantify variability in a variety of ways. This chapter discusses three measures that are commonly used: range, variance, and standard deviation.

Range

Range is defined simply as the difference between the highest and lowest scores in a distribution.[1] This measures the spread of the scores. The number of new probation cases in 1990, for example, went from a low of 19 to a high of 26. Thus the range is 26 cases minus 19 cases equals 7 cases. Likewise, the number of new probation cases in 1991 went from 6 cases to 56 cases, which is a range of 50 cases. The range communicates that these two distributions are quite different in terms of spread or variability. The range is measured in the units of the variable that is being reported. All measures of variability, like those of central tendency, carry the unit of the variable.

One problem with using range as a measure of variability is that it describes only the end (i.e., highest and lowest) scores of a distribution. The range tells us nothing about the other scores. To see what we mean by this, examine the following two sets of scores.[2]

$$1, 2, 2, 3, 4, 5, 6, 24$$

$$1, 5, 8, 15, 19, 20, 24$$

Although these data sets consist of different scores, the range is the same for both. The lowest value in each distribution is 1 and the highest is 24. Thus the range in both cases is $24 - 1 = 23$. This example shows that the range, although somewhat useful, is a crude measure of variability.

Exercise 4–1   Range

In an effort to explain to Dave and Mike why one was promoted and the other wasn't, you start by explaining the range of test scores. What is the range for each? Dave's group (highest possible score was 100)

$$96, 64, 67, 80, 56, 94, 92, 48, 50, 87, 77, 23$$

Mike's group (highest possible score was 60)

$$37, 21, 10, 25, 17, 20, 14, 47, 38, 58, 46, 30$$

Measures of Deviation

Variability is the extent to which scores in a distribution differ from central tendency. The range tells us something about the differences among scores but it only provides limited information. Other measures have been developed that correspond more closely to the definition of variability. The measures presented in this section of the chapter are called *variance* and *standard deviation*. These measures are derived by an equation that computes the difference between each score in a data set and the central tendency of those scores. In this way, variability is measured by considering all the scores, not just the highest and lowest ones.

Variance

The variance of scores in a population is measured with the following equation and is denoted as σ^2 (lower case Greek letter sigma squared).

$$\sigma^2 = \frac{\Sigma(X - \mu)^2}{N} \qquad \text{Equation 4.1}$$

The variance is computed by subtracting the mean from each score in a distribution. The equation uses the Greek letter mu (μ) to designate the population mean. Differences between scores and the mean reflect the degree to which scores deviate above or below the central tendency of those scores. These differences are squared, summed, and then divided by the number of scores in the distribution. Hence variance represents the average squared deviation of scores from their mean.

An example of a variance computation is provided in Table 4.2, which shows hypothetical data on the number of murders during one week in six precincts. For the sake of the example, assume that the six precincts are the regions under the responsibility of one police chief, thus constituting a population.[3]

The values in column A of Table 4.2 are the number of murders (X). The numbers in column B show the difference between the value in column A and the

Table 4.2 Steps in Measuring the Variance of the Number of Murders During One Week in Six Precincts (a Population)

	(A) X	(B) $X - \mu$	(C) $(X - \mu)^2$
	4	1	1
	0	−3	9
	3	0	0
	5	2	4
	4	1	1
	2	−1	1
Sum	18	0	16

Note: The data in column A are the number of murders. The mean number of murders is $\mu = 18/6 = 3$.

mean (which is $18/6 = 3$). The numbers in column C are the square of the differences. The variance is found by dividing the sum of column C by the number of scores in the distribution. Therefore, σ^2 is $16/6 = 2.67$ murders-squared. This tells us that the values in column A vary around their mean an average of 2.67 units-squared.

Another look at Table 4.2 reveals why the difference between scores and the mean are squared. Column B shows that when the mean is subtracted from each score in a distribution, the sum of the differences equals zero. This, in fact, is a mathematical principle that occurs with any group of scores.[4] Differences are squared to prevent the sum from always equaling zero. If Equation 4.1 is used properly, the sum of squared differences equals zero only when there is no variability among the scores.

A situation in which there is no variation is displayed in Table 4.3. Again, we present hypothetical data that show the number of murders during one week in six precincts. This time, however, all the precincts show that there are four murders; no variation occurs among the precincts. In this case, the variance is

Table 4.3 Measuring the Variance of the Number of Murders During One Week in Six Precincts When There Is No Variation

	X	$X - \mu$	$(X - \mu)^2$
	4	0	0
	4	0	0
	4	0	0
	4	0	0
	4	0	0
	4	0	0
Sum	24	0	0

Note: The data in the first column are the number of murders. The mean number of murders is $\mu = 24/6 = 4$.

0/6 = 0, which, of course, makes sense. The variance is zero when there is no variation among the measurements.

Standard Deviation

The variance expresses variation in terms of squared units (e.g., murders-squared). We can also see that squared units are difficult for us to comprehend. We can convert square units into original units by taking the square root of the variance. This gives us the *standard deviation* and is represented as σ (lower case Greek letter sigma without the square notation).

$$\sigma = \sqrt{\frac{\Sigma(X - \mu)^2}{N}}$$ Equation 4.2

The standard deviation for the data in Table 4.2 is

$$\sqrt{2.67 \text{ murders}^2} = 1.63 \text{ murders}.$$

This tells us that murders in the six precincts deviate from the mean about 1.63 units, on average.

Exercise 4–2   Variance and Standard Deviation
Using the data sets from Exercise 4–1, determine the variance and standard deviation for test scores in both groups. Assume the groups constitute a population.

Fine Tuning the Standard Deviation
The standard deviation is the most commonly used measure of variation. As such, statisticians have devoted a great deal of time to studying the behavior of the standard deviation equation. One of the main problems that they found is that the standard deviation of scores in a sample tends to be a poor estimator of the standard deviation of the scores in the population from which the sample was selected. A minor adjustment corrects this problem. Instead of dividing the sum of squared deviations by N, we simply divide by $N - 1$. The standard deviation equation with this correction is used exclusively with samples and is symbolized with the letter s (as opposed to σ). Also, μ is replaced with $\bar{X}$, the mean of a sample.

$$s = \sqrt{\frac{\Sigma(X - \bar{X})^2}{N - 1}}$$ Equation 4.3

Statisticians also found that the standard deviation equation (with or without the correction) is somewhat cumbersome to use. The equation is simple in appearance and clearly conveys the concept of variation, but the repetitious subtraction of the mean from each score is tedious. Therefore, a computational formula for the standard deviation was devised (Equation 4.4).

$$s = \sqrt{\frac{N\Sigma X^2 - (\Sigma X)^2}{N(N - 1)}}$$ Equation 4.4

Although the computational formula appears to be more complex than the original or conceptual formula, the computational formula is easier to use. In Equation 4.4 the left term in the numerator is found by multiplying N by the sum of the squared scores. From this quantity, the square of the sum of the scores is subtracted. The difference is divided by N times $N - 1$. Finally, the square root is

Table 4.4 Measuring the Standard Deviation of Twelve Scores from a Criminal Justice Examination

	X	X^2
	27	729
	42	1,764
	38	1,444
	30	900
	31	961
	42	1,764
	42	1,764
	31	961
	38	1,444
	38	1,444
	38	1,444
	30	900
Sum	427	15,519

taken. Equations 4.3 and 4.4 both yield the same answer for the standard deviation, but the latter is easier to use.[5]

We can see how to use the computational formula for the standard deviation by considering Table 4.4, which presents the scores of 12 randomly selected criminal justice students who agreed to complete a test version of a new examination that is being considered by the faculty in a criminal justice department.

Table 4.4 has two columns of information. The column labeled X shows the original datum or score for each student. The column labeled X^2 contains the square of each score. The number of scores along with the sum of the columns in Table 4.4 are used in the computational formula as follows:

$$s = \sqrt{\frac{12(15,519) - (427)^2}{12(12 - 1)}}$$

this equals

$$s = \sqrt{\frac{186,228 - 182,329}{132}}$$

which finally gives

$$s = \sqrt{\frac{3,899}{132}} = \sqrt{29.54} = 5.43$$

This result tells us that the standard deviation of the test scores is 5.43 units. The computation also gives a good estimate of what the standard deviation would be if all the criminal justice students in the department were to have taken the test, not just the 12 in the sample.

Computing the Standard Deviation with Grouped Data

Chapter 3 showed that a mean can be computed if one has scores that are grouped by frequencies. The same is true for the computation of the standard deviation. Table 4.5 presents the test scores from Table 4.4, except that unique scores are

Table 4.5   Measuring the Standard Deviation of Twelve Scores from a Criminal Justice Examination Grouped by Frequency

X	f	fX	fX²
27	1	27	729
42	3	126	5,292
38	4	152	5,776
30	2	60	1,800
31	2	62	1,922
Sum	12	427	15,519

listed with their frequency of occurrence. The column label X indicates a score and f represents the frequency of that score. We can see that there is one score of 27, there are three scores of 42, and so on. The label fX stands for the product of a score and its frequency, and fX^2 is the product of the squared score and its frequency. Equation 4.4 can be modified to account for score grouping and is presented as Equation 4.5.

$$s = \sqrt{\frac{N\Sigma fx^2 - (\Sigma fx)^2}{N(N-1)}}$$ Equation 4.5

We can use Equation 4.5 to compute the standard deviation of the grouped scores in Table 4.5. The sum of the frequencies is N, and the other terms are taken directly from the table.

$$s = \sqrt{\frac{12(15,519) - (427)^2}{12(12-1)}} = 5.43$$

A Final Word About Variation Equations

The discussion of the different types of equations that measure variation may be somewhat confusing. Therefore, we present the computational formulas for variance and standard deviation that you should use with this textbook and your data. The equations for both variance and the standard deviation are presented because they are really two forms of the same basic equation. We realize, however, that you will probably use standard deviation more than variance.

Equations 4.6 and 4.7 are used to measure the variance (σ^2) and the standard deviation (σ) of scores in a *population*. Note how these equations are identified with the lower case Greek letter sigma.

$$\sigma^2 = \frac{N\Sigma X^2 - (\Sigma X)^2}{N^2}$$ Equation 4.6

$$\sigma = \sqrt{\frac{N\Sigma X^2 - (\Sigma X)^2}{N^2}}$$ Equation 4.7

Equations 4.8 and 4.9 are used to measure the variance (s^2) and the standard deviation (s) of scores in a *sample*. Note how these equations are identified with a small English letter s.

$$s^2 = \frac{N\Sigma X^2 - (\Sigma X)^2}{N(N-1)}$$ Equation 4.8

$$s = \sqrt{\frac{N\Sigma X^2 - (\Sigma X)^2}{N(N-1)}}$$

Equation 4.9

A Brief Review

We have discussed how scores in most distributions differ from their mean. This is known as variability and, like good statisticians, we want to measure it. Three measures of variability have been presented: range, variance, and standard deviation. The most commonly used measure of variability is standard deviation.

We began our discussion of variability by examining two distributions—the number of new probation cases from January to June in 1990 and in 1991. On visual inspection, it was surmised that the 1991 distribution had more variability than that for 1990. Our supposition can now be tested by calculating standard deviations for both distributions.

Table 4.6 shows the number of new probation cases during the target months of 1990 (a sample). These are the same data that appear in Table 4.1. Table 4.6 also shows the information needed to compute the standard deviation. Using Equation 4.9 we have

$$s = \sqrt{\frac{6(2,762) - (128)^2}{6(6-1)}}$$

leading to

$$s = \sqrt{\frac{16,572 - 16,384}{30}}$$

which finally gives

$$s = \sqrt{\frac{188}{30}} = \sqrt{6.27} = 2.50$$

The standard deviation for the 1990 data is 2.50 cases. Therefore, on average, the new probation cases in the months of January to June deviate from their mean by about 2.50 cases. Given that the mean for 1990 is 21.33 cases, the standard deviation of 2.50 cases appears to be correct.

Table 4.6　Measuring the Standard Deviation of New Probation Cases from January to June in 1990 for Alex County Using the Computational Formula

Month	X	X²
January	20	400
February	26	676
March	19	361
April	21	441
May	22	484
June	20	400
Sum	128	2,762

Exercise 4–3   Standard Deviation

Calculate the standard deviation for the number of new probation cases in 1991, which are displayed in Table 4.1 (assume these data constitute a sample). Compare that standard deviation with the one we computed for 1990. If our intuition is correct, we expect to find that the standard deviation for 1991 is larger than that for 1990. Is it?[6]

Mean, Standard Deviation, and Chebyshev's Theorem

We know a lot about the details of a distribution when we have all the scores in front of us. For example, we can count the number of test scores that are above a certain value to grant an award to graduating police cadets. There are times, however, when we want to know some details of a distribution but do not have access to the individual scores. A nineteenth century Russian mathematician by the name of Pafnuti Lvovich Chebyshev was concerned about this issue and formulated what is commonly referred to as *Chebyshev's theorem.* In essence, the theorem states that *at least 75% of scores in a distribution fall between scores that are two standard deviations above and below the mean, and at least 89% of scores fall between scores that are three standard deviations above and below the mean.*

This can be illustrated in an example. Assume that a national study of police officers reports that the mean age is 28 years with a standard deviation of 1.6 years. Using Chebyshev's theorem we can estimate that at least 75% of the officers have an age of 28 years $\pm$ (2 $\times$ 1.6 years) (the symbol $\pm$ stands for *plus or minus*). This tells us that at least 75% of the officers have an age of 28 years $\pm$ 3.2 years; the range is 24.8 years to 31.2 years.

Likewise, at least 89% of the officers have an age of 28 years $\pm$ (3 $\times$ 1.6 years), ranging from 23.2 years to 32.8 years. Although Chebyshev's theorem yields only conservative estimates, it provides some details about a distribution of scores when one knows nothing more than the mean and standard deviation.

Exercise 4–4   Application of Chebyshev's Theorem

Assume that the average sentence for sexual assault is 9 years with a standard deviation of 2.3 years. Use Chebyshev's theorem to compute sentences that include at least 75% of the sentences above and below the mean. Then compute the sentences that include at least 89% of the sentences above and below the mean.

Mean, Standard Deviation, and z Scores

Another useful, but more precise, statistical tool that uses the mean and standard deviation is called a *standard score transformation,* also known as a *z score transformation.* Equation 4.10 shows how a z score is computed.

$$z = \frac{X - \bar{X}}{s}$$ Equation 4.10

A z score is constructed from one or more raw scores in a population or sample. A z score is formed by subtracting the mean from a raw score and then dividing by the standard deviation. This produces a transformed score that expresses the number of standard deviations a raw score is above or below the mean. For example, assume that we have recorded the ages of a sample of police chiefs and found that the mean is 55 years and the standard deviation is 5 years. If Chief Smith is 60 years of age, the z score for his age is

$$z_{Smith} = \frac{60 \text{ years} - 55 \text{ years}}{5 \text{ years}} = 1.00$$

This means that the chief's age is 1.00 standard deviation above the mean. This makes sense because we can calculate Chief Smith's age by adding 1.00 standard deviation to the mean age (55 years + 5 years = 60 years).

If another person, say Chief Jones, is 40 years of age, the z score for his age is

$$z_{Jones} = \frac{40 \text{ years} - 55 \text{ years}}{5 \text{ years}} = -3.00$$

Here we can see that this chief's age is 3.00 standard deviations below the mean. This is why the z score bears a negative sign. We can compute Chief Jone's age by subtracting 3.00 standard deviations from the mean age (55 years $- 3 \times 5$ years = 40 years).

Properties of z Scores

A z score possesses three important properties. First, z scores are numbers that do not carry any units of the variable being measured. The units of variables are canceled in the formation of z scores. This is why the z scores for the police chiefs in the prior example are 1.00 and -3.00, not 1.00 year or -3.00 years. As a consequence, all z scores are completely comparable with one another, even if their corresponding raw scores have dissimilar units.

Second, z scores express how far a raw score is above or below the mean in terms of standard deviations. A z score of 1.58 means that the corresponding raw score is 1.58 standard deviations above the mean. A z score of -2.19 refers to a raw score that is 2.19 standard deviations below the mean. Raw scores that are above the mean have positive z scores and those that are below the mean have negative z scores. A raw score that is equal to the mean has a z score of zero.

Third, if an entire group of raw scores have been transformed into z scores, the mean of the z scores is 0.00 and the standard deviation is 1.00. This result occurs with any group of scores. For example, Table 4.7 presents the ages and job tenure

Table 4.7   Age and Job Tenure of Eight Police Officers with Corresponding z Transformations

	Age	$z_{(age)}$	Tenure	$z_{(tenure)}$
	41	1.705	20.1	1.715
	20	−1.131	0.5	−1.075
	35	0.895	15.6	1.075
	25	−0.456	3.9	−0.591
	23	−0.726	3.2	−0.690
	30	0.219	10.8	0.391
	21	−0.996	1.9	−0.875
	32	0.490	8.4	0.050
$\bar{X}$	28.375	0.000	8.050	0.000
s	7.405	1.000	7.025	1.000

of eight police officers with the corresponding z transformations. It is shown that the mean for both sets of z scores is 0.00 and the standard deviation is 1.00. This illustrates how a z score transformation takes a raw score from a distribution (with its own mean and standard deviation) and computes a corresponding score in a distribution in which the mean is 0.00 and the standard deviation is 1.00.[7]

Use of z Scores Transformations for Comparing Scores from Different Distributions

A z score is useful in comparing scores from different distributions. The following example is both a description of a common problem encountered by criminal justice administrators and an illustration of how z scores can be applied in a meaningful way.

Because of budget reductions, a supervisor is able to recommend a salary increase for only one or two probation officers. One officer is working in the juvenile division, and the other is in the adult division. The caseloads are similar, but the nature of the work is quite different. The juvenile officer has less serious cases in terms of criminal offense, but each case is demanding in terms of supervision and treatment requirements. The adult division officer has a caseload that contains more cases with serious criminal offense and criminal history.

The juvenile officer has been successful with 59 cases in the last year. The juvenile division's mean success rate is 50 cases with a standard deviation of 6.3 cases. During the same time period, the adult division officer has been successful with 45 cases. The mean adult division success rate is 35 cases with a standard deviation of 2.8 cases.

So far, we can see that both officers performed above the average. However, the question for the supervisor is "Which officer, if either, performed better than the other?" A simplistic (and quite unfair) approach to this problem is to compare the number of successful cases for each officer. If we do this, the juvenile officer receives the salary increase because the 59 successful cases is greater than the 45 cases completed by the adult division officer. However, making this comparison assumes that one successful case in the juvenile caseload is equal to one in the adult division caseload. It is easy to see that this is not true given what we have said about the difference in the nature of juvenile and adult probation cases. A better approach for comparing the officers is to convert their raw scores into z scores. This tells us how far each officer is above the respective mean in terms of standard deviation. In essence, the z score transformations take the raw scores from two separate distributions (each with their own units, means, and standard deviations) and compute corresponding standard scores that are in a distribution in which the mean is 0.00 and the standard deviation is 1.00. Hence the z scores of the two officers are directly comparable.

The z scores for the juvenile and adult probation officers are computed with Equation 4.10 in the following way.

$$z_{(Juvenile)} = \frac{59 - 50}{6.3} = 1.43$$

$$z_{(Adult)} = \frac{45 - 35}{2.8} = 3.57$$

The z score for the adult division probation officer is substantially higher than that for the juvenile probation officer, even though the former had a fewer number of successful cases. The z score for the adult division officer tells us that the officer successfully completed a number of cases that is 3.57 standard deviations above the mean for the adult probation division. In comparison, the juvenile officer successfully completed a number of cases that is only 1.43 standard deviations above the mean for the juvenile probation division. Relatively speaking, the adult probation officer outperformed the juvenile officer and, barring any impediments, probably will be the recipient of the merit salary increase.

Exercise 4–5   z Scores

Part of the promotion process includes comparing certain aspects of officers' performances with the performance of the officers in each test group. With respect to Dave and Mike, who was the better ticket writer? Use z scores to determine whose performance is better.

	Mike	Dave
No. of tickets	110	75
Test group mean	95	67
Standard deviation	4.7	2.9

---

z Scores and Normal Distribution

The previous section discusses the utility of z scores. However, if we are working with a population of normally distributed scores, z scores provide an additional benefit. With a normal distribution, z scores can be used to help answer difficult questions.

The z transformation of a population of raw scores is computed as any other z score, except that the equation has slightly different terms in it.

$$z = \frac{X - \mu}{\sigma}$$

Equation 4.11

Equation 4.11 differs from Equation 4.10 only in that Equation 4.11 contains the terms μ and σ, which represent the mean and the standard deviation of population scores. z transformations of normally distributed population raw scores are called *standard normal deviates*. The distribution of standard normal deviates is referred to as the *standard normal curve*. Like all distributions of z scores, it has a mean of 0.00 and a standard deviation of 1.00.

A full discussion of the mathematical properties of the standard normal curve is beyond the scope of this text. However, one basic property is that the area under the curve between two z scores reflects the percentage or proportion of scores in the population that is between the corresponding raw scores.[8] Although this sounds a bit complex, it is not that difficult to understand or apply.

Figure 4.1 presents the standard normal curve and identifies z scores that are one standard deviation apart. The area between the z scores also is shown. One can see that the area under the curve between z scores of 0.00 and 1.00 is .3413, which means that 34.13% of the z scores in a population distribution are between 0.00 and 1.00. Because the tails of the curve drop off rapidly as one gets farther from the mean, so does the area. Thus the area under the curve between z scores of 1.00 and 2.00 is .1359 or 13.59%.

Table A in the Appendix helps us use *z* scores to solve problems that we encounter with normal distributions of raw scores. Table A presents a series of six panels. Within each panel are three columns. The first column lists a *z* score. The second column provides the area under the standard normal curve from 0.00 (i.e., the mean) to that *z* score. The third column provides the area from the *z* score to the tail of the distribution. For example, for a *z* score of 1.00, we see that the area from 0.00 to the *z* score is .3413 (see Figure 4.1). This can be read as 34.13%. The area from a *z* score of 1.00 to the tail is .1587, which is 15.87%. This tells us that 34.13% of the scores in a normal distribution are between the mean and a score that is 1.00 standard deviation above the mean. Beyond that point lie 15.87% of the scores. The two areas for any *z* score in Table A add to .500 or 50%.

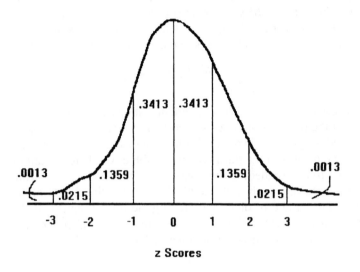

z Scores

Figure 4.1 Areas under the standard normal curve.

Table A only presents information about the right-hand side of the standard normal curve (which has only positive *z* scores). This is not an oversight. There is no reason to expand the table to include the left-hand side of the curve, which has negative *z* scores, because normal distributions are symmetric. The information presented in Table A applies equally to the right- and left-hand sides of the standard normal curve. Therefore, if 34.13% of the scores in a normal distribution are between the mean and a score that is 1.00 standard deviation above the mean, 34.13% of the scores are between the mean and a score that is 1.00 standard deviation below the mean. In total, 68.26% of the scores are between scores that are 1.00 standard deviation above and below the mean.

Using Table A, with similar reasoning we can compute that 95.44% of the scores in a normal distribution fall between scores that are ±2.00 standard deviations around the mean, and that 99.74% fall between scores that are ±3.00 standard deviations around the mean. Thus we can see how use of standard normal deviates greatly improves our estimate of the percentages of scores around the mean over use of Chebyshev's theorem. (The theorem states that at least 75% of the scores in a distribution are within ±2.00 standard deviations around the mean and at least 89% are within ±3.00 standard deviations.)

How does the standard normal curve benefit us? Let us consider two related examples. First, assume that a national survey of police departments has just revealed that the current mean age of police staff is 48.02 years with a standard deviation of 8.33 years. If age is a normally distributed variable, we can estimate that about 68% of the staff is between the ages of 39.7 and 56.4 years (± 1.00 standard deviation). Likewise, about 95% of the staff is between the ages of 31.4 and 64.7 years (± 2.00 standard deviations). Nearly all staff are between the ages of 23.0 and 73.0 years (± 3.00 standard deviations). Therefore we can make reasonably accurate estimates about age in the population of police staff without having any other statistical information except for the mean and standard deviation.

Using the same survey results, assume that you are working on a committee that is concerned with police retirement benefits. If staff members typically retire at age 65 years or older, what percentage of the nation's police staff might be considering retirement this year?

One can answer this question by examining a list of the nation's police officers and counting the number who are 65 years of age or older. If such a list were not available (or impractical to work with), the standard normal curve is useful for providing an estimate. First, we need to compute the z score for 65 years of age.

$$z_{65} = \frac{65 \text{ years} - 48.02 \text{ years}}{8.33 \text{ years}} = 2.04$$

This tells us that the age of 65 years is 2.04 standard deviations above the national mean. Assuming that the distribution of ages is normal, we can refer to Table A (see Appendix) to find the percentage of ages with a z score of 2.04 and beyond.

The information we need is in the third column of Table A (where the tail of the standard normal curve is shaded) at the z score of 2.04. Reading over from the z score we find that the area in the tail is .0207. This means that 2.07% of the police staff are 65 years of age or older and are eligible for retirement. If the national police staff consists of 200,000 officers, we estimate the number of potential retirees at about 4,140. This analysis is summarized in Figure 4.2.

Summary

Variability is defined as the extent to which scores differ from central tendency. Three measures of variability are range, variance, and standard deviation. The *range* is the crudest of these measures because it takes into account only the lowest and highest scores in a distribution. The other measures are much better because they incorporate all scores.

The most commonly used measure of variability is *standard deviation*. This is because standard deviation presents variation in the original unit of the variables.

Even though standard deviation is preferred over variance, one should keep in mind that the two measures are based on the same root equation and therefore are related terms. *Variance* is important to keep in mind. Chapter 10 shows how the variance is preferred over the standard deviation in a particular context.

Useful statistical tools that incorporate standard deviation are Chebyshev's theorem and z score transformations. *Chebyshev's theorem* basically states that at least 75% of the scores in a group fall within ± 2.00 standard deviations of the mean and that at least 89% fall within ± 3.00 standard deviations. The theorem helps us to know useful details about a distribution from simply knowing the mean and the standard deviation.

A *z score transformation* produces standardized scores. A z score is unitless and tells us how many standard deviations a raw score is above or below its mean. If z scores have been calculated from a sample or a population of raw scores, the mean of the z scores is 0.00 and the standard deviation is 1.00.

1. Horizontal Axis is drawn with mean (48.02 years) and intervals of one standard deviation (8.33 years). Shaded area represents the unknown percentage of police staff who are eligible for retirement (those 65 and older).

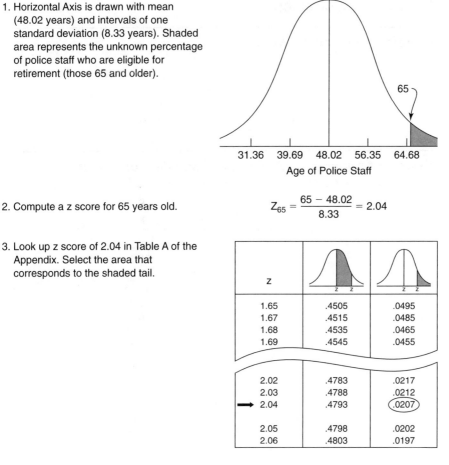

31.36   39.69   48.02   56.35   64.68

Age of Police Staff

2. Compute a z score for 65 years old.

$$Z_{65} = \frac{65 - 48.02}{8.33} = 2.04$$

3. Look up z score of 2.04 in Table A of the Appendix. Select the area that corresponds to the shaded tail.

z		
1.65	.4505	.0495
1.67	.4515	.0485
1.68	.4535	.0465
1.69	.4545	.0455
2.02	.4783	.0217
2.03	.4788	.0212
2.04	.4793	.0207
2.05	.4798	.0202
2.06	.4803	.0197

4. The value of .0207 means that 2.07% of the police staff ages are 65 and beyond.

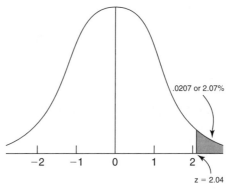

.0207 or 2.07%

z = 2.04

5. Multiply 200,000 by .0207 for the estimate of retirement-eligible police staff.

$200,00 \times 0.0207 = 4,140$

Figure 4.2   Steps in Using the Standard Normal Curve for the Police Staff Retirement Example

A *z* score based on raw scores from a normal distribution is called a *standard normal deviate*. The frequency distribution of standard normal deviates is called the *standard normal curve*. This curve is useful for answering a number of questions about population distributions.

Answers to Exercises

Exercise Answer 4–1   Range

Group	Range	
Dave's	73	(96–23)
Mike's	48	(58–10)

Exercise Answer 4–2   Variance and Standard Deviation

Variance and standard deviation for Dave's group

X	$X - \mu$	$(X - \mu)^2$
96	26.5	702.25
64	−5.5	30.25
67	−2.5	6.25
80	10.5	110.25
56	−13.5	182.25
94	24.5	600.25
92	22.5	506.25
48	−21.5	462.25
50	−19.5	380.25
87	17.5	306.25
77	7.5	56.25
23	−46.5	2,162.25
Sum 834	0	5,505.00

$\mu = 834/12 = 69.5$

$$\text{Variance} = \sigma^2 = \frac{5,505}{12} = 458.75$$

$$\text{Standard deviation} = \sigma = \sqrt{458.75} = 21.42$$

Variance and standard deviation for Mike's group

X	$X - \mu$	$(X - \mu)^2$
37	6.75	45.56
21	−9.25	85.56
10	−20.25	410.06
25	−5.25	27.56
17	−13.25	175.56
20	−10.25	105.06
14	−16.25	264.06
47	16.75	280.56
38	7.75	60.06
58	27.75	770.06
46	15.75	248.06
30	−.25	.06
Sum 363	0	2,472.22

$\mu = 363/12 = 30.25$

$$\text{Variance} = \sigma^2 = \frac{2472.22}{12} = 206.02$$

$$\text{Standard deviation} = \sigma = \sqrt{206.02} = 14.35$$

Exercise Answer 4–3 Standard Deviation for New Probation Cases in the First Six Months of 1991

x	x^2
20	400
15	225
30	900
6	36
56	3,136
10	100
Sum 137	4,797

$$\text{Standard deviation} = s = \sqrt{\frac{6(4,797) - (137)^2}{6(5)}}$$

$$s = \sqrt{\frac{10,013}{30}} = \sqrt{333.77} = 18.27$$

Our suspicion was correct. There is more variation in the new probation cases during the first six months of 1991 as compared with the same period of 1990.

Exercise Answer 4–4 Application of Chebyshev's Theorem

At least 75 percent of the prisoners will have sentences between

$$9 - 2(2.3) = 4.4 \text{ years}$$

and

$$9 + 2(2.23) = 13.6 \text{ years}$$

At least 89% of the prisoners will have sentences between

$$9 - 3(2.3) = 2.1 \text{ years}$$

and

$$9 + 3(2.3) = 15.9 \text{ years}$$

Exercise Answer 4–5 z Scores

$$z_{(\text{Mike})} = \frac{110 - 95}{4.7} = 3.19$$

$$z_{(\text{Dave})} = \frac{75 - 67}{2.9} = 2.76$$

Relatively speaking, Mike was more productive than Dave.

Computer Applications for Selected Exercises

Exercise Answer 4–1   Range

It would be easy to do this exercise by hand, but we show you how to use the computer to do it so you know what to do if you ever have a large data set. Set up the first column to show whose text score you are entering. Set up a code of *1* for Dave and a code of *2* for Mike. This is shown in the `Define Labels:` dialog box in Figure 4.3.

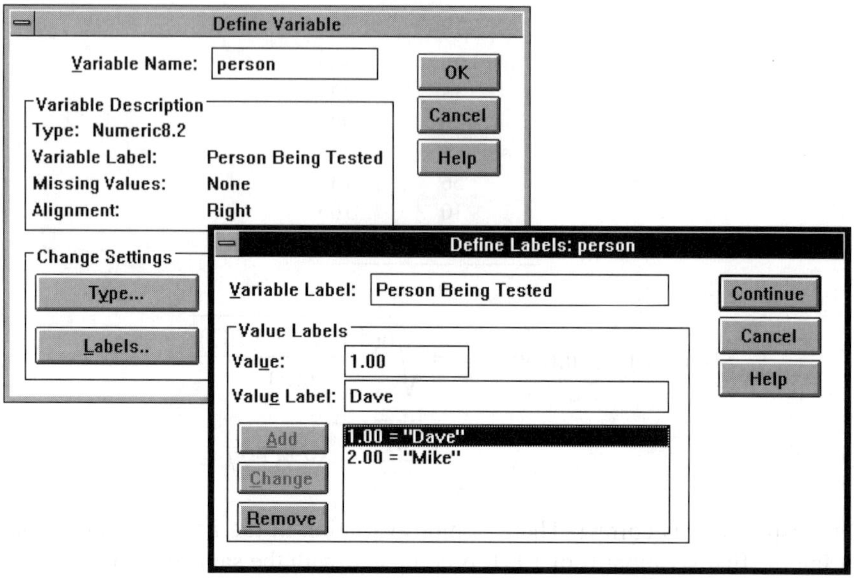

Figure 4.3

Type a *1* or a *2* in the Data Editor to indicate whose score is being entered. If you forget which number to type while entering the data, click the right mouse button in the cell and *SPSS* shows the defined data values. Double-click on the choice you want (Figure 4.4).

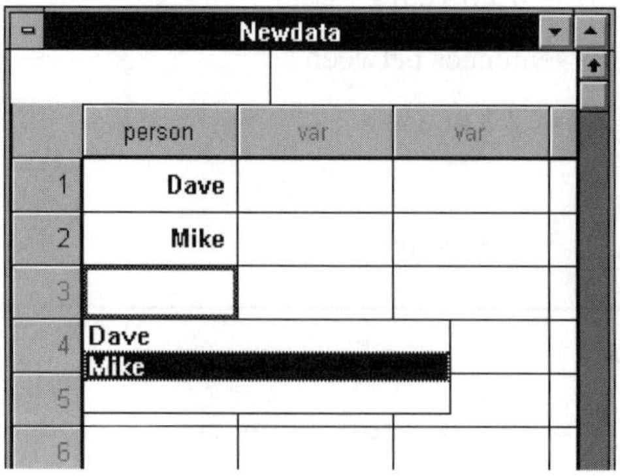

Figure 4.4

If this feature is not working for you, look on the toolbar in the upper right to see if the label icon (Figure 4.5) is highlighted. Click on it once if it is not highlighted.

Figure 4.5

You need one column for each test. Because the tests have different maximum values, you know they are different tests. Each test measures something different; therefore each test has its own column. Because the tests are completely different and Dave took only the 100-point test and Mike took only the 60-point test, skip the `person` column. You have a smaller data set, but you always have to remember whose scores are in which column. Such a data entry scheme also violates the one row per person data entry scheme usually used in statistical software. If you were to add a third variable, for example, the time it took to take each test, a two-column scheme would not provide a way to place each test time and keep it separate by person but together by score.

The final data set should look something like the one in Figure 4.6. The scores for the test that had 100 as the highest possible score (Dave's group) are in the column labeled `scr_100`. The scores for the test that had a high score of 60 (Mike's group) are in the column labeled `scr_60`.

		d:\justice\chapter4\41.sav	
1:person		1	
	person	scr_100	scr_60
9	Dave	50.00	.
10	Dave	87.00	.
11	Dave	77.00	.
12	Dave	23.00	.
13	Mike	.	37.00
14	Mike	.	21.00
15	Mike	.	10.00
16	Mike	.	25.00
17	Mike	.	17.00
18	Mike	.	20.00
19	Mike	.	14.00
20	Mike	.	47.00
21	Mike	.	38.00
	Mike		50.00

Figure 4.6

Remember that variable (column) names can only be eight characters long and cannot contain spaces. You could have labeled the columns *test1* and *test2*, but the names used give more information in the Data Editor screen. Use an underscore (_) as a space to make the variable names easier to read.

The `scr_100` column shows the results of a test that has a maximum score of 100. The `scr_60` column shows the results of a test that has a maximum score of 60. The values in the `person` column (Dave and Mike) tell us who took each test.

The data for Dave end in row 12. This is because Dave took the test 12 times. Mike also took his test 12 times. His data are in rows 13 through 24.

Now that you have the data in place, use the `Frequencies` dialog box to determine the range for each test. Put the two test variables in position. Uncheck the option for displaying frequency tables in the lower left corner of the box. A message lets you know that if you do not perform the next step, you will not have any output. Click on `OK`.

Click on the `Statistics` button at the bottom left of the dialog box. Click in the box that reads `Range` (Figure 4.7). It is in the lower left of the dialog box in

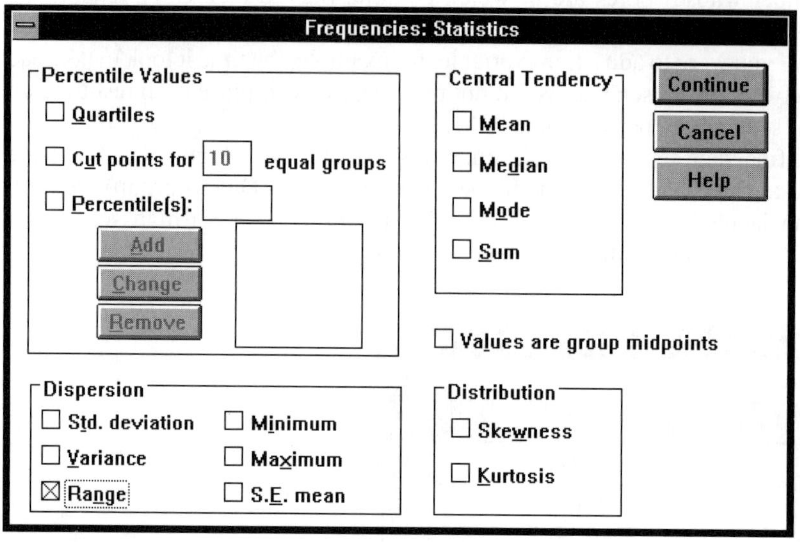

Figure 4.7

the area labeled `Dispersion`. The output is shown in Figure 4.8. If you forgot to uncheck the display tables option, you will see the output for `scr_100`. To find the range, subtract the lowest score from the highest score, or look at the bottom of that section to see the range calculated for you. The value is 73.

If you remembered to uncheck the display frequency tables option, you receive output such as that depicted in Figure 4.9 for `scr_60`. The range for Mike's scores was 48.

Exercise Answer 4–2   Variance and Standard Deviation

In this exercise, use the same data set as for Exercise 4–1. Open the `Frequencies:` dialog box and put the two test variables in the `Variable(s)` area at the center of the box. Make sure the `Display frequency tables` box in the lower left corner of the dialog box is blank. Click on the `Statistics` button. Choose `Variance` and `Std. deviation` from the `Dispersion` area of the dialog box (Figure 4.10). Uncheck `Range` if it is still marked from Exercise 4–1. Your dialog box should look like Figure 4.11.

Click on `Continue` and then `OK` in the main `Frequencies` dialog box. The output should look like Figure 4.12.

Each test has 12 valid cases and 12 missing cases. This is an artifact of how the data were entered. Only the valid cases are used in the calculation of the statistics. The test with a possible perfect score of 100 showed a standard deviation of 22.371 and a total variance of 500.455. The other test showed a standard devia-

```
SCR_100    Test Score (perfect= 100)
```

Value Label	Value	Frequency	Percent	Valid Percent	Cum Percent
	23.00	1	4.2	8.3	8.3
	48.00	1	4.2	8.3	16.7
	50.00	1	4.2	8.3	25.0
	56.00	1	4.2	8.3	33.3
	64.00	1	4.2	8.3	41.7
	67.00	1	4.2	8.3	50.0
	77.00	1	4.2	8.3	58.3
	80.00	1	4.2	8.3	66.7
	87.00	1	4.2	8.3	75.0
	92.00	1	4.2	8.3	83.3
	94.00	1	4.2	8.3	91.7
	96.00	1	4.2	8.3	100.0
		12	50.0	Missing	
	Total	24	100.0	100.0	

```
Range          73.000
```

Figure 4.8

```
SCR_60     Test Score (perfect = 60)


Range          48.000


Valid cases      12      Missing cases      12
```

Figure 4.9

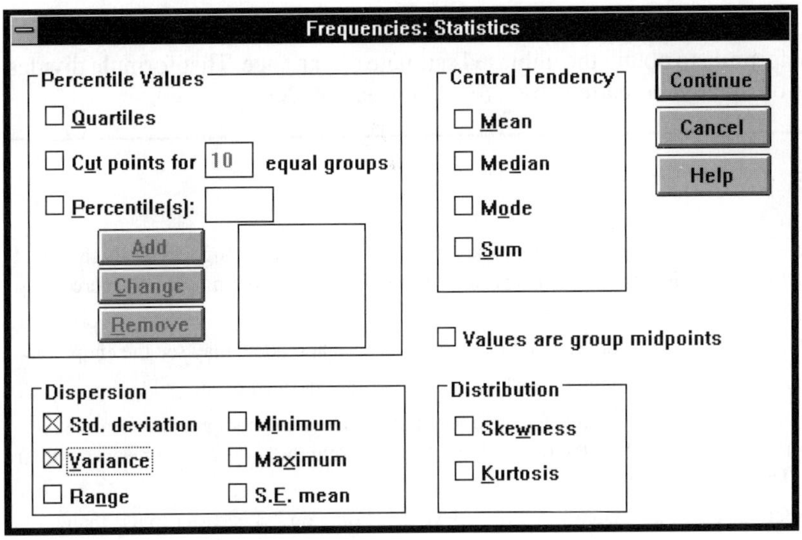

Figure 4.10

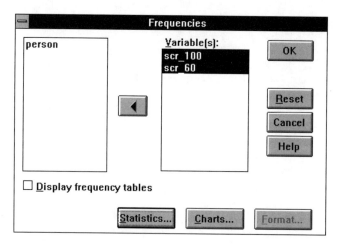

Figure 4.11

```
SCR_100    Test Score (perfect= 100)


Std dev      22.371      Variance     500.455


Valid cases     12       Missing cases     12

- - - - - - - - - - - - - - - - - - - - - - - - - - - - - - - - - - -

SCR_60     Test Score (perfect = 60)


Std dev      14.992      Variance     224.750


Valid cases     12       Missing cases     12
```

Figure 4.12

tion of 14.992 and a total variance of 224.750. In performing the analysis, *SPSS* uses the formula to obtain the unbiased estimate of variance. That formula divides the sum of squared deviations by $(N - 1)$ instead of (N).

Notes

1. There are different ways to formulate the range. We opted to use range equals high score minus low score. Some statisticians prefer range equals high score minus low score plus one.

2. These two sets of scores have been placed in order so that readers may see the endpoints.

3. The point was made in chapter 1 that a population is not defined by size.

4. We invite the reader to test this. Create a batch of numbers and compute the mean. Subtract the mean from each of the original numbers and sum the differences preserving their signs. The total equals zero.

5. It is often the case that students do not believe that Equation 4.4 is easier to use than Equation 4.3. We ask that doubting students use both equations on the same set of data to discover the utility of Equation 4.4.

6. We can only compare standard deviations between distributions in which the same variable is measured, in this case the number of new probation cases. If, for example, we measure the standard deviations in the age of new probationers and the number of new probation cases, we cannot simply compare the two computations and say that one was larger or smaller than the other. This is because standard deviations have units. The unit for one variable is years; the unit for the other is cases.

7. We encourage readers to compute z score transformations for any group of raw scores to prove to themselves that the mean and standard deviation of the former equal 0 and 1, respectively. Keep in mind, however, that small group sizes and rounding error may keep one from computing the exact values of 0 and 1. However, the mean and standard deviation of z scores are always close to the values specified.

8. Actually, the area under any normal curve between two scores reflects the percentage of scores in the population between those two scores.

5. Comparative Statistics

The County Prosecutor: Re-election Time

It's that time again! Another young hotshot wants to take your place. It doesn't seem that long ago that you were a young assistant prosecuting attorney who decided you could do a better job as county prosecutor than your boss. You campaigned endlessly on issues and change rather than the numbers that your opponent relied on. Now it's twelve years later and your challenger is running a tough campaign that focuses on your record, using the statistics you try to avoid. You are disturbed by a knock on the door. It's your campaign manager, who has been with you since the very beginning. He advises you that there are some problems with this campaign. You had wanted to avoid the numbers game, but your opponent is using them to her advantage. Your campaign manager once again tries to persuade you that the numbers are what will win or lose this election for you. So you ask, what should I use? What numbers will be beneficial to my campaign?

Your manager advises you to use crime rate and percentage change in crime since you first took office. These are believed to be your strongest statistics. You advise your manager that you'll come up with some figures, discuss them with him, and the two of you will make a decision. As your campaign manager leaves the office, you realize you will need some assistance in pulling together the proper figures. You turn to your old criminal justice statistics book for guidance.

Comparative Statistics

According to the 1990 Uniform Crime Reports ([UCR] 1991), there were 1,820,130 violent crimes in the United States in 1990 compared with only 1,361,820 in 1981. This change is an increase of 458,310 violent crimes (33.7%). The report also indicates that the rate of violent crime per 100,000 inhabitants of the United States was 594.3 in 1981 and 731.8 in 1990, or an increase of 23.1%. In addition, the report states that the U.S. population in 1981 was approximately 229 million and had increased to approximately 249 million by 1990 for an increase of 8.7%. These data suggest that the number of violent crimes and the rate of violent crime per 100,000 inhabitants increased at a greater rate than the U.S. population in the past 10 years.

Two of the statistics reported are perhaps the two most frequently used statistics in criminal justice. These are crime rate and percentage change. Both of these statistics help us to compare crime statistics over time and to compare crime statistics in relation to population size and other statistics. Another statistic illustrated in the foregoing data is so simple that we are likely to ignore it. That statistic is referred to as the *difference*. The number of crimes was different in one time period compared with another. We are interested not only in noting difference but also in measuring it and comparing it with other differences. The essence of comparative statistics is the study of differences. In this chapter, we review these measures and present a general discussion of comparative statistical procedures.

Crime Rates

The use of crime rates allows us to compare crime across vastly different settings. This is shown with an examination of the data in Table 5.1.

In a comparison of states only on the number of index crimes, Hawaii comes out "best" and California "worst." However, this is not a fair comparison because these states are very different from each other in terms of population. Hawaii is a small state whereas California is a huge one. One expects the number of crimes to be much higher in California owing to the population difference alone, because more people means more criminals, more victims, more residences, more autos, and more businesses. Comparisons among the other states in Table 5.1 also takes population into account. Because of these large population differences, it is misleading to compare these states on the absolute number of index crimes. One solution to this problem is to make the populations the same, that is, to standardize the populations. If, for example, each of these states had a population of 100,000, how many index crimes are there according to the data? To answer this question and, more important, to help us compare crime rates between different states (or cities or counties), we calculate a population-based crime rate as follows:

$$\text{Crime rate} = \frac{\text{Number of index crimes}}{\text{Population}} \times 100,000$$

For example, the index crime rate for Hawaii in 1990 was

$$\text{Index crime rate} = \frac{67,676}{1,108,229} \times 100,000 = 6,106.7$$

For California in 1990, the index crime rate was

$$\text{Index crime rate} = \frac{1,965,237}{29,760,021} \times 100,000 = 6,603$$

Table 5.1   Number of Index Crimes and Population in Selected States, 1990

State	No. of Index Crimes	Population
Hawaii	67,676	1,108,229
Colorado	199,434	3,294,394
Arizona	298,140	3,665,228
Michigan	557,232	9,259,297
Florida	1,139,934	12,937,926
New York	1,144,874	17,990,455
California	1,965,237	29,760,021

Source: *Uniform Crime Reports,* 1990

The remaining crime rates are as follows:

Colorado	6,053.7
Arizona	7,887.7
Michigan	5,995.8
Florida	8,810.8
New York	6,603.6

These rates may be interpreted as follows: For every 100,000 inhabitants of Hawaii in 1990, there were 6,106.7 index crimes; for every 100,000 inhabitants of Colorado in 1990, there were 6,053.7 index crimes; and for every 100,000 inhabitants of California in 1990, there were 6,603 index crimes.

We can see that in terms of crime rate Michigan comes out "best" and Florida "worst." In addition, the data show that Hawaii and California are quite similar and that Arizona surprisingly has a higher crime rate than all the other states except Florida. What these crime rates allow us to do is to compare states with differing populations in a manner that standardizes the populations. Rates are useful because they allow us to take an important variable, in this case population, and reduce it to a common standard.

The most common standard for population-based crime rate is the rate per 100,000 people; however, we can just as easily use 1,000 or 10,000 or even 1,000,000. In instances in which the population is small, it makes more sense to use a smaller standard. For example, the number of index crimes in Beaver Falls, Pennsylvania, in 1990 was 410. The population was 10,687 (UCR 1990). Dividing 410 by 10,687 then multiplying by a standard of 100,000 yields an index crime rate of 3,836.4. This is interpreted as "for every 100,000 inhabitants of Beaver Falls, Pennsylvania, in 1990, there were 3,836.4 index crimes." This is accurate, but it might be more meaningful, especially to the residents of Beaver Falls, to use a standard of 1,000. Dividing 410 by 10,687 and multiplying by 1,000 yields a crime rate of 38.3. This means that for every 1,000 inhabitants of Beaver Falls in 1990 there were 38.3 index crimes.

The foregoing example is useful in drawing attention to a simpler way to calculate rates using a variety of standards. Dividing 410 by 10,687 yields a quotient that looks like the following:

$$0.0383643$$

We simply need to move the decimal point to determine the rate per 100 (3.8) or per 1,000 (38.3) or per 10,000 (383.6) or per 100,000 (3,836.4) or per 1,000,000 (38,364.3).

There are a number of points to keep in mind when using crime rates. First, crime rates are most useful when comparing cities, states, or counties of comparable size. Comparing the crime rate in Beaver Falls with the crime rate in Philadelphia makes little sense. Second, population-based crime rates use the number of people that officially reside in a jurisdiction as the population figure. This can produce unusually large crime rates for some jurisdictions that have large nonresident populations. Two examples are Washington, D.C., and Las Vegas, Nevada. The number of index crimes in Washington, D.C., in 1990 was reported to be 65,389, and the resident population was 606,900 (UCR, 1990). This yields an index crime rate of 10,744 per 100,000 inhabitants. However, the actual number of people in Washington, D.C., on any given day far exceeds 606,900. Most of the daily population lives outside the city. Similarly, in Las Vegas the index crime rate of 7,130.9 per 100,000 inhabitants is affected by the fact that a sizable portion of the daily population is made up of nonresidents from other states and countries. When we read that any particular jurisdiction has an unusually high crime rate, it is wise to question the population figure.

Exercise 5–1   Crime Rates

Although you have been the prosecutor for twelve years, you decide to examine crime rates (per 100,000) in your county for the last six years. What year appears to have been the safest? Least safe?

Year	Crime Index	Population
1988	88,241	426,482
1989	70,003	400,095*
1990	75,687	410,599
1991	85,334	413,499
1992	79,097	441,449†
1993	72,359	441,948

*Lost a city to the next county.

†Incorporated two cities.

Crime-specific Rates

Most crime rates are population based. That is, they use the number of people in the population as the denominator in the equation. This produces the ratio of crimes to people and gives some idea of the risk of crime in a jurisdiction. In some instances, it is useful to use a different base that is tied more closely to the nature of the offense. For example, it can be helpful to calculate the auto theft rate based on the number of registered autos rather than the number of people. The resultant crime-specific rate yields a better estimate of the risk of auto theft because it is based not on people but on the number of autos. According to the 1990 UCR, there were 1,635,907 auto thefts in the United States in 1990. This yields a population-based auto theft rate of 657.8. For every 100,000 people in the United States in 1990, there were 657.8 auto thefts. According to the Bureau of the Census (1992), there were 143,026,000 registered autos in the United States in 1990. The crime-specific auto theft rate per 100,000 registered autos (1,635,907 divided by 143,026,000 × 100,000) is 1,143.8. This is a much higher rate and is more indicative of the risk of auto theft in this nation.

A study of bank robberies in midwestern states (Seng 1991) found clear differences in the risk of bank robbery among population-based rates and bank robbery rates based on the number of financial institutions in a state. For example, the population-based rate of bank robbery in Michigan, calculated as a ten year average, was 9.1 per 100,000 people, but 144.8 per 100,000 financial institutions. Similarly, we obtain a better sense of the risk of residential burglary using the number of housing units as a base and a much better sense of the risk of rape based on the number of women and girls between the ages of 12 and 65 years rather than the total population, which includes babies as well as 90-year-old men.

The use of rates is a common practice in criminal justice. In addition to index crime and crime-specific rates, you find victimization rates, which are an expression of the number of victimizations usually per 1,000 persons 12 years of age and older. A variety of system rates also gives some indication of how the various parts of the criminal justice system are performing. For example, arrest rates show the number of arrests per 100 reported crimes, and clearance rates show the number of crimes cleared by arrest per 100 reported crimes. Conviction rates deal with the number of convictions per 100 arraignments, and recidivism rates show the number of rearrested offenders per 100 parolees. System rates are essentially percentages because they usually use 100 as a base.

Exercise 5–2 Crime-specific Rates

Having examined the crime rates for the previous six years, you decide to look at individual offenses. What are the crime-specific rates for the following offenses: auto theft, convenience store robberies, and business burglaries? (Use per 1,000.)

2,347 Auto thefts	12,695 Registered autos
21 Robberies	1,176 Convenience stores
1,960 Burglaries	7,328 Businesses

Percentage Change

The number of violent crimes in the United States increased 33.7% between 1981 and 1990. Percentage change is a useful statistic because it allows us to compare data over time and in different jurisdictions. The calculation of percentage change is quite simple. Let us take the earlier example and see how the 33.7% figure was produced. The number of violent crimes in the first time period, 1981, is 1,361,820. We call this a. The number of violent crimes in the second time period, 1990, is 1,820,130. We call this b. This yields an increase of $1,820,130 - 1,361,820$ ($b - a$), or 458,310. How many is that per hundred? To answer that question we divide the difference (458,310) by the number we started with and multiply by 100. That is

$$\frac{458,310}{1,361,820} \times 100 = 33.7$$

What we did is subtract the number in the first time period (a) from the number in the second time period (b) and divide the difference by the number in the first time period (a) then multiply by 100. Stated as a formula:

$$\frac{b - a}{a} \times 100$$

This is the formula for percentage change. When we say that the number of violent crimes increased 33.7% between 1981 and 1990, we are saying that for every 100 violent crimes in 1981, there were 133.7 in 1990.

It is also possible for the number of crimes (or the number of persons, objects, or events we are studying) to decrease, which yields a negative change. The number of burglaries in the United States in 1981 was 3,779,700 (a) and in 1990 was 3,073,900 (b). Putting these figures into the formula we get

$$\frac{3,073,900 - 3,779,700}{3,779,700} = \frac{-705,800}{3,779,700} \times 100 = -18.7\%$$

The foregoing examples deal with change in the same jurisdiction over time. However, criminal justice data often compare jurisdictions. A comparison of prison populations among states is such an example. Table 5.2 presents data on

Table 5.2   Percentage Change in Prison Populations in Selected States, 1981–1990

State	Prison Population 1981	1990	Percentage Change
New York	25,494	54,859	115.2
Vermont	361	1,046	189.8
Illinois	13,669	27,516	101.3
North Dakota	238	482	102.5
Texas	31,504	50,042	58.8
Delaware	984	3,506	256.3
California	27,913	97,309	248.6
Alaska	510	2,622	414.1

Source: *Historical Statistics on Prisoners in State and Federal Institutions, Yearend 1925–1986,* Washington, D.C.: Bureau of Justice Statistics, May 1988, and *Prisoners in 1990,* Washington, D.C.: Bureau of Justice Statistics, May 1991.

changes in prison populations of selected states between 1981 and 1990. We can see that the prison population in each of these states increased in the past ten years. However, it is difficult to compare the various states because of the large differences in the size of their prison populations, especially the starting point in 1981. For example, how does a change from 25,494 to 54,859, an increase of 29,365 inmates, compare with a change from 361 to 1,046, or 685 inmates? Percentage change allows us to make such comparisons by reducing the starting point in each state to 100 and asking, If each state had 100 inmates in 1981, how many would it have in 1990 according to the data? Using this common standard, we can see that the sharpest increases are in the smaller states, led by Alaska with a 414.1 percent change in prison population in ten years. One way to appreciate what this indicates is to realize that a percentage change of 414.1% means that if there were 100 inmates in a room in 1981, according to the data, there would be 514.1 inmates in that room in 1990.

Exercise 5–3   Percentage Change

What is the percentage change of the three offenses in Exercise 5–2 from your first year as prosecuting attorney (1982) to the year before re-election?

Crime	1982	1993
Auto theft	3,359	2,347
Robbery	9	21
Burglary	2,111	1,960

Trend Analyses

Comparative statistics are techniques or procedures that allow us to compare differences over time. We have discussed the idea of difference and examined two useful statistics, rate and percentage change, as comparative techniques. However, when comparing data over fairly long time periods of ten years or more, it is useful to use graphs to present the data, because graphs more clearly indicate the trend of change over time (Figure 5.1). Such techniques are classified under

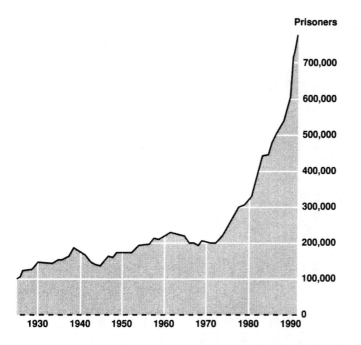

Figure 5.1A Sentenced prisoners in state and federal institutions on December 31 (United States, 1925–1991).

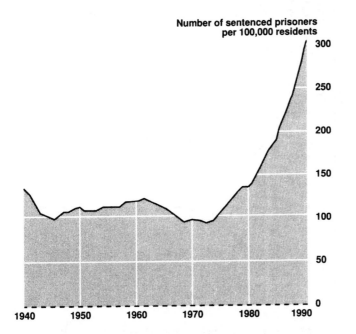

Figure 5.1B Rate (per 100,000 resident population) of sentenced prisoners in state and federal institutions on December 31 (United States 1940–1991).

the rubric of trend analysis. Some basic points of trend analysis are presented in this chapter.

In May 1988, the Bureau of Justice Statistics published a report on the number of prisoners sentenced to federal and state prisons for each year from 1925 through 1986. We have updated this table to include 1987 through 1991. A

Table 5.3 Number and Rate (per 100,00 Resident Population of Each Sex) of Sentenced Prisoners in State and Federal Institutions on December 31 (United States, 1925–1991)

Year	Total	Rate	Males Number	Rate	Females Number	Rate
1925	91,669	79	88,231	149	3,438	6
1926	97,991	83	94,287	157	3,704	6
1927	109,983	91	104,983	173	4,363	7
1928	116,390	96	111,836	182	4,554	8
1929	120,496	98	115,876	187	4,620	8
1930	129,453	104	124,785	200	4,668	8
1931	137,082	110	132,638	211	4,444	7
1932	137,997	110	133,573	211	4,424	7
1933	136,810	109	132,520	209	4,290	7
1934	138,316	109	133,769	209	4,547	7
1935	144,180	113	139,278	217	4,902	8
1936	145,038	113	139,990	217	5,048	8
1937	152,741	118	147,375	227	5,368	8
1938	160,285	123	154,826	236	5,459	8
1939	179,818	137	173,143	263	6,675	10
1940	173,706	131	167,345	252	6,361	10
1941	165,439	124	159,228	239	6,211	9

Year	Total	Rate	Males Number	Rate	Females Number	Rate
1960	212,953	117	205,265	230	7,688	8
1961	220,149	119	212,268	234	7,881	8
1962	218,830	117	210,823	229	8,007	8
1963	217,283	114	209,538	225	7,745	8
1964	214,336	111	206,632	219	7,704	8
1965	210,895	108	203,327	213	7,568	8
1966	199,654	102	192,703	201	6,951	7
1967	194,896	98	188,661	195	6,235	6
1968	187,914	94	182,102	187	5,812	6
1969	196,007	97	189,413	192	6,594	6
1970	196,429	96	190,794	191	5,635	5
1971	198,061	95	191,732	189	6,329	6
1972	196,092	93	189,823	185	6,269	6
1973	204,211	96	197,523	191	6,004	6
1974	218,466	102	211,077	202	7,389	7
1975	240,593	111	231,918	220	8,675	8
1976	262,833	120	252,794	238	10,039	9
1977[a]	278,141	126	267,097	249	11,044	10

Year						
1942	150,384	112	144,167	217	6,217	9
1943	137,220	103	131,054	202	6,166	9
1944	132,456	100	126,350	200	6,106	9
1945	133,649	98	127,609	193	6,040	9
1946	140,079	99	134,075	191	6,004	8
1947	151,304	105	144,961	202	6,343	9
1948	155,977	106	149,739	205	6,238	8
1949	163,749	109	157,663	211	6,086	8
1950	166,123	109	160,309	211	5,814	8
1951	165,680	107	159,610	208	6,070	8
1952	168,233	107	161,994	208	6,239	8
1953	173,579	108	166,909	211	6,670	8
1954	182,901	112	175,907	218	6,994	8
1955	185,780	112	178,655	217	7,125	8
1956	189,565	112	182,190	218	7,375	9
1957	195,414	113	188,113	221	7,301	8
1958	205,643	117	198,208	229	7,435	8
1959	208,105	117	200,469	228	7,636	8
1977[b]	285,456	129	274,244	255	11,212	10
1978	294,396	132	282,813	261	11,583	10
1979	301,470	133	289,465	264	12,005	10
1980	315,974	138	303,643	274	12,331	11
1981	353,167	153	338,940	302	14,227	12
1982	394,374	170	378,045	336	16,329	14
1983	419,820	179	402,391	352	17,429	14
1984	443,398	188	424,193	NA	19,205	NA
1985	480,568	200	458,972	NA	21,296	NA
1986	522,084	216	497,540	NA	24,544	NA
1987	560,812	228	533,990	NA	26,822	NA
1988	603,732	244	573,587	NA	30,145	NA
1989	680,907	271	643,643	NA	37,264	NA
1990	739,980	292	699,416	NA	40,564	NA
1991	789,347	310	745,520	NA	43,827	NA

Note: Both custody and jurisdiction figures are shown for 1977 to facilitate year to year comparison. Data for 1984–90 have been revised from previous presentations.

Source: U.S. Department of Justice, Bureau of Justice Statistics. *Prisoners 1925–81*, Bulletin NCJ-85861, p. 2; *Prisoners in 1983*, Bulletin NCJ-92949, p. 2; *Prisoners in 1985*, Bulletin NCJ-101384, p. 2; *Prisoners in 1986*, Bulletin NCJ-104864, p. 3, Table 5 (Washington, DC: U.S. Department of Justice); and U.S. Department of Justice, Bureau of Justice Statistics. *Correctional Populations in the United States, 1985*, NCJ-103957, Tables 5.1–5.4; *1986* NCJ-111611, Tables 5.1–5.4; *1987*, NCJ-118762, Tables 5.1–5.4; *1988*, NCJ-124280, Tables 5.1–5.4; *1989*, NCJ-130445, Tables 5.1–5.4; *1990*, NCJ-135946, Tables 5.1–5.4; *1991*, NCJ-142729, Tables 5.1–5.4; *1991*, NCJ-142729, Tables 5.1–5.4 (Washington, DC: USGPO). Table adapted by SOURCEBOOK staff.

[a]Custody counts.

[b]Jurisdiction counts.

summary of these data is presented in Table 5.3. Inspection of the data confirms that the prison population in the United States increased sharply in the years since 1925, when there were 91,669 prisoners in state and federal prisons, to 1991 when there were a total of 789,347. The report notes that this amounts to a 761 percent increase.

Closer inspection shows interesting fluctuations in the data. There is an apparent overall upward trend, but there are interesting declines in some years. This information can be presented in a graph that plots the yearly change in prison population since 1925. This graph is presented in Figure 5.1A.

This picture shows the gradual upward trend in prison population through 1986 and the sharp increase in the last few years. There also are declines in prison populations during World War II and the Vietnam War. The data are plotted on a year to year basis. With large data sets, as is the case with the 67 years of prison population data, plotting each year can be time consuming.

Another, and more useful, technique is to group the data into five-year intervals, for example 1925 to 1929 and 1930 to 1934, and calculate the mean number of prisoners in the interval and draw a graph of the means placing these values at the midpoint of the interval. An example of this method is presented in Figure 5.2. The overall trend is still apparent but the picture has less jagged peaks and valleys. This is known as *smoothing the data* using simple averages.

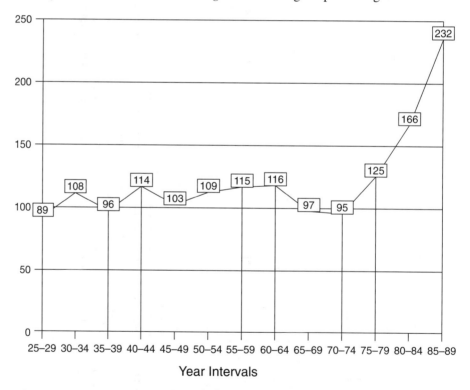

Figure 5.2   Mean rate (per 100,000) of sentenced prisoners in state and federal institutions by interval, 1925–1989.

Another procedure particularly useful for data that cover long periods is called a *moving average*. We select a time interval as we did for the simple average, for example, the five years 1925–1929, and calculate the average number of inmates during this period, which is 107,178.4. The next interval in the moving average technique drops the first year of the preceding interval and adds the next year to the list. Thus the second interval drops 1925 and adds 1930, for an interval that contains the years 1926, 1927, 1928, 1929, and 1930. The third interval drops 1926 and adds 1931 for an interval that contains the years 1927, 1928, 1929, 1930, and 1931. This procedure is repeated until all the years have been included. The result is a smooth trend line. A general rule in using data to indicate trends is to use no less than five years of data. This is particularly important in criminal justice because of the many factors that change from year to year in the variables we measure. Although the UCR indicate change over a one-year period for various index crimes, the trend analysis contained in the reports is for a five-year period.

Summary

Chapter 5 discusses comparative techniques that are especially important to the field of criminal justice. Change is an integral part of all elements of criminal justice, so it is quite common to note *differences* in various measures from one year to the next. The essence of comparative statistics is the study of differences. Exploration of such differences is sometimes difficult because the jurisdictions studied are dissimilar in regard to important variables. Calculation of various *rates* is a useful technique in making such comparisons; these rates include *crime rates*, *crime-specific rates*, and *system rates*. *Percentage change* is an important measure of difference over time. *Trend analysis* and simple *graphs* are used to compare data that concern long periods of time.

Answers to Exercises

Exercise Answer 5–1 Crime Rates
1988 Crime Rate

$$\frac{88,241}{426,482} \times 100,000 = 20,690.44$$

1989 Crime Rate

$$\frac{70,003}{400,095} \times 100,000 = 17,496.59$$

1990 Crime Rate

$$\frac{75,687}{410,599} \times 100,000 = 18,433.31$$

1991 Crime Rate

$$\frac{85,334}{413,499} \times 100,000 = 20,638.70$$

1992 Crime Rate

$$\frac{79,097}{441,449} \times 100,000 = 17,917.59$$

1993 Crime Rate

$$\frac{72,359}{441,948} \times 100,000 = 16,372.74$$

Safest Year: 1993
Least Safe Year: 1988

Exercise Answer 5–2   Crime-specific Rates
Auto Thefts (per 1,000 registered autos)

$$\frac{2,347}{12,695} \times 1,000 = 184.88$$

Convenience Store Robberies (per 1,000 stores)

$$\frac{21}{1,176} \times 1,000 = 17.86$$

Business Burglaries (per 1,000 businesses)

$$\frac{1,960}{7,328} \times 1,000 = 267.47$$

Exercise Answer 5–3   Percentage Change
Auto Thefts

$$\frac{2,347 - 3,359}{3,359} \times 100 = -30.13\%$$

Robberies

$$\frac{21 - 9}{9} \times 100 = +133.33\%$$

Burglaries

$$\frac{1,960 - 2,111}{2,111} \times 100 = -7.15\%$$

Computer Applications for Selected Exercises

Exercise Answer 5–2   Crime-specific Rates
The formula for crime-specific rate per 1,000 is

(Number of crimes ÷ Base population) × 1,000

Determining the rate is easy with a calculator if there are only one or two rates. If there are more than that, you can enter the formula into *SPSS* and have the result placed in a new data column.

Set up one column for the number of crimes and one for the base population in which the crimes were committed. Each row is a different type of crime.

Click once on the gray column head for the first variable. Click on the insert variable icon on the toolbar to add a column to the left of the one you have highlighted (Figure 5.3).

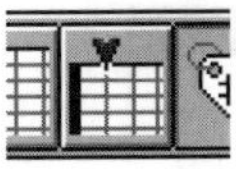

Figure 5.3

Use this column as a label for the rows in the Data Editor (Figure 5.4). Double-click on the column head. Click on `Type` in the lower left corner to bring up the `Define Variable Type` dialog box. Choose `String` as the variable type. String columns can contain letters, numbers, and spaces. They are sometimes referred to as *alphanumeric* fields because they can contain letters (alpha) and numbers (numeric). Set the width to 20.

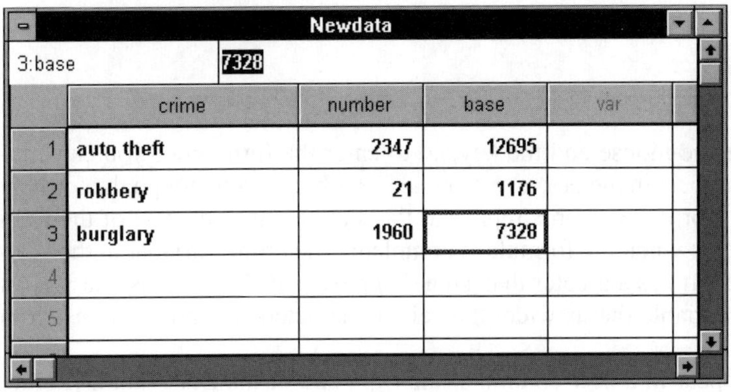

	crime	number	base	var
1	auto theft	2347	12695	
2	robbery	21	1176	
3	burglary	1960	7328	
4				
5				

Newdata — 3:base 7328

Figure 5.4

You can set up the formula using the `Compute` function in the `Transform` menu (Figure 5.5).

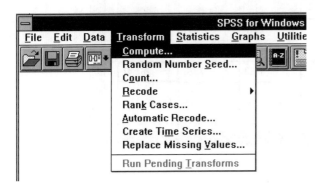

Figure 5.5

This dialog box has several features, but you need only a few. Start by clicking your mouse in the `Target Variable:` field in the upper left corner of the dialog box (Figure 5.6). Type in the column name for the result of this formula. Click on `Type&Label` and add a variable label.

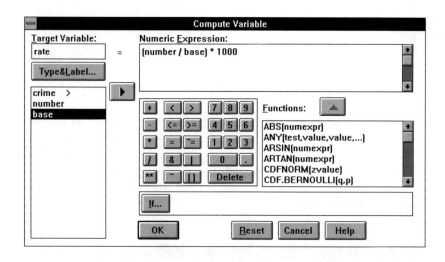

Figure 5.6

You can use the mouse and the keypad to enter the formula or you can simply type the numbers in the Numeric Expression: box. Even though the formula is made up of words, the words represent the numbers in each row of the Data Editor. Choose OK when the formula is complete. The crime variable in the variable list on the left has a greater than sign (>) next to it. This means that it is an alphanumeric variable that is wider than eight characters. Do not try to use it in the formula.

The rates appear in a new column at the right end of the Data Editor (Figure 5.7). The rates are rounded to two decimal places. On the data entry line, you can see that the stored value of the highlighted cell is a much longer number.

	crime	number	base	rate
1	auto theft	2347	12695	184.88
2	robbery	21	1176	17.86
3	burglary	1960	7328	267.47
4				
5				

Newdata

3:rate   267.467248908297

Figure 5.7

You can change the rounding by changing the number of displayed decimal places in the Define Variable Type dialog box for this column. Double-click on the column head and choose Type. Change the number of decimal places (Figure 5.8). Choose Continue and then OK. Look at the results in the Data Editor. The number stored by *SPSS* has not changed. You have only changed what is being displayed.

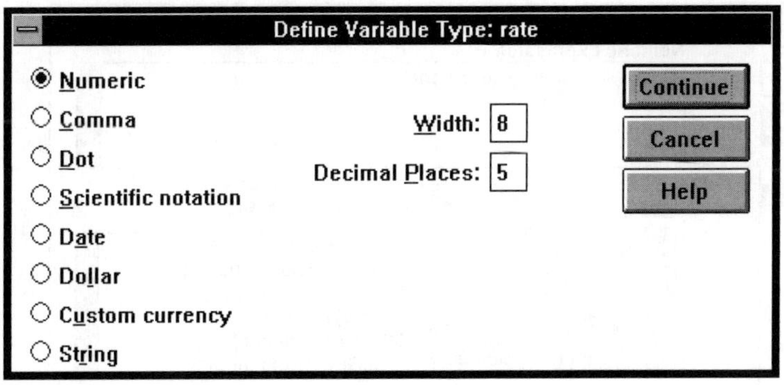

Define Variable Type: rate

- ⦿ **N**umeric
- ○ **C**omma
- ○ **D**ot
- ○ **S**cientific notation
- ○ D**a**te
- ○ Do**l**lar
- ○ C**u**stom currency
- ○ Str**i**ng

Width: 8

Decimal **P**laces: 5

[Continue] [Cancel] [Help]

Figure 5.8

Exercise Answer 5–3   Percentage Change

Enter the data in this exercise in the same way as for Exercise 5–2. The data are shown in Figure 5.9.

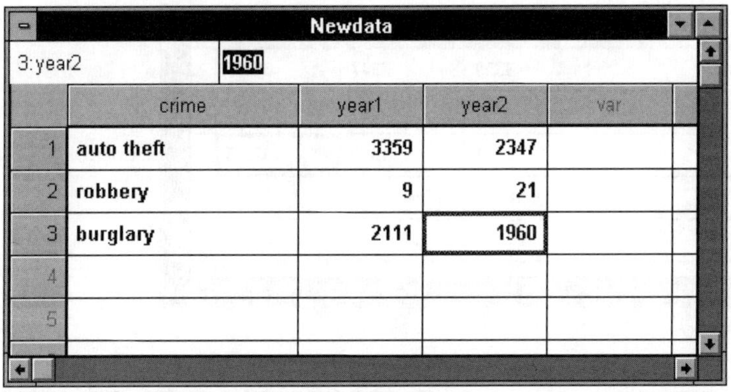

Newdata

3:year2   1960

	crime	year1	year2	var
1	auto theft	3359	2347	
2	robbery	9	21	
3	burglary	2111	1960	
4				
5				

Figure 5.9

You can use the Compute Variable function to calculate the percentage change. The formula for percentage change is

$$[(\text{new} - \text{old}) \div \text{old}] \times 100\%$$

Always divide by the old value because you are comparing it with the new information. A positive new change variable indicates an increase in crime rate. A negative value indicates a decrease. If there is no change, the numerator is zero, and so is the percentage. Figure 5.10 shows the formula as it appears in the Compute Variable dialog box.

Click on OK when the formula is ready. The result is placed in a new column on the right-hand side of the Data Editor (Figure 5.11).

You cannot display the percent sign (%) in the student version of *SPSS for Windows,* but you included 100 in the formula, so the values appear in the correct scale. It looks like there has been a dramatic decrease in auto theft rate (30.13%), a small decrease in burglary rate (7.15%), and an extremely large increase in robbery rate (133.33%).

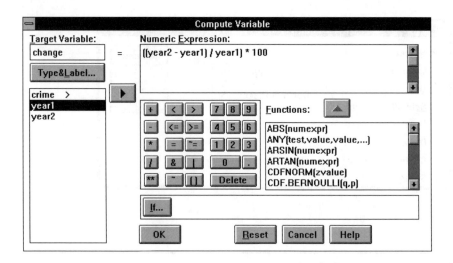

Figure 5.10

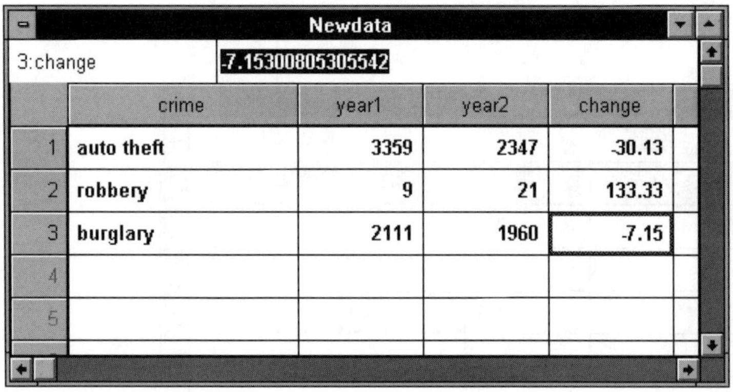

Figure 5.11

References

Bureau of the Census (1992). *Statistical Abstracts of the United States.* Washington, DC: U.S. Department of Commerce. p. 606.

Crime in America, 1990. 1991. (Uniform Crime Reports.) Washington, DC: Federal Bureau of Investigation.

Historical Statistics on Prisoners in State and Federal Institutions, Yearend 1925–1986. 1988. Washington, DC: Bureau of Justice Statistics.

Prisoners in 1990. 1991. Washington, DC: Bureau of Justice Statistics.

Seng, M. J. 1991. Bank robbery in midwestern states: 1980–1989. Paper presented at Annual Conference of the Midwestern Criminal Justice Association, 16–18 October, Chicago.

Part Two
Explanation

6. Relationships Between Nominal Variables

The Rookie Probation Officer

Even though you graduated with honors, you knew starting out as a rookie probation officer would not be easy. You knew there would be procedures and reports you would have to learn. That was expected. What came as a big surprise were the statistical reports you would have to provide every month. The number of cases, calls, reports, and court appearances had to be tracked. You were told this was done more for administrative purposes, such as budgeting requests or additional officers, than anything else, but it had to be done.

The first few weeks you are quite busy learning the ropes. One day your supervisor comes to you for advice. Because you have taken a statistics course more recently than the other staff members have, your assistance is needed to put together a report for the chief judge. Apparently there has been some discussion in the local newspapers that there is a growing disparity among judges as to the types of probation sentences being imposed on juvenile offenders. The chief judge wants to know whether there is any truth to this observation. The probation department has been asked to examine the sentencing patterns of judges during the past year. In particular, the judge wants to know (1) whether the race or ethnicity of the juvenile is related to the type of sentence given; (2) whether there is a relationship between a judge's race or ethnicity and the type of sentence imposed; and (3) whether the type of offense makes a difference in the sentence.

You feel somewhat honored, yet scared, that you have been asked to assist with such a report. However, because the statistics course was one of the last courses you took before graduation, and you did well in it, you readily agree to assist. Your supervisor, who is not very strong in statistics, asks you where to begin and what should be the main focus of the project. You easily recall your course and reply, "Because the primary questions that the judge wants answered deal with the relationship between nominal variables, that's where we'll begin."

Relationships Between Nominal Variables

Chapters 1 through 5 deal with the basic statistical procedures used in organizing data and in comparing various aspects of two or more data sets. These procedures allow us to gain a preliminary understanding of our data and are used in everyday practice in criminal justice. However, criminal justice practitioners not only describe and compare crime and system phenomena but also attempt to explain them. For example, we are not satisfied in merely noting differences in crime rates between two or more communities. We want to explore why the rates differ. Are the rates related to police presence, target availability, or social makeup? Similarly, one can ask what variables are related to outcomes such as prison crowding, bank robbery rates, judges' use of court time, probation officers' acceptance of caseload classification schemes, court clerk efficiency, or police officers' job satisfaction.

Answers to these and hundreds of other similar questions all are used to explain phenomena by identifying the variables related to the phenomena. To measure the degree to which variables are related, however, one must first understand the statistical meaning of a relationship. This leads to a discussion of dependent and independent variables, the concept of statistical significance, and hypothesis testing. Although these topics may be difficult to grasp, they all deal with three basic questions: (1) How can we tell if two or more variables are related? (2) How can we assess the strength of the relationship? (3) How can we tell if the relationship is statistically significant (i.e., has a low probability of having occurred by chance)?

The Meaning of a Statistical Relationship

Two or more variables are related when measurable changes in one variable correspond with measurable changes in another variable (Handel 1978). For example, it is common to see that prison sentences tend to be short for less serious crimes and long for more serious crimes. This shows that length of sentence is related to seriousness of offense. We also might hypothesize that age is related to type of offense, that political affiliation is not related to judicial decisions, or that the tendency to abuse children is related to parents' experiences of their own childhood abuse. In each of these statements, we are suggesting that a change in one of these variables goes along with, or corresponds to, a change in another variable. This means that we try to explain one variable in terms of another. We try to explain length of sentence by seriousness of offense, type of offense by age, judicial decision by political affiliation, or child abuse by parents' experiences of abuse. In this context, the variable that we are attempting to explain is called the *dependent variable*. The variable we use to explain the dependent variable is called the *independent variable*.

Criminal justice practitioners study relationships that differ in type. At times, one simply needs to document that an association exists between two variables. At other times, one needs to establish that one variable causes the other.[1] Regardless of the type of explanation that is sought, measuring a relationship involves explaining one or more dependent variables with one or more independent variables.

How can we tell if variables are related? The answer to that question differs in terms of the type of variables under study. The procedure for examining relationships between nominal variables is different from that for interval or ratio variables. This chapter discusses the former, and chapter 7 discusses the latter.

Let us begin with a simple example. Suppose we want to see if defendants' court appearances are related to electronic monitoring. We know that some defendants appear for their scheduled court appearance and some do not. Do the defendants who are wearing an electronic monitor appear in court more frequently than those who are not wearing such a device?

For our example, we have a small group of 30 defendants; some are on electronic monitoring and some are not. Likewise, some of the defendants have appeared in court as scheduled and some have not. These data are presented in Table 6.1.

Given the way the information in Table 6.1 is displayed, we cannot tell whether electronic monitoring is related to court appearance. We need to cross reference the two variables to see if they are related. We can do this by constructing a joint frequency distribution of the two variables in a format called a *contingency table* (Table 6.2).

A contingency table is a set of interrelated boxes called *cells*. The frequency in each cell indicates the number of defendants who possess a joint characteristic. The upper-left cell in Table 6.2 indicates that there are nine defendants who are on electronic monitoring *and* who appeared in court as scheduled. The lower-left cell indicates that there are seven persons on electronic monitoring *and* who did not appear as scheduled. The upper- and lower-right cells show the numbers of defendants not on electronic monitoring who did and did not appear in court as scheduled.

Table 6.1   Frequency of Court Appearance for Thirty Defendants, Some of Whom Are on Electronic Monitoring

Defendant	On Electronic Monitoring	Appeared in Court as Scheduled
1	Yes	No
2	Yes	No
3	No	Yes
4	Yes	Yes
5	No	No
6	Yes	Yes
7	No	No
8	Yes	No
9	No	No
10	Yes	Yes
11	No	Yes
12	Yes	No
13	No	Yes
14	Yes	No
15	No	No
16	Yes	Yes
17	No	No
18	Yes	Yes
19	No	Yes
20	Yes	No
21	No	No
22	Yes	No
23	No	No
24	Yes	Yes
25	No	Yes
26	Yes	Yes
27	No	No
28	Yes	Yes
29	No	Yes
30	Yes	Yes

**Table 6.2   Contingency Table of Defendants'
Court Appearance and Electronic
Monitoring Status**

		Defendant on Electronic Monitoring		
		Yes	**No**	
Appeared in Court as Scheduled	**Yes**	9	6	15
	No	7	8	15
		16	14	30

The numbers that appear on the outside of the contingency table are called *marginal frequencies*. Summing cell frequencies from left to right gives us row totals. Fifteen defendants appeared in court as scheduled, and 15 did not. Summing cell frequencies from top to bottom gives us column totals. These tell us that 16 defendants are on electronic monitoring and 14 are not. The sum of the row totals (15 + 15), the sum of the column totals (16 + 14), and the sum of the cell frequencies (9 + 6 + 7 + 8) each gives us *N*, which is 30.

When constructing a contingency table, it is useful to place the *independent variable* on the *top* of the table and the *dependent variable* along the *side*. You can configure the table the opposite way, but we have found that the specified layout is easier to use.

Table 6.2 shows that of the 16 defendants on electronic monitoring, 9 appeared in court as scheduled and 7 did not. Of the 14 defendants who are not monitored, 6 appeared as scheduled and 8 did not. Although one can easily switch the placement of the independent and dependent variables, the structure of the table makes it easy for us to see what happens to court appearance when defendants are and are not monitored electronically.

The design of Table 6.2 is effective for describing the joint occurrence of electronic monitoring and court appearance, but it does not readily help us to see if the two variables are related. For this, we need to create column percentages, that is, percentages of the cell frequencies using the column totals. Column percentages have been added to the information in Table 6.2 and are shown in Table 6.3.[2]

The column percentages for the defendants on electronic monitoring are formed by dividing the cell frequencies by 16 and multiplying by 100 percent (e.g., $9/16 \times 100\% = 56\%$). Likewise, the column percentages for those not on electric monitoring are found by dividing the cell frequencies by 14 and multiplying by 100 percent (e.g., $8/14 \times 100\% = 57\%$). Each percentage is rounded to the nearest unit.[3]

With column percentages in place, one can begin to see if a relationship exists between electronic monitoring and court appearance. Table 6.3 shows that 56 percent of the defendants on electronic monitoring appeared in court as scheduled, whereas 44 percent did not. This finding is essentially reversed for the defendants who are not being monitored; 43 percent appeared in court and 57 percent did not. The difference in the distribution of the column percentages for the monitored and nonmonitored defendants leads us to believe that there is a relationship between the dependent and independent variables. Although the information in Table 6.3 is not striking, the findings indicate that monitored defendants tend to appear in court more frequently than nonmonitored defendants.

Table 6.3   Contingency Table from Table 6.2 with Column Percentages Added

		Defendant on Electronic Monitoring		
		Yes	No	
Appeared in Court as Scheduled	Yes	9 56%	6 43%	15
	No	7 44%	8 57%	15
		16	14	30

Why does a difference in the distribution of column percentages lead us to believe that there is a relationship between electronic monitoring and court appearance? Because the difference tells us that the percentage of defendants appearing in court (or not appearing in court) depends on whether they are being monitored (or not being monitored).

This idea probably can be seen more readily in a situation in which the dependent and independent variables are related perfectly. For example, Table 6.4 presents a case in which all of the monitored defendants and none of the non-monitored defendants appeared in court as scheduled. One can easily see how court appearance clearly depends on monitoring status. Although this type of perfect situation is unlikely to occur in reality, the distributions of the column percentages are as different as they can be, and thus illustrate a perfect relationship.

If no relationship was present in the example, the distribution of column percentages for court appearance would be the same for those who were and those who were not being monitored. This indicates that the tendency to appear in court does not depend on electronic monitoring. This is the situation depicted in Table 6.5. The cell frequencies have been arranged to illustrate a case in which 50 percent of the monitored defendants appeared in court and 50 percent did not. The same behavior is seen among defendants who are not monitored. Thus, the similarity of the distribution of column percentages in Table 6.5 shows that court appearance is not related to electronic monitoring. Given these data, one can see

Table 6.4   Contingency Table in Which There Is a Perfect Relationship Between Court Appearance and Electronic Monitoring

		Defendant on Electronic Monitoring		
		Yes	No	
Appeared in Court as Scheduled	Yes	16 100%	0 0%	16
	No	0 0%	14 100%	14
		16	14	30

that there is a 50 percent chance of a defendant's appearing in court whether or not he or she is being monitored.

Table 6.5   Contingency Table in Which There Is No Relationship Between Court Appearance and Electronic Monitoring

		Defendant on Electronic Monitoring		
		Yes	**No**	
Appeared in Court as Scheduled	**Yes**	8 50%	7 50%	15
	No	8 50%	7 50%	15
		16	14	30

Exercise 6–1   Relationships Between Variables: Contingency Tables

Using the following data, construct a contingency table to determine if a relationship exists between the race of the juvenile (white or non-white) and whether probation was received for a first-time offense of auto theft.

Juvenile	Race	Received Probation	Juvenile	Race	Received Probation
1	White	Yes	15	Non-white	Yes
2	White	No	16	White	Yes
3	White	Yes	17	White	No
4	Non-white	Yes	18	White	No
5	Non-white	Yes	19	White	Yes
6	White	Yes	20	White	Yes
7	White	Yes	21	Non-white	Yes
8	White	No	22	White	Yes
9	White	No	23	Non-white	Yes
10	Non-white	No	24	White	No
11	Non-white	No	25	Non-white	Yes
12	Non-white	No	26	Non-white	Yes
13	Non-white	Yes	27	White	Yes
14	Non-white	Yes	28	White	Yes

Significance and Strength of Relationships

The procedure discussed so far merely helps one visualize a relationship between dependent and independent variables. It does not tell us if the relationship is statistically significant (i.e., if it can be explained by something other than chance), nor does it tell us the strength of that relationship. Therefore, we need to augment our skills in exploring and interpreting relationships.

The Meaning of Statistical Significance

Statistical significance is a term used to indicate that an observed relationship is not due to chance. The traditional way to test significance is a component of a method known as *hypothesis testing*.[4]

In hypothesis testing, one establishes two opposing hypotheses. The first hypothesis states that there is no relationship between two variables such as *X* and *Y*. This is called the *null hypothesis* (the word *null* is Latin for *not any*). The second hypothesis states that there is a relationship. This is called the *rival* or *research hypothesis*. It is logical to presume that there either is or is not a relationship between *X* and *Y*. Although it may seem counterintuitive, we presume that the null hypothesis is true and decide to reject it only if there is evidence to persuade us to do so. This is similar to due process of law, in which we presume someone is innocent until there is evidence to suggest otherwise (Hy, Feig, and Regoli 1983).[5]

In our discussion of the relationship between monitoring and court appearance, we stated that differences in the column percentages of the contingency table suggested that there is a relationship between the dependent and independent variables. In reality, however, such differences can be explained by a genuine relationship or by chance. The hypothesis testing process helps us decide which of these is the case. If differences in column percentages are due to chance, we are unable to reject the null hypothesis and conclude that the data do not indicate a relationship. If differences are due to a systematic association between the dependent and independent variables, we reject the null hypothesis in favor of the rival hypothesis and conclude that the data do indicate a relationship.

Consider the far-fetched example in Table 6.6 that examines a relationship between eye color and career choice among a group of hypothetical criminal justice students. Most of us would probably guess that there is no relationship between these two variables. As such, we expect the column percentages of career choices to be the same for each eye color. However, Table 6.6 shows that some differences exist. Is this difference indicative of a real relationship or of a chance occurrence?

Table 6.6 Contingency Table to Examine the Relationship Between Eye Color and Career Choice Among 150 Hypothetical Criminal Justice Students

		Eye Color			
		Blue	**Brown**	**Green**	
	Law Enforcement	2 4%	3 6%	3 6%	8
Career Choice	**Prosecution**	30 60%	29 58%	32 64%	91
	Defense	15 30%	14 28%	13 26%	42
	Corrections	3 6%	4 8%	2 4%	9
		50	50	50	150

In the hypothesis testing process, a statistical test is used to help answer our question. In the case of nominal variables (such as those in all of the contingency tables in this chapter), a procedure known as the *chi-square test* is performed, and its results are evaluated. A chi-square test of Table 6.6 indicates that the difference in the column percentages can be explained by chance.

In the sections that follow, we explain how the chi-square test is calculated and used to determine statistical significance. In addition, we discuss the related concepts of *degrees of freedom* and *level of significance*.

The Chi-square Test and Statistical Significance

Let us now turn to another example in our discussion of significance testing. Table 6.7 presents data on offenses and dispositions (sentences) for a sample of juvenile cases. The question is, Do the data in Table 6.7 describe a statistically significant relationship?

It is generally recognized that the seriousness of an offense is related to sentences for adult offenders. However, this relationship may not be true for juvenile offenders because the court acts in accordance with the best interests of the child.

We begin to answer our question by specifying the null and rival hypotheses. The null hypothesis (symbolized as H_0) states that there is no relationship between the dependent and independent variables; that is, any observed difference in the column percentages is due to chance. The rival hypothesis (symbolized as H_1) states that there is a relationship. Remember that in the hypothesis testing process, H_0 is assumed to be true until we have evidence to suggest that it is false, in which case we reject H_0 in favor of H_1. The evidence that we need to reject or not reject H_0 comes from the chi-square test (χ^2). The chi-square equation has the following form:

$$\chi^2 = \sum \frac{(o - e)^2}{e}$$

Equation 6.1

This equation may appear to be complex, but it is very easy to use once you understand the terminology. The o and e stand for observed and expected frequencies. *Observed frequencies* are those that are in the cells when we construct a contingency table. For example, Table 6.7 reveals that 80 children committed

Table 6.7   Contingency Table to Examine the Relationship Between Seriousness of Offense and Disposition for Juvenile Cases

		Serious	Not Serious	
	Dismissal	22 15%	48 29%	70
Disposition	Probation	80 54%	93 57%	173
	Incarceration	46 31%	22 13%	68
		148	163	311

Seriousness of Offense

Note: Table adapted from Seng (1970).

serious crimes and were placed on probation. This and all the other cell frequencies are observed because they are derived from the actual data collected. The *expected frequencies* are the cell frequencies that we anticipate or expect to find in the cells if H_0 was true, that is, in this case, if disposition and offense seriousness were not related. In every situation, the expected frequencies must be computed.

The chi-square equation tells us to subtract the expected frequency from the observed frequency within a cell and divide by the expected frequency. This process is done for each cell. The capital Greek letter sigma (Σ) tells us to sum our computations across all the cells. The result is called chi-square, which, symbolically, is represented as χ^2.

Computing Expected Frequencies

The expected frequencies for the cells in a contingency table are based on the assumption that H_0 is true. Given this, how does one compute these frequencies?

The *expected frequencies* are computed from the *marginal frequencies*. In other words, we use the row totals and column totals to help us estimate what the cell frequencies are if the null hypothesis is true. As an example, let us compute the expected frequency for the upper-left cell—the cell that identifies the juveniles who committed a serious crime and whose cases were dismissed by the court.

Remember that H_0 states that there is no relationship between seriousness of crime and sentencing of juvenile offenders. If that is the case, the ratio of the frequency of juveniles whose cases were dismissed to all juveniles who committed a serious crime should be the same as the ratio of the number of juveniles whose cases were dismissed to the total number of juveniles. If we allow e_d to represent the expected frequency of dismissed juveniles, our ratios can be expressed in the following way:

$$\frac{e_d}{148} = \frac{70}{311}$$

Solving for e_d, we then have

$$e_d = \frac{70 \times 148}{311} = 33.31$$

This means that we expect there to be 33.31 incarcerated juveniles if the null hypothesis is true.

The value of 33.31 may cause some people to ask, "How can there be .31 juveniles?" If this concerns you, keep in mind that an expected frequency is a computed entity and thus can take on decimal places. It is an estimate. In addition, it is good practice to have decimal places with expected frequencies to differentiate them from observed frequencies.

Using the same reasoning, let us compute the expected frequency for the lower-right cell—the cell that identifies the juveniles who committed a nonserious crime and who were incarcerated by the court.

According to H_0, the ratio of the frequency of incarcerated juveniles to all the juveniles who committed a nonserious crime should be the same as the ratio of the number of juveniles who were incarcerated to the total number of juveniles. If we allow e_i to represent the expected frequency of incarcerated juveniles, these ratios can be expressed as follows:

$$\frac{e_i}{163} = \frac{68}{311}$$

Solving for e_i, we then have

$$e_i = \frac{68 \times 163}{311} = 35.64$$

From these computations, it is possible to see that expected frequencies can be found with a routine procedure. The expected frequency for any cell equals the product of the row total of a cell and the column total, divided by N. If the terms RT and CT stand for the row and column totals of a cell, the formula for computing an expected frequency is

$$e = \frac{RT \times CT}{N} \qquad \text{Equation 6.2}$$

Table 6.8 presents all the expected frequencies for the data in Table 6.7. We encourage you to compute each of the expected frequencies using Equation 6.2.

Computing the Chi-square Statistic

After the expected frequencies have been determined, χ^2 can be computed. Table 6.9 shows the cell-by-cell calculations. The overall test statistic is determined by summing the individual computations: $\chi^2 = 3.84 + 3.49 + 0.07 + 0.06 + 5.75 + 5.22 = 18.43$.

At this point, we need to determine if a χ^2 value of 18.43 is large enough to reject the null hypothesis. To do this, we compare the computed χ^2 with a reference value that has been obtained from what is called the *chi-square distribution*.[6] These values are presented in Table B of the Appendix. To find the correct reference value, we first need to know the degrees of freedom of the contingency table and the desired level of significance.

Degrees of Freedom

The size of a χ^2 value is influenced by the size of the contingency table from which the value is computed. A table with many cells tends to yield a χ^2 value that is larger than that of a table that has a few cells. Table size needs to be taken into account when one decides whether a χ^2 value is large enough to reject the null hypothesis. In statistical terms, the size of a contingency table is referred to as *degrees of freedom*. Intuition may tell you that this is simply the total number

Table 6.8   Observed Frequencies from Table 6.7 with Expected Frequencies Included

		Serious	Not Serious	
	Dismissal	22 (33.31)	48 (36.69)	70
Disposition	**Probation**	80 (82.33)	93 (90.67)	173
	Incarceration	46 (32.36)	22 (35.64)	68
		148	163	311

Seriousness of Offense

Table 6.9 Cell Computations for the χ^2 Test That Examines the Relationship Between Crime Seriousness and Sentencing for Juvenile Offenders

$$\frac{(22 - 33.31)^2}{33.31} = 3.84$$

$$\frac{(48 - 36.69)^2}{36.69} = 3.49$$

$$\frac{(80 - 82.33)^2}{82.33} = 0.07$$

$$\frac{(93 - 90.67)^2}{90.67} = 0.06$$

$$\frac{(46 - 32.36)^2}{32.36} = 5.75$$

$$\frac{(22 - 35.64)^2}{32.36} = 5.75$$

of cells in a table. In reality, however, *degrees of freedom* refers to the number of *unrestricted* cells. These are the cells in a contingency table that do not have restrictions on the size of frequencies other those imposed by the marginal totals.

Table 6.10 presents the contingency table that relates sentencing to crime seriousness for juvenile offenders. Only two of the six cells are unrestricted (except by the marginal totals). Once these two cells are determined, the frequencies in the remaining cells are automatically determined. These frequencies can be computed from existing information. For example, we know that the frequency in the upper-right cell has to be 48 because $70 - 22 = 48$. Likewise, the frequency in the lower-left cell has to be $148 - (80 + 22) = 46$, and so on. The frequency for every cell, except the two shown in Table 6.10, can be computed. The table has 2 degrees of freedom.

If the letters r and c stand for the number of rows and columns in a contingency table, the degree of freedom (df) is computed in the following way:

$$df = (r - 1) \times (c - 1) \qquad \text{Equation 6.3}$$

Table 6.10 Contingency Table from Table 6.7 with Cell Frequencies Removed to Illustrate Degrees of Freedom

		Seriousness of Offense		
		Serious	**Not Serious**	
	Dismissal	22		70
Disposition	**Probation**	80		173
	Incarceration			68
		148	163	311

The table in the example has three rows and two columns; the degrees of freedom are $(3 - 1) \times (2 - 1) = 2 \times 1 = 2$. This follows exactly the pattern discussed earlier.

Level of Significance

Hypothesis testing is based on the presumption that H_0 is true. Statistical procedures test the null hypothesis. We are inclined to reject the null hypothesis in favor of the rival hypothesis if there is evidence to suggest that the former may be untrue. What, then, is the evidence to make us reject H_0?

To help answer this question, consider a situation in which you have enrolled in a difficult class and are concerned that you may fail it. When you talk with the teacher, she confirms that you are having difficulty, but there is only about a 10 percent chance that you will fail. When you hear this news, you are inclined to reject your initial concern because the probability of failure is so small.

This is exactly the basis of the reasoning for rejecting H_0. After computing the value of a test statistic (which is χ^2 in this case), we evaluate the chance probability of finding a value that is as large or larger than the one we computed from our data. If this probability is small, say 5 percent, we can presume that the outcome of the analysis is probably not due to chance. We then have the evidence to reject H_0 in favor of H_1 (the logical alternative). When the chance of finding a test statistic with a large value is very small, H_0 is probably false.

In hypothesis testing, you must select a chance probability for rejecting H_0. Although a number of such probabilities can (and should) be chosen, most statisticians select 5 percent (Cohen 1990). This is called the *level of significance*. If someone chooses a 5 percent chance probability for rejecting H_0, they are selecting a .05 level of significance.

Evaluating the χ^2 Result

In the example of crime seriousness and sentencing for juvenile offenders, do we have the evidence to reject H_0 or must we retain it? To answer this question, turn to Table B in the Appendix. There you find critical values of χ^2. On the left-hand side of the table are degrees of freedom (*df*), and across the top are various levels of significance. We find a critical value of χ^2 for our example by locating the intersection of the row and column that correspond to the *df* of our contingency table and the desired level of significance.[7]

The contingency table in the example has 2 degrees of freedom, and we can select (as a matter of convention) a .05 level of significance. Table B tells us that our critical χ^2 is 5.99. This means that there is 5 percent chance of finding a χ^2 value of 5.99 or higher in a contingency table with 2 degrees of freedom. We can reject H_0 in favor of H_1 if the computed χ^2 value is 5.99 or higher.

Our earlier computations showed that the χ^2 value for the data in Table 6.8 is 18.43. However, all we need to reject H_0 is a χ^2 of 5.99. We can reject H_0 in favor of H_1. This means that the data in the study suggest that we probably have found a relationship between crime seriousness and sentencing for juvenile offenders.[8]

Interpreting the Relationship

The χ^2 analysis informs us that the relationship between juvenile crime seriousness and sentencing is statistically significant. How then do we describe the relationship? The first step is realizing that the significance of the χ^2 analysis indicates that juveniles in the study who committed serious and nonserious crimes were, overall, sentenced in different ways. We can describe that difference by using the column percentages in Table 6.7.

Just over half of the juveniles who committed both serious and nonserious crimes were given probation (54% and 57%, respectively). Of the remaining juveniles, those who committed serious crimes were incarcerated at a rate of about 2-to-1 over those who were dismissed (31% versus 15%). Those who committed nonserious crimes were dismissed at a rate of about 2-to-1 over those who were incarcerated (29% versus 13%). Thus the data indicate that judges gave probation to about half of the juvenile offenders irrespective of the seriousness of the crime. Of the remaining half, juveniles who committed serious crimes tended to be incarcerated, whereas those who committed nonserious crimes tended to be dismissed.

Assumptions of the χ^2 Test

To use the χ^2 test appropriately, one needs to be sure that the data meet basic assumptions. The description of these assumptions varies somewhat among texts (McCall 1990; Siegel and Castellan 1988). There are three assumptions that one should generally heed. First, the categories of the dependent and independent variables must be mutually exclusive. This means that observations may be classified in one and only one cell of a contingency table. A review of Table 6.8 shows that juveniles can occupy only one of the six cells. The crime they committed was either serious or not serious. Likewise, their sentence can be dismissal, probation, or incarceration. These are mutually exclusive categories because no juvenile can be placed in more than one cell.

The second and third assumptions are that no more than 20 percent of the expected frequencies are less than five, and that *none* is less than one. These assumptions are necessary because the χ^2 equation divides the term $(o - e)^2$ by e, the expected frequency of the cell. Because of this quotient, χ^2 is inflated if expected frequencies tend to be small. This can incorrectly lead to the rejection of H_0 when it should be retained. In the case of Table 6.8, we can see that none of the expected frequencies was less than five. The second and third assumptions have been met.

Exercise 6–2   Chi-square Analysis

One hundred seventy-five persons were arrested and convicted for burglary (all first-time offenders). At conviction, each offender received deferred prosecution, probation, or a jail sentence. Using the data in Exercise Table 6.2, examine the possible relationship between race and the type of sentences issued.

		Race		
		White	Black	Other
	Deferred Prosecution	23	15	13
Sentence	**Probation**	40	20	17
	Jail	15	22	10

1. What is H_0?
2. What is H_1?
3. Calculate χ^2. Is it significant at .05?
4. Can we reject H_0?

Strength of Statistical Relationships

The statistical significance of a relationship often is confused with the *strength* of that relationship. There is a tendency to believe that the larger the χ^2 value, the stronger the relationship between the dependent and independent variables. This is not true.

Larger contingency tables tend to yield larger χ^2 values. Sample size has the same effect. For example, we found that the χ^2 value for the data in Table 6.8 was 18.43 with a sample size of 311 juveniles. If the column percentages remain the same but we double the sample size to 622, the χ^2 value doubles, even though the nature of the relationship between crime seriousness and sentencing is unchanged. This shows that larger χ^2 values do not necessarily indicate stronger relationships.

The Phi Coefficient

Although the χ^2 value by itself does not measure the magnitude of a relationship in a contingency table, the value is important to use in other equations. For example, an equation that measures the association between variables in a 2×2 (read *two by two*) table is called ϕ (lower case Greek phi) and is found with the following equation:

$$\phi = \sqrt{\frac{\chi^2}{N}} \qquad \text{Equation 6.4}$$

Phi produces a coefficient of 0 when there is no relationship between the dependent and independent variables and 1.00 when the relationship is perfect.

Let us compare two values of ϕ by computing the association between variables in Tables 6.3 and 6.4. Table 6.3 examines the relationship between electronic monitoring and appearance in court. In an earlier discussion, we noted that defendants who were monitored tended to appear in court more often than those who were not, but the difference was not striking. Not surprisingly, the χ^2 value for this table is 0.54 and is not statistically significant at the .05 level.[9] The association between variables in Table 6.3 is as follows:

$$\phi = \sqrt{\frac{\chi^2}{N}} = \sqrt{\frac{0.54}{30}} = 0.13$$

The value of 0.13 is very close to 0.00 and indicates a very weak relationship.

Table 6.4 is an example of a perfect relationship. The table shows a situation in which all monitored defendants appeared in court and all nonmonitored defendants did not. In this case, the χ^2 value is 30.00 and is statistically significant at the .05 level. Phi for this significant association is as follows:

$$\phi = \sqrt{\frac{\chi^2}{N}} = \sqrt{\frac{30.00}{30}} = 1.00$$

This value reflects the perfect relationship described in Table 6.4.

The Cramér Coefficient *V*

For tables that are larger than 2×2, the ϕ coefficient can range beyond 1.00. This causes difficulty in its use. The following equation, called *Cramér's V*, is used:

$$V = \sqrt{\frac{\chi^2}{N(J - 1)}} \qquad \text{Equation 6.5}$$

It is not difficult to see that V is a modification of ϕ and is therefore the same basic equation. However, the V coefficient includes the term J, which stands for the number of rows or columns in a contingency table, whichever is smaller.[10] Like ϕ, the V coefficient has a minimum value of 0.00 and a maximum value of 1.00.

Let us compute Cramér's V for the 3×2 contingency table used to examine the relationship between crime seriousness and sentencing for juvenile offenders (Table 6.8). In our earlier computations, we found that the χ^2 value was 18.43, which was statistically significant at the .05 level. We need to use Cramér's V to measure the strength of this relationship because the table is larger than 2×2. Here, $J = 2$ because 2 is the smaller value of two columns and three rows.

$$V = \sqrt{\frac{\chi^2}{N(J-1)}} = \sqrt{\frac{18.43}{311(2-1)}} = 0.24$$

Although the relationship is statistically significant, V tells us that it is weak. One possible explanation is that many factors are involved in sentencing juvenile offenders. The data suggest that crime seriousness is one of those factors, but there are probably many others.

There are no hard-and-fast rules for interpreting ϕ or V. Table 6.11 provides a guideline for classifying the strength of relationships based on values of the ϕ and V coefficients.

The ϕ and V coefficients are extremely useful measures of association. There may be times, however, when V can equal 1.00, even though the data in a contingency table do not appear to be perfectly related. For the way we have taught you to interpret contingency tables, this can happen when there are more rows than columns.

A perfect relationship is found when the dependent variable relies completely on the independent variable, as in Table 6.4. The table shows that all defendants on electronic monitoring appeared in court as scheduled, whereas all nonmonitored defendants did not.

When there are more rows than columns in a contingency table, complete reliance of one variable on another occurs when at least one category of the independent variable is associated with more than one category of the dependent variable. For example, Table 6.12 displays hypothetical data about the relationship between career choice and gender of 100 hypothetical criminal justice students.

With Table 6.4 it was easy to see that one category of the independent variable was associated with one and only one category of the dependent variable. Table 6.12, however, shows that each gender is associated with two career choices. This depicts a perfect relationship, even though it may not seem like one. The hypothetical data tell us that all men prefer law enforcement *and* defense, whereas all women choose prosecution and corrections. The χ^2 value for Table 6.12 is 100.00, and Cramér's V is 1.00.

Table 6.11 Strength of Relationships in Terms of the Value of the ϕ and V Coefficients

Value	Strength
Up to .25	Weak
.26–.50	Weak to moderate
.51–.75	Moderate to strong
.75–1.00	Strong

Table 6.12 Contingency Table That Displays a Relationship Between Gender and Career Choice Among 100 Hypothetical Criminal Justice Students

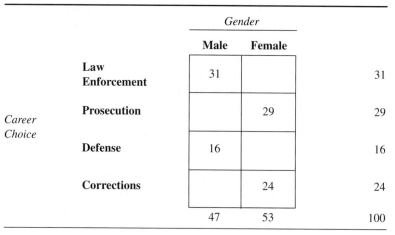

		Gender		
		Male	Female	
Career Choice	Law Enforcement	31		31
	Prosecution		29	29
	Defense	16		16
	Corrections		24	24
		47	53	100

Exercise 6–3   Phi and Cramér's V

For the data in Exercises 6.1 and 6.2, determine the strength of the relationships. Be sure to use the proper statistic, ϕ or Cramér's V.

Summary

A relationship exists when changes in one variable systematically correspond with changes in another. In situations in which one wishes to explain one *variable* in terms of another, it is customary to label these variables as *dependent* and *independent*.

Relationships between *nominal variables* are studied by means of a *contingency table*. It is beneficial (but not necessary) to arrange these tables by having the independent variable placed on the top and the dependent variable along the side. To visualize a relationship, *column percentages* are computed by means of division of the *cell frequencies* by the *column totals*.

The *statistical significance* of a relationship is assessed within the context of a formal process called *hypothesis testing*. In this process, we specify the null and rival hypotheses, which are denoted H_0 and H_1, respectively. The *null hypothesis* asserts that a relationship does not exist between the variables in a study. The *rival hypothesis* states that a relationship does exist. A statistical analysis of the data is used to test the *probability* that the null hypothesis is true. If that probability is small, for example, 5 percent or less, H_0 is rejected in favor of H_1. If the probability is higher, for example, more than 5 percent, H_0 is retained. *Level of significance* denotes the probability that leads us to reject that hypothesis.

The χ^2 equation is most commonly used to test the null hypothesis with data in a contingency table. In essence, the equation compares the observed frequencies of the cells in the table with the frequencies one expects if H_0 is true. Expected frequencies are computed from the row and column totals of the contingency table.

A *critical* χ^2 *value* is found in Table B of the Appendix. A level of significance and the degrees of freedom of a contingency table are needed to find the critical value. Within this context, *degrees of freedom* are the number of cells that do not have restrictions on the size of frequencies other than those imposed by the marginal totals. The χ^2 value is statistically significant if it equals or exceeds the critical value found in Table B.

The statistical significance of the χ^2 test reflects only the probability of finding one's results by *chance*. The significance of a χ^2 test can tell us that there probably is a relationship between two variables, but it does not tell us directly about the strength of that relationship. Other equations are needed for that.

The *strength of a relationship* in a 2 × 2 contingency table is computed with an equation called φ. Larger tables require *Cramér's V*. In both cases, a coefficient is computed that ranges from 0.00 to 1.00. A coefficient of 0.00 indicates that there is no relationship between two variables. A coefficient of 1.00 indicates a perfect relationship. The larger the values of φ and V, the stronger is the relationship between the variables in a contingency table.

Answers to Exercises

Exercise Answer 6–1   Contingency Tables

		Race of Juvenile		
		White	**Non-white**	
Received Probation	**Yes**	10 63%	9 75%	19
	No	6 37%	3 25%	9
		16	12	28

It does appear that race makes some difference in whether a juvenile receives probation.

Exercise Answer 6–2   Chi-square Test

		Race			
		White	**Black**	**Other**	
	Deferred Prosecution	23 (22.73) .003	15 (16.61) .16	13 (11.66) .15	51
Sentence	**Probation**	40 (34.32) .94	20 (25.08) 1.03	17 (17.60) .02	77
	Jail	15 (20.95) 1.69	22 (15.31) 2.92	10 (10.74) .05	47
		78	57	40	175

H_0: Race is not related to type of punishment.
H_1: Race is related to type of punishment.
$\chi^2 = 6.97$; not significant at the .05 level.
The data do not suggest that race is related to the type of punishment given.

Note (Exercise Answer 6–2): Each cell has three numbers in it. The top number is the observed frequency. The number in parentheses is the expected frequency. The bottom number is the χ^2 value for that cell.

Exercise Answer 6–3   Phi and Cramér's V

		Race		
		White	**Non-white**	
Received Probation	**Yes**	10 (10.86) .07	9 (8.14) .09	19
	No	6 (5.14) .14	3 (3.86) .19	9
		16	12	28

$\chi^2 = .49$; not statistically significant.

$$\phi = \sqrt{\frac{\chi^2}{N}} = \sqrt{\frac{0.49}{28}} = 0.132$$

$\phi = 0.132$; very weak relationship.

		Race			
		White	**Black**	**Other**	
Sentence	**Deferred Prosecution**	23 (22.73) .003	15 (16.61) .16	13 (11.66) .15	51
	Probation	40 (34.32) .94	20 (25.08) 1.03	17 (17.60) .02	77
	Jail	15 (20.95) 1.69	22 (15.31) 2.92	10 (10.74) .05	47
		78	57	40	175

$$\text{Cramér's } V = \sqrt{\frac{\chi^2}{N(J-1)}} = \sqrt{\frac{6.87}{172(2)}} = 0.141$$

Cramér's $V = .141$; very weak relationship.

Computer Applications for Selected Exercises

Exercise Answer 6–2   Chi-square Test

Use the same strategy for entering data in this exercise that you used in Exercise 2.1. The table is a summary of offender-level data. Let *SPSS* know that the original data were collected at that level. Make one column in the Data Editor sen–

`tence` and one `race`. Assign each cell in the grid a coordinate pair that consists of sentence and race. For example, the upper-left cell is `Deferred Prosecution` and the cell to the right of it is `White`. The lower-left cell is `Jail` and the cell to the right of it is `Other`. Fill in all possible pairs of sentence and race. Then go back and fill in the corresponding number of offenders for each cell in the grid. Your data set should look like Figure 6.1.

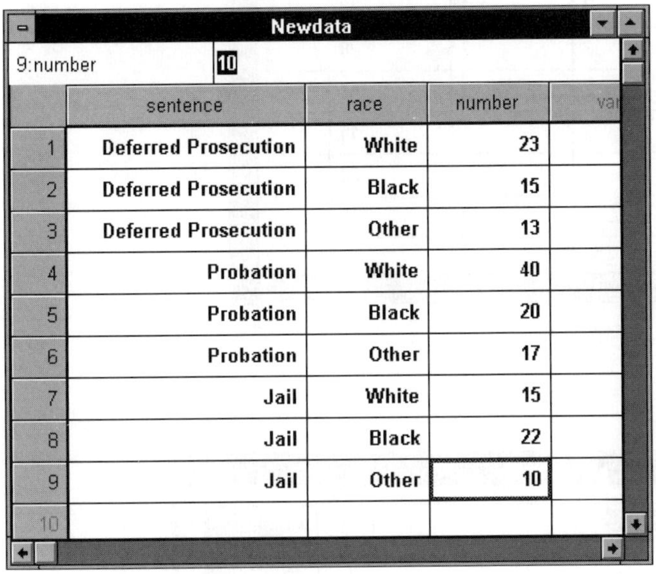

	sentence	race	number	va
1	Deferred Prosecution	White	23	
2	Deferred Prosecution	Black	15	
3	Deferred Prosecution	Other	13	
4	Probation	White	40	
5	Probation	Black	20	
6	Probation	Other	17	
7	Jail	White	15	
8	Jail	Black	22	
9	Jail	Other	10	
10				

Newdata — 9:number 10

Figure 6.1

The data shown for sentence and race show the *value labels*. You have the option of entering numeric codes or using alphanumeric fields to store these labels. Statisticians usually use numbers and then assign labels. This strategy allows more flexibility later in the analytic process. In particular, if the data are stored numerically, they are much easier to regroup, as in Exercise 2.2.

Figure 6.2 shows the actual numbers stored in the Data Editor. You can toggle to the view of the Data Editor that shows labels instead of values by clicking once on the label button on the toolbar. The underlying data in both views are the same.

The `Define Labels:` dialog box is in the `Define Variable` dialog box for each variable. Double-click on the column heading for `sentence` and then click on `Label` at the lower left of the dialog box. Fill in the information for the value labels. Figure 6.3 shows how the dialog box looks for the example.

Weight the data so that *SPSS* recognizes the true number of offenders in the sample (see the instructions for Exercise 2.1). Weight the data by the number variable. This column holds the number of offenders in each cell in the grid. *SPSS* sees from what kind of data distribution this sample was drawn. Remember to check to see the `Weight On` message in the lower-right corner of the *SPSS for Windows* display. If that message does not appear, your analysis will not run properly.

After the data are weighted, run the analysis. The χ^2 is calculated with the Crosstabs procedure. Crosstabs is in the Statistics menu under `Summarize` (Figure 6.4).

For this analysis, use `sentence` as the row variable and `race` as the column variable (Figure 6.5).

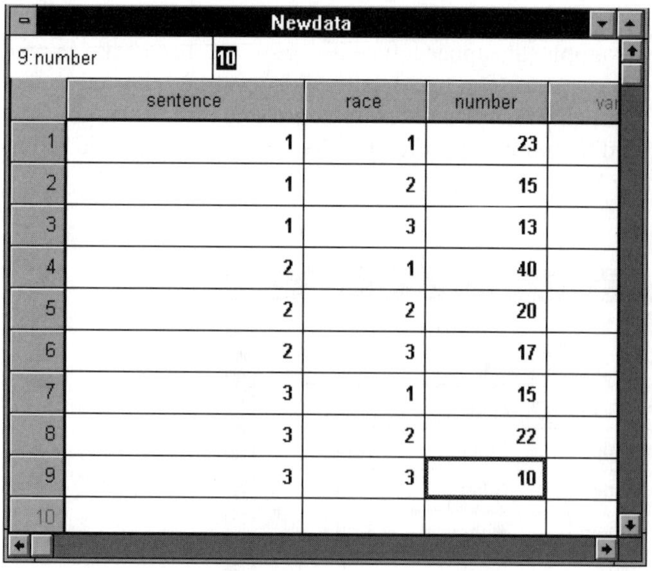

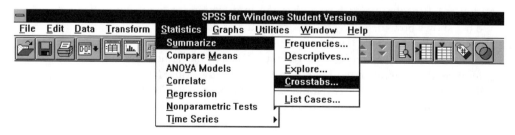

Newdata			
9:number		10	

	sentence	race	number	va
1	1	1	23	
2	1	2	15	
3	1	3	13	
4	2	1	40	
5	2	2	20	
6	2	3	17	
7	3	1	15	
8	3	2	22	
9	3	3	10	
10				

Figure 6.2

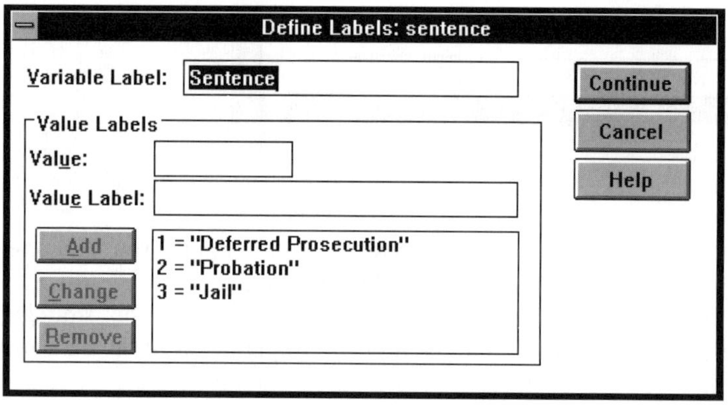

Define Labels: sentence

Variable Label: Sentence

Value Labels
Value:
Value Label:

Add
Change
Remove

1 = "Deferred Prosecution"
2 = "Probation"
3 = "Jail"

Continue
Cancel
Help

Figure 6.3

SPSS for Windows Student Version

File   Edit   Data   Transform   Statistics   Graphs   Utilities   Window   Help

Summarize   Frequencies...
Compare Means   Descriptives...
ANOVA Models   Explore...
Correlate   Crosstabs...
Regression   List Cases...
Nonparametric Tests
Time Series

Figure 6.4

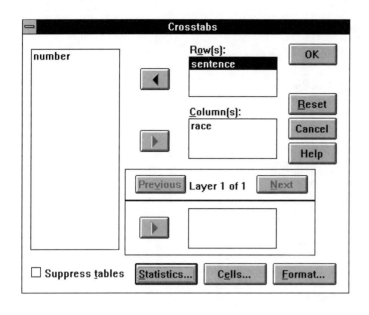

Figure 6.5

If you choose OK now, you get a table that looks like the one from which you drew the data. You need to calculate the χ^2 statistic. Click on Statistics at the bottom center of the dialog box. Choose Chi-square in the upper-left corner of this box (Figure 6.6).

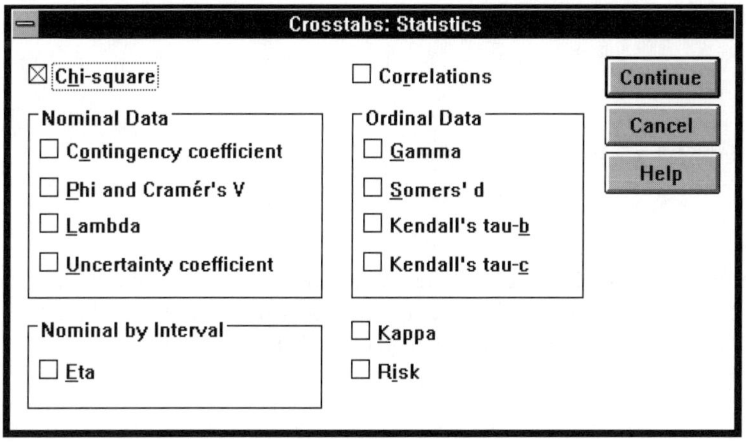

Figure 6.6

Choose Continue and then choose OK in the main Crosstabs dialog box to view the output (Figure 6.7). There is a lot of information, so look at some of the individual pieces first. The counts appear in a table at the top of the output. The statistics are printed at the bottom. The statistics help you determine if you can reject the null hypothesis, but you still need the cross tabulation table to describe any relationship you find.

Start at the top and look at the first line of the output (Figure 6.8). It is a title that identifies exactly which analysis you are conducting. You are looking at a cross tabulation of sentence and race.

```
SENTENCE   Sentence   by   RACE   Race
```

Count	RACE White 1	Black 2	Other 3	Page 1 of 1 Row Total
SENTENCE				
1 Deferred Prosecu	23	15	13	51 29.1
2 Probation	40	20	17	77 44.0
3 Jail	15	22	10	47 26.9
Column Total	78 44.6	57 32.6	40 22.9	175 100.0

Chi-Square	Value	DF	Significance
Pearson	6.96902	4	.13753
Likelihood Ratio	6.83509	4	.14486
Mantel-Haenszel test for linear association	.27639	1	.59907

```
Minimum Expected Frequency -    10.743


Number of Missing Observations:   0
```

Figure 6.7

```
             SENTENCE   Sentence   by   RACE   Race
```

Figure 6.8

Below that is the body of the table. The counts in the middle of the table are the same ones in the exercise text. Look at the information around the table. The upper-left corner of the table tells what is in each cell (Figure 6.9).

```
Count   |
        |
        |
        |
 _____|_____
        |
```

Figure 6.9

This is a simple cross tabulation. You are looking only at counts in the cells. To see some of the other things you can add, use the dialog recall button on the toolbar to retrieve the Crosstabs dialog box. Choose Cells at the bottom. Observed is already checked under Counts when you get into the dialog box. That is because the table already shows the observed sample count for each cell.

Choose `Expected Count` and `Unstandardized Residual`. The *expected count* tells how many cases to expect in the cell if there is no relationship between the variables. The *unstandardized residual* is the difference between the observed and expected counts.

Rerun the analysis and look at this upper-left cell as a key to understanding the information in the table. What does this information reveal to you?

The left and top of the cross tabulation table provide the other labels (Figure 6.10).

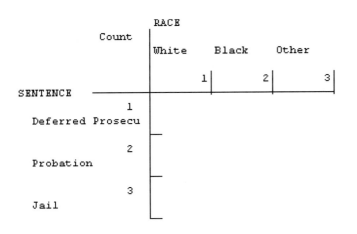

Figure 6.10

The variable names (column names) are in all caps. SENTENCE defines the rows and is on the left. RACE defines the columns and is on the top. The individual values are printed with whatever part of the label fits. Under SENTENCE, deferred prosecution has a value of 1. The label is longer than the format allows, but enough of it shows so that the table is still understandable. The top of the table shows that the value entered in the Data Editor for black was 2. The information on the top and left of the cross tabulation is for labeling only.

The information on the right and bottom of the table is used in the analysis (Figure 6.11). The numbers on the right and bottom are different kinds of totals. They are often referred to as the *marginals* because they appear as totals in the margins of the table.

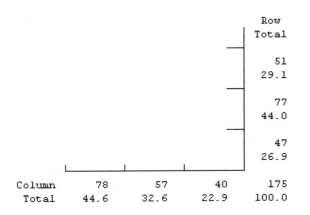

Figure 6.11

The top number in each pair is the total count for that row or column. The bottom number is the percentage of the table total the count represents. The total number of offenders in the first row is 51. The total number offenders in the first column is 78.

The lower-right corner shows the total number of valid observations and the total percentage. There were 175 offenders in this sample. The percentage totals 100.

The statistics are printed at the bottom of the table (Figure 6.12).

Chi-Square	Value	DF	Significance
Pearson	6.96902	4	.13753
Likelihood Ratio	6.83509	4	.14486
Mantel-Haenszel test for linear association	.27639	1	.59907

Minimum Expected Frequency -   10.743

Figure 6.12

The χ^2 formula you are using is the *Pearson* version. Look at that line. The Value column gives the actual χ^2 value. The DF column shows the degrees of freedom to use if you want to find this χ^2 value in a table. You can do that to determine if the χ^2 is significant at the .05 level.

The program does you a favor, though, and uses an algorithm (formula) to calculate the exact significance of this χ^2 value with these degrees of freedom. The value for this table is approximately .13. Because .13 is greater than .05, you cannot reject the null hypothesis that there is no relationship between race and sentence. The data in this exercise suggest that there is no relationship between race and sentence.

Exercise Answer 6–3   Phi and Cramér's V

Use the same data as for Exercise 6–2. Go to the Crosstabs dialog box by using the dialog recall button or by going through the Statistics menu to Summarize. Make sure that sentence is still the row variable and race is still the column variable. Choose Statistics at the bottom. Choose Phi and Cramér's V from the Nominal Data area (Figure 6.13).

You can leave Chi-square selected. Now choose Continue and then OK in the main Crosstabs dialog box.

The output includes all the information from Exercise 6–2 followed by a new statistics table that summarizes φ and Cramér's *V* (Figure 6.14).

Both φ and Cramér's *V* are zero when there is no relationship between the two variables. They are both 1 when the variables are perfectly related.

The φ statistic is appropriate for 2×2 tables. This table is 3×3, so use Cramér's *V* to assess the strength of the relationship. The Cramér's value is .14111. This value is close to zero, so there is not a strong relationship between race and sentence. The approximate significance value is also outside the range generally considered significant.

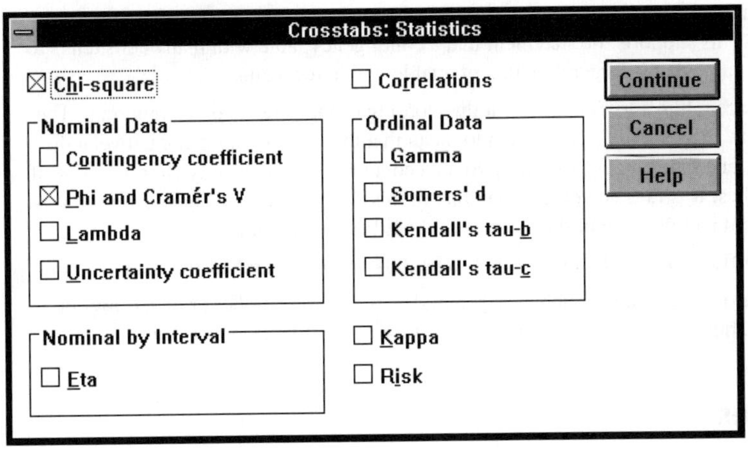

Figure 6.13

Statistic	Value	ASE1	Val/ASE0	Approximate Significance
Phi	.19956			.13753 *1
Cramer's V	.14111			.13753 *1

*1 Pearson chi-square probability

Figure 6.14

Notes

1. The method for establishing a causal relationship is important but is beyond the scope of this book. Readers interested in causal relationships are encouraged to read a research methodology text such as Mitchell and Jolley (1992).

2. In tables where frequencies and percentages are displayed, the latter are offset to enhance visualization.

3. In general, decimal places in the percentage calculations unnecessarily complicate the information in the contingency table. Therefore, column percentages are rounded to the nearest unit to facilitate the process of looking for a relationship.

4. The process of hypothesis testing is a form of statistical analysis that was pioneered by the statistician Sir Ronald A. Fisher. Hypothesis testing is not the only way in which relationships are studied statistically. However, the method has gained popularity among modern research practitioners.

5. It often seems backward to many people that one presumes the truth of the null hypothesis unless there is evidence to the contrary. However, developing a statistical test that presumes the truth of the research hypothesis requires detailed knowledge of the relationship under study. If such detailed knowledge were available, there would be no need for the research.

6. The chi-square distribution is actually a family of theoretical frequency distributions of χ^2 values based on the assumption that the null hypothesis is true. These distributions are determined mathematically and are based on probability theory.

7. Table B in the Appendix shows that significant values of χ^2 increase as *df* (table size) increases. This supports the statement that a contingency table with many cells tends to yield a χ^2 value that is larger than that of a table with a few cells.

8. This may seem like a trivial point, but the wording of the conclusion is important. The significance of χ^2 should *not* be taken to mean that there is a relationship between the dependent and independent variables. Such a conclusion is made only after a review of many studies. It is fair, however, to say that in this study a relationship was found. It is possible that a replication of the study would not lead to the same results.

9. To be significant at the .05 level, χ^2 has to be 3.84 for one degree of freedom.

10. In the case of square tables such as 3×3 or 4×4, *J* is the number of equal rows or columns. Thus, $J = 3$ for a 3×3 table; $J = 4$ for a 4×4 table, and so on.

References

Cohen, J. 1990. "Things I Have Learned (So Far)." *American Psychologist* 45:1304–11.

Handel, J. D. 1978. *Introductory Statistics for Sociology*. Englewood Cliffs, N.J.: Prentice-Hall.

Hy, R., Feig, D. G., and Regoli, R. M. 1983. *Research Methods and Statistics*. Cincinnati: Anderson Publishing.

McCall, R. B. 1990. *Fundamental Statistics for the Behavioral Sciences*. 5th ed. New York: Harcourt, Brace, Jovanovich.

Mitchell, M., and Jolley, J. 1992. *Research Design Explained*. 2d ed. New York: Harcourt, Brace, Jovanovich.

Seng, M. 1970. "Disposition of Delinquent Children." Ph.D. diss., University of Chicago.

Siegel, S., and Castellan, N. J. 1988. *Nonparametric Statistics for the Behavioral Sciences*. New York: McGraw-Hill.

7. Correlation

Working in Research and Development

When you began pursuing your criminal justice degree, you had no idea what you would do with it. By the time you graduated, you had decided to become a police officer. However, working in the Research and Development (R & D) Unit was not really what you had in mind. But because you were injured in a foot chase several weeks ago and placed on light duty, there have not been many choices. So here you are in R & D.

As a member of R & D you find that the work of this unit is very important, providing information that can assist other units in doing their jobs better. For example, an auto theft ring was apprehended two weeks ago because of information from R & D. This new awareness has caused you to view R & D with a whole new perspective. Actually, you are beginning to see a way for your college education to be put to good use, particularly your statistics and research methodology classes.

Your current project is a priority. The new budget is about to go into effect, and with it 100 new police officers are to be added. The chief has asked R & D for a report on the assignment of patrol officers. In particular, the chief wants to know if there is a relationship between the number of officers assigned to given areas and the number of calls answered, crimes reported, and arrests made. This information is meant to assist the chief in assigning the new officers.

When you were first given this project, you were somewhat apprehensive about your ability to provide the proper data. However, a review of your statistics notes refreshed your memory about what you would need to do to examine the type of data the chief wants. The relationships the chief is interested in necessitate a report that examines the correlation of the variables in question.

Correlation

Earlier chapters examined the statistical relationship between nominal variables. Chapters 7, 8, and 9 focus on analytic techniques designed to handle two or more interval or ratio variables. We begin with problems that focus on questions about the relationship between two ratio variables. For example, what is the relationship between height and weight? Everyday observation and common sense tell us that taller people weigh more than shorter people. However, we do not expect every tall person to weigh more than every short person or that a perfect correspondence exists between height and weight, such that the tallest person always weighs the most, followed by the next tallest person, and so on. The variables, height and weight, are clearly associated, but what is the precise magnitude and nature of that relationship?

In the field of criminal justice, questions regarding the association between variables can become more complicated than the height and weight problem. For example, are staff turnover rates in jails related to the numbers of inmate attacks on guards?

Are probationers' ages associated with how many times they violate their conditions of probation? Are parolees' risk scale scores at release related to the number of times they are arrested in the community? These questions concerning the relationship between two variables illustrate problems in correlation. When interval or ratio variables are related, they are said to be correlated, and their relationship is generally referred to as a *correlation*.

This chapter discusses correlation by first examining how relationships are diagrammed (scatter diagrams). It then focuses on the most widely used correlational technique, the Pearson product-moment correlation coefficient.[1] This statistic is denoted *r*.

Scatter Diagrams

The examination of two variables is often referred to as *bivariate analysis*. Bivariate correlational problems designate one variable in the relationship X and the other Y. The first step in determining a correlation is the creation of a bivariate distribution. Table 7.1 presents data on two variables. As shown, X represents police officer applicants' intelligence quotients (IQs) based on the Wechsler Adult Intelligence Scale (WAIS), and Y represents their scores on a police aptitude test (PAT). Assume that investigators in the police department's R & D unit have collected data to examine whether PAT scores are related to scores on the WAIS, an established test of intelligence. Because the concepts of intelligence and aptitude are similar, applicants' PAT scores should be related to their IQs, that is, the scores should be correlated.

The data in Table 7.1 do not readily show whether X and Y are associated. A more informative way to tell at a glance whether two variables are related is to create a scatter diagram, which is done in Figure 7.1. The X axis is called the *abscissa*, and the Y axis is called the *ordinate*. The actual points presented in the

Table 7.1   Police Applicants' WAIS and PAT Scores

Applicant	WAIS Score(X)	PAT Score (Y)
Joan	125	46
Susan	115	42
Robert	100	36
Matthew	105	39
Bill	95	42
Fred	98	34
Joe	90	25
Mary	110	40
Nancy	103	37
Carol	93	20

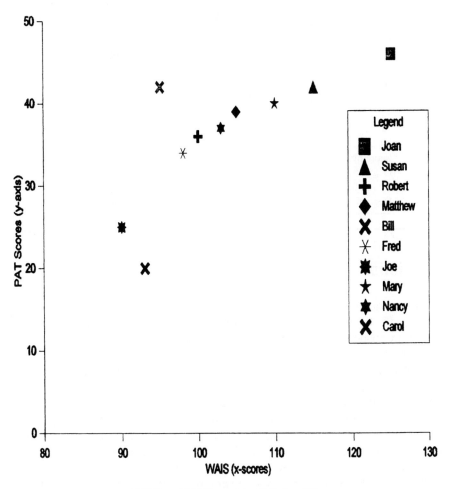

Figure 7.1   Scatterplot of WAIS and PAT Scores for 10 Police Officers

diagram are the locations of ordered pairs of X and Y scores for each police officer applicant. For example, officer no. 1 (Joan) scored 125 on the WAIS and
46 on the PAT. Her ordered pair is written as (125, 46). X scores always precede
Y scores in any ordered pair. To graph Joan's ordered pair (or any ordered pair)
in the bivariate distribution of IQs and PAT scores, simply locate her score on the
X axis (125), then find her score on the Y axis (46), and plot the points where
these two scores intersect. This intersection is Joan's performance on both tests,
which is plotted as one point or ordered pair on the scatter diagram. When this
has been done for all the test takers, the scatter diagram for WAIS and PAT scores
is complete.

Exercise 7–1   Scattergrams
While working on the report for the chief, you realize that this might be a
good time to examine a hunch of yours. You believe that there might be a relationship between residential burglaries (X) and sexual assaults (Y) in your
community. Using the following data, construct a scattergram to see if a relationship exists.

Month	No. of Burglaries	No. of Sexual Assaults
January	42	21
February	36	15
March	74	50
April	38	20
May	56	46
June	84	41
July	74	40
August	88	36
September	75	56
October	66	40
November	48	44
December	44	34

Covariation

The scatter diagram presented in Figure 7.1 provides a visual display of the data that suggests how the variables are correlated. When we examine how the points or dots are dispersed in the diagram, we can see that the scores tend to change together, or covary, with one another in a particular way. Covariation is a basic concept in correlation. *Covariation* is another way of saying that as changes occur in one variable (X), changes also occur in another variable (Y); that is, as X values change, Y values change or fluctuate in a particular pattern.

An inspection of the points in the scatterplot in Figure 7.1 shows that IQ (WAIS scores) and PAT scores do covary. Specifically, as X values increase, Y values increase. In other words, police applicants who score high on the WAIS tend also to score high on the PAT, and those who score low on the WAIS tend also to score low on the PAT. These variables covary and therefore are related to each other. However, the data indicate that the relationship is not perfect. For example, Bill scored relatively low on the WAIS and relatively high on the PAT. Overall, the covariation of X and Y is consistent (i.e., higher and lower values on the WAIS go with higher and lower values on the PAT), but not every pair of scores behaves in exactly that way.

It is useful at this point to review some important mathematical concepts involved in correlation, since an understanding of covariation and other measures proves useful later. To see how the various measures discussed in the following pages are applied to the WAIS-PAT example, refer to Table 7.2 at appropriate points.

How strongly related are X and Y? We can begin to answer this question by calculating the covariation between the two variables. We construct our measure of covariation by finding deviation scores for every X and Y value in each of the ordered pairs.[2] *Deviation scores* are simply the difference between a score value and its respective mean. To find the deviation scores for PAT scores, we have to find the mean of the scores. The same applies to the WAIS scores. A person's standing relative to the others in a group on $\underline{X}$ and Y is reflected in the size and algebraic sign of the deviation scores $(X - \overline{X})$ and $(Y - \overline{Y})$. If a person scores high on both variables, as Joan did (Table 7.1), the product of $(X - \overline{X})$ and $(Y - \overline{Y})$ is large and positive. Similarly, if a person scores relatively low on both X and Y, as Joe did, the product of $(X - \overline{X})$ and $(Y - \overline{Y})$ also is large and positive. (Remember that the product of two negative numbers is a positive number.) If most high values of X are paired with high values of Y and most low values of

Table 7.2 Definitional Formula for Calculating Pearson's *r* for the Data in Table 7.1

Applicant	WAIS Score (X)	Deviation Score (X − X̄)	PAT Score (Y)	Deviation Score (Y − Ȳ)	Cross Product (X − X̄)(Y − Ȳ)
Joan	125	21.6	46	9.9	213.84
Susan	115	11.6	42	5.9	68.44
Robert	100	−3.4	36	−.1	.34
Matthew	105	1.6	39	2.9	4.64
Bill	95	−8.4	42	5.9	−49.56
Fred	98	−5.4	34	−2.1	11.34
Joe	90	−13.4	25	−11.1	148.74
Mary	110	6.6	40	3.9	25.74
Nancy	103	−.4	37	.9	−.36
Carol	93	−10.4	20	−16.1	167.44
Sum	1034		361		590.60
Mean	103.4		36.1		
SD	10.78		8.02		

X are paired with low values of Y, then the sum of these products across all persons would be large and positive (Equation 7.1).

$$\Sigma(X - \overline{X})(Y - \overline{Y}) \qquad\qquad \text{Equation 7.1}$$

On the other hand, if most high values of X are paired with low values of Y and most low values of X are paired with high values of Y, then the product $(X - \overline{X})(Y - \overline{Y})$ is large and negative as is the sum of these products. The sum of the products of the X and Y deviation scores is called the *sum of the cross products*, which is calculated with Equation 7.1. If the sum of the cross products is positive, then X and Y are said to be *positively* or *directly related*. If the sum of the cross products is negative, then X and Y are said to be *negatively* or *inversely related*. What happens when X and Y have no relationship? In that case, high values of X are likely to be paired with both high and low values of Y, and low values of X are also likely to be paired with both high and low values of Y. Some persons with positive $(X - \overline{X})$ scores are paired with positive $(Y - \overline{Y})$ scores, whereas others are paired with negative $(Y - \overline{Y})$ scores. When the cross products $(X - \overline{X})(Y - \overline{Y})$ are calculated, some are positive and others are negative. The sum of the cross products, that is, $\Sigma (X - \overline{X})(Y - \overline{Y})$, contains a fairly even number of positive and negative terms of the same size and therefore is relatively close to zero. If the sum of the cross products is close to zero, then X and Y are said to be *unrelated*.

The sum of the cross products alone is not really a suitable measure of association. With large numbers of scores, this sum usually is large because many numbers are subtracted from their means. With a small number of scores, the opposite is true. As a measure of association, the sum of the cross products is influenced by the size of a group of scores and does not allow us to compare relationships between X and Y in groups of varying sizes. However, if we take the average of the sum of the cross products, then the group size effect is eliminated. The average of the cross products is the covariance of the X and Y scores, which is symbolized *Cov(x,y)*. As shown in Equation 7.2, we divide the sum of the cross products by $N - 1$, instead of N, for the same reason we divide the sum of the squared deviations by $N - 1$ when we calculate S^2 (the variance of a set of scores). In Equation 7.2, N is the number of people and not the total number of X and Y scores.

$$Cov(x,y) = \frac{\Sigma(X - \overline{X})(Y - \overline{Y})}{N - 1} \qquad \text{Equation 7.2}$$

Exercise 7–2   Cross Products and Covariances

Using the data from Exercise 7–1, calculate the cross products and covariance.

Pearson Product-Moment Correlation

The covariance equation is useful for determining the extent to which two variables vary together. We should not overlook the fact, however, that Equation 7.2 carries the measurement units of the X and Y variables. This can cause a problem with interpretation. For example, assume that we computed the covariance for data in a study on the relationship of height, measured in feet, and weight, measured in pounds. If the computational result of Equation 7.2 were 350, it would mean that the covariance was 350 feet-pounds. *Feet-pounds* is an odd sounding unit but is the natural result of multiplying $(X - \overline{X})$ and $(Y - \overline{Y})$. What is worse is that it is difficult for one to acquire a feeling for or an understanding of what a foot-pound is. Therefore, it is impossible to know if 350 feet-pounds represents a strong or a weak relationship.

To our benefit, Pearson found that covariance has an upper limit. In other words, there is a point that the covariance of two variables cannot exceed. This upper limit is found when the variables relate perfectly. In such a case, the computation from Equation 7.2 equals the product of the standard deviations of the X and Y variables, S_xS_y.

This gives us a way to handle the problem of uninterpretable units. Equation 7.2 measures the covariance that exists between two variables, and S_xS_y tells us how much covariance there would be if the relationship were perfect. A ratio of the former to the latter causes cancellation of the units and gives a general measure of association. This ratio is the *Pearson product-moment correlation coefficient*, which is symbolized by r and is shown in Equation 7.3:

$$r = \frac{Cov(x,y)}{S_xS_y} \qquad \text{Equation 7.3}$$

Table 7.2 provides the data needed to calculate r for the data presented in Table 7.1. The X variable is police officer applicants' scores on WAIS and the Y variable is their scores on PAT. To calculate the Pearson r for these two variables, we first have to determine their covariance, which is the sum of the cross products divided by $N - 1$. We do this by finding X and Y, subtracting every score from their respective means, and adding the resultant cross products. We then divide the sum of the cross products by $N - 1$. As you can see, covariance is equal to 590.60 ÷ 9 = 65.62. Next, we find the standard deviations of X and Y, which are 10.78 and 8.02, respectively. Finally, we divide the covariance of X and Y ($Cov(x,y)$) by the product of the standard deviations of X and Y (S_xS_y). This gives the following:

$$r = \frac{65.62}{(10.78)(8.02)} = \frac{65.62}{86.46} = 0.76$$

Table 7.3 Computational Formula for Calculating Pearson's *r* for the Data in Table 7.1

Applicant	WAIS Score	PAT Score	X^2	Y^2	XY
Joan	125	46	15,625	2,116	5,750
Susan	115	42	13,225	1,764	4,830
Robert	100	36	10,000	1,296	3,600
Matthew	105	39	11,025	1,521	4,095
Bill	95	42	9,025	1,764	3,990
Fred	98	34	9,604	1,156	3,332
Joe	90	25	8,100	625	2,250
Mary	110	40	12,100	1,600	4,400
Nancy	103	37	10,609	1,369	3,811
Carol	93	20	8,649	400	1,860
Sum	1,034	361	107,962	13,611	37,918

This calculation involves the *definitional* formula for Pearson's *r*, which is rather unwieldy.[3] The following formula has been derived for *computational* use. The computation is much simpler and less time-consuming and produces the same result as the definitional formula.

$$r = \frac{N\sum XY - (\sum X)(\sum Y)}{\sqrt{[N\sum X^2 - (\sum X)^2][N\sum Y^2 - (\sum Y)^2]}} \qquad \text{Equation 7.4}$$

At first glance, this formula may appear frightening, but it is easy to use. Using this computational formula, we calculated the Pearson *r* for the data set that contains IQ (WAIS) and PAT score (Table 7.3).

We first summed the X and Y scores, and then squared the totals to obtain the sum of X quantity squared, $(\sum X)^2$, and the sum of Y quantity squared, $(\sum Y)^2$. Next, we squared each of the X and Y scores and summed the resultant squared values to obtain $\sum X^2$ and $\sum Y^2$. Then we multiplied each X score with its corresponding Y score and added the results to obtain the sum of the products, $\sum XY$. The *N* in correlational problems refers to the number of people, not the number of X and Y scores. By plugging in the correct quantities in Equation 7.4 and performing the required calculations, we find that *r* = .76, which is the same value we found with the definitional formula for *r*.

$$r = \frac{10(37,918) - (1,034)(361)}{\sqrt{[10(107,962) - (1,034)^2][10(13,611) - (361)^2]}} = 0.76$$

Exercise 7–3 Pearson's *r*
For the data from Exercise 7–1, calculate the Pearson *r*.

Pearson's *r* as a General Measure of Association

A correlation coefficient is an index of both the strength and direction of the relationship between X and Y. The Pearson *r* has no units; one finds it by dividing the covariance of X and Y by the product of the standard deviations of X and Y. The correlation coefficient is actually a pure number that does not depend on the units of measurement chosen for X and Y. To illustrate, let us return to

Table 7.4 Hypothetical Data for Measuring the Correlation of Height (in Inches) and Weight (in Pounds)

Person	Height (X)	Weight (Y)	X²	Y²	XY
1	68	155	4,624	24,025	1,054
2	72	175	5,184	30,625	12,600
3	66	140	4,356	19,600	9,240
4	75	210	5,625	44,100	15,750
5	62	125	3,844	15,625	7,750
6	65	170	4,225	28,900	11,050
Sum	408	975	27,858	162,875	66,930

Table 7.5 Hypothetical Data for Measuring the Correlation of Height (in Meters) and Weight (in Kilograms)

Person	Height (X)	Weight (Y)	X²	Y²	XY
1	1.73	70.31	2.9929	4,943.4961	121.6363
2	1.83	79.38	3.3489	6,301.1844	145.2654
3	1.68	63.50	2.8224	4,032.2500	106.6800
4	1.91	95.25	3.6481	9,072.5625	181.9275
5	1.57	56.70	2.4649	3,214.8900	89.0190
6	1.65	77.11	2.7225	5,945.9521	127.2315
Sum	10.37	442.25	17.9997	33,510.3351	771.7597

Note: The height and weight data for this table were converted from the data in Table 7.4.

the example of height and weight. Table 7.4 presents data on six persons whose heights and weights were measured in inches and pounds. The correlation is .88.

$$r = \frac{6(66,930) - (408)(975)}{\sqrt{[6(27,858) - (408)^2][6(162,875) - (975)^2]}} = 0.88$$

We measured the same six people again, but this time measured height in meters and weight in kilograms. These data are shown in Table 7.5. As it can be seen, the correlation between the variables is unchanged. The formula for Pearson's r makes adjustments for differences in units of measurement, which leave intact the fundamental relationship between X and Y.

$$r = \frac{6(771.7597) - (10.37)(442.25)}{\sqrt{[6(17.9997) - (10.37)^2][6(33,510.3351) - (442.25)^2]}} = 0.88$$

The Direction of r

As we suggested in our discussion of covariance, r can capture either a positive or negative relationship between X and Y. The nature of the association is given by the sign of the correlation coefficient. When the sign is *positive*, r indicates that X and Y have a *direct* relationship. In other words, when X values increase, Y values increase, and when X values decrease, Y values decrease. The opposite is true when the sign for *r* is *negative*, which indicates that X and Y have an *inverse* relationship. When X and Y have a negative or inverse relationship, increases in X are paired with decreases in Y and decreases in X with increases in Y.

The Strength of *r*

Values for Pearson's *r* range from -1.00 to $+1.00$. The closer *r* is to 1.00, the stronger the relationship is between X and Y. The closer *r* is to 0.00, the weaker is the relationship. Pearson's *r* can never be larger than 1.00, irrespective of its sign.[4] When $r = \pm1.00$, the relationship between X and Y is perfect. However, when we say that a Pearson product-moment correlation indicates a perfect relationship between X and Y (i.e., when $|r| = 1.00$),[5] we really mean that X and Y have a perfect linear or straight-line relationship. Pearson's *r* was designed to measure the association between variables that bear a linear relationship to each other; that is, when the values of the variables X and Y are depicted in a scatterplot, their joint values or ordered pairs either form a straight line or approximate a straight line. When $|r| = 1.00$, the points fall exactly on the line; when $|r|$ is close to 1.00, the points fall close to a straight line; and when $r = 0.00$, the points are dispersed throughout the scatterplot in more of a random or circular pattern (Figure 7.2). As shown in Figure 7.2, when $r = +1.00$, all the points fall exactly on a straight line with a positive slope (i.e., the line slants upward), when $r = -1.00$, all the points fall exactly on a straight line with a negative slope (i.e., the line slants downward).

In terms of graphic presentation, the size of *r* is the extent to which the points in a scatterplot hug a straight line. When $|r| = 1.00$, the points lie exactly on the line, when $|r|$ is greater than 0.00 but less than 1.00, the points start to form a cluster that approximates a straight line. In general, as the points become closer and closer to forming a straight line, the size of $|r|$ increases until it reaches 1.00. As the points become more and more scattered or dispersed and diverge farther and farther away from a straight line, the size of *r* decreases until it reaches 0.00.

The absolute value of *r* tells us about the relative strength of a relationship. It is important to remember that *r*s with the same absolute value but different signs are equal in strength, and that a negative *r* that is larger in absolute value than a positive *r* indicates a stronger linear relationship. For example, *r*s of $-.40$ and $+.40$ both reflect relationships of the same magnitude. Likewise, these coefficients indicate relationships that are of greater magnitude than when $r = .35$. In addition, an *r* of .80 reveals a stronger relationship than when *r* is .40, but how much larger is it?

Mathematicians have devised a simple statistic to help us interpret the size of a correlation coefficient; it is called the *coefficient of determination* (r^2). Squaring the correlation coefficient tells us the proportion of variance in one variable (Y) that is explained by its linear relationship to another variable (X). Squaring a number eliminates its negative sign; r^2 tells us about the strength of a relationship but not about its direction. Values of r^2 range from 0.00 to 1.00 and are a proportion. An r^2 of .80 tells us that 80% of the variance in Y is attributable to its relationship with X. Likewise, the coefficient tells us that 80% of the variance in X is attributable to its relationship with Y.

When $r = 1.00$, $r^2 = 1.00$, which means that all of the variability in Y is explained by Y's relationship to X. As X values change, Y values change and all the points (X, Y) move (i.e., fall) exactly on a straight line. In instances in which

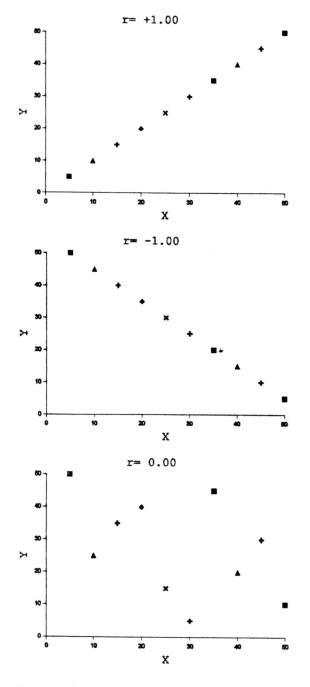

Figure 7.2   Scatterplots when $r = +1.00$, $r = -1.00$, and $r = 0.00$.

$|r|$ is less than 1.00, r^2 is less than 1.00, and the variability of X explains only a part of the variability of Y. Only a portion (less than 100%) of Y's variability is explained by the its relationship with X. To illustrate, when $r = .90$, 81% of Y's variance is explained by its relationship to X (i.e., $r^2 = .81$); when $r = .70$, 49% of Y's variance is explained by its relationship to X; when $r = .50$, 25% of Y's variance is explained by its relationship to X; and when $r = 0.00$ (i.e., where there is no linear relationship between X and Y), none of Y's variance is explained by its relationship to X. In the example of the WAIS and PAT scores, if $r = .76$, then $r^2 = .58$. This means that 58% of the variance in the PAT scores is explained by the WAIS scores.

Exercise 7–4 Coefficient of Determination

For the data from Exercise 7–1, what is the coefficient of determination? What does it mean?

The Effect of Outlying Scores on the Pearson *r*

Chapters 3 and 4 explain that the mean and variance can be greatly influenced when outlier (i.e., extreme) scores are included in a distribution. The size of *r* is also affected when outliers appear in an X or Y distribution. Table 7.6 displays hypothetical X and Y scores for four people. The correlation coefficient for the first three people is $r = -.33$, and $r^2 = .11$. If the fourth person (who is notably different from the other three) is included, the correlation becomes $r = .99$ and $r^2 = .99$.

Testing the Statistical Significance of *r*

Pearson's *r* is a descriptive measure of the relationship between two variables in a sample. By itself, *r* does not indicate whether a relationship actually exists in the bivariate population distribution of X and Y. To make that determination, we need to test the null hypothesis (H_0) that the correlation in the bivariate population distribution is equal to zero. The population correlation coefficient is symbolized ρ, the lower case Greek letter rho. How do we decide to reject or not reject H_0? In other words, how large does the sample *r* have to be before we can conclude that there is a bivariate relationship in the population (i.e., ρ ≠ 0.00)?

   A correlation coefficient is deemed sufficiently large when it reaches a predetermined level of *statistical significance*.[6] Traditionally, the .05 *confidence level* is used as the reference point or standard that guides decisions regarding H_0. For

Table 7.6 Hypothetical X and Y Scores That Demonstrate the Effect of Outlying Scores on the Computation of Pearson's *r*

Person	*X*	*Y*
1	2	7
2	4	9
3	5	5
4	80	40

example, we found that the relationship between police applicants' IQ (WAIS score) and PAT score was .76. It is possible that the correlation in the police applicant population is actually zero (i.e., PAT score and IQ are unrelated). If that is the case, a sample r of .76 would have occurred as a result of sampling error or by chance.

Table C in the Appendix provides the critical values of r that are needed to reach the .05 and .01 levels of significance for samples of different sizes. The values of r required for statistical significance are defined specifically by *degrees of freedom* (*df*), which are equal to the number of individuals minus two ($N - 2$). As Table C shows, for 8 *df*, an r of .63 is required to reach statistical significance at the .05 level. The r of .76 is larger than the table value. We reject the null hypothesis (H_0: $\rho = 0.00$) in favor of the rival hypothesis (H_1: $\rho \neq 0.00$) and conclude that a statistically significant positive correlation exists in the population of police applicants from which the current sample was selected. Another way of saying this is to conclude that the relationship in the population is not likely to be zero. In fact, the probability of finding a sample r as large as .76 when the population r is really zero is less than 5 percent.

Exercise 7–5   Strength of Pearson's r

Is the Pearson's r from the data set you have been using statistically significant at the .05 level?

More About the Interpretation of *r*

Although we have a great deal of confidence that WAIS and PAT scores are associated, we have only explored the extent to which they are linearly related. Pearson's r was designed to measure linear or straight-line relationships between two variables. It is quite conceivable that X and Y can have an r of zero and yet be perfectly related in another way. Figure 7.3 presents the curvilinear relationship between X (anxiety) and Y (percentage of time police officers hit the middle of the target during weapons qualifications). The worst shooting is done by officers who are so relaxed they are not even concentrating on the target and by those who are too nervous to hold the gun straight. These data illustrate that Pearson's r can be close to zero when two variables are strongly related in a nonlinear manner. For the data in Figure 7.3, $r = -.13$, in spite of the apparent strong curvilinear relationship between anxiety and target accuracy.[7]

Another factor that must be considered in the interpretation of r is sample size. With larger and larger sample sizes, smaller and smaller values of r are needed to reach statistical significance. For example, with 100 *df*, an r of .19 is all you need to attain statistical significance at the .05 level, which explains less than 4 percent of the variance in Y. This is clearly an instance in which r has statistical significance but no real practical significance or usefulness in explaining the relationship between X and Y.

Finally, we leave you with an important caveat about correlations: correlation implies covariation, not causality. Correlation is a necessary, but not a sufficient, condition to infer a causal relationship between X and Y. If X and Y are corre-

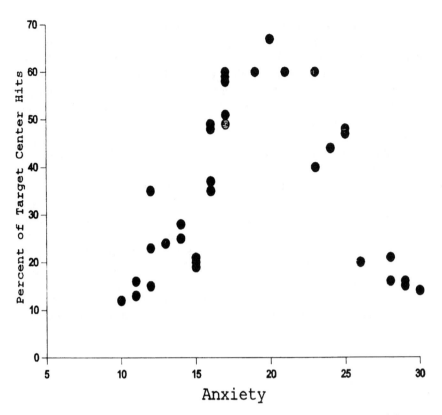

Figure 7.3 Scatterplot depicting the nonlinear relationship between anxiety and the percentage of target center hits during weapons qualification.

lated, X may cause Y, Y may cause X, or Z may cause both X and Y, which would produce a spurious or false correlation between X and Y.

Summary

From time to time, criminal justice practitioners study important relationships. *Pearson's r* is based on the concept of variation discussed in chapter 4. If two variables are related, they covary. This means they vary with each other in a systematic way. Pearson's r is a statistical method used to quantify the extent to which two variables vary together.

Pearson's r is a proportion formed by dividing the observed *covariance* of two variables, Cov(x,y), by the covariance that would be evidenced if there was a perfect relationship, S_xS_y. As such, the coefficient carries no measurement units and cannot exceed 1.00. In a perfect positive or direct relationship, $r = +1.00$. In a perfect negative or inverse relationship, $r = -1.00$.

It should not be forgotten that r measures the degree of linear relationship between two variables. Thus, when $r = 1.00$ it means that there is a perfect linear relationship. Likewise, when $r = 0.00$ it means that there is no linear relationship. Pearson's r is not designed to measure nonlinear or curvilinear relationships.

It is important to interpret properly both the *sign* and *magnitude* of *r*. The sign denotes the nature of a relationship (positive or negative), and the magnitude denotes the strength (weak, moderate, strong). For example, *rs* of .63 and −.32 describe two different relationships. The first is positive and the second is negative. The first relationship is stronger than the second because the value of .63 is greater than the value of .32. Remember, you should not consider the sign of *r* when interpreting the strength of a relationship.

The square of *r*, or r^2, is the *coefficient of determination* and tells us the percentage of the variance of one variable that is attributable to the variance of the other. For example, if $r = .58$, $r^2 = .34$. This tells us that 34% of the variance of one variable is attributable to its relationship to the other.

In testing the *statistical significance* of *r*, we are looking for the likelihood that the null hypothesis is true. In the case of correlations, the null hypothesis is that the population coefficient, ρ, is 0.00. If the sample *r* is large enough, we can reject H_0, and we have evidence that *r* estimates a relationship that exists in the population from which our sample has been drawn. Significant values of *r* can be found in Table C of the Appendix.

A strong correlation between two variables as measured by *r* does not imply causality. Causal relationships are a special form of association that require the application of specific research designs.

Answers to Exercises

Exercise Answer 7–1   Scattergram

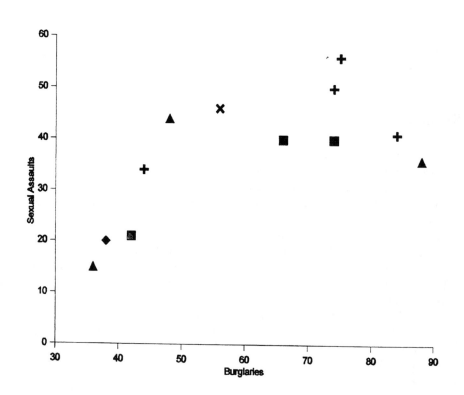

Exercise Answer 7–2   Cross Products and Covariance

Month	No. of Burglaries (X)	Deviation Score $(X - \bar{X})$	No. of Sexual Assaults (Y)	Deviation Score $(Y - \bar{Y})$	Cross Product $(X - \bar{X})(Y - \bar{Y})$
Jan	42	−18.42	21	−15.92	293.25
Feb	36	−24.42	15	−21.92	535.29
Mar	74	13.58	50	13.08	177.63
Apr	38	−22.42	20	−16.92	379.35
May	56	−4.42	46	9.08	−40.13
June	84	23.58	41	4.08	96.21
July	74	13.58	40	3.08	41.83
Aug	88	27.58	36	−.92	−25.37
Sept	75	14.58	56	19.08	278.19
Oct	66	5.58	40	3.08	17.19
Nov	48	−12.42	44	7.08	−87.93
Dec	44	−16.42	34	−2.92	47.95
SUM	725		443		1,713.46
Mean	60.42		36.92		
SD	18.61		12.55		

$$Covariance \ (x,y) = \frac{(1,713.46)}{(11)} = 155.77$$

Exercise Answer 7–3   Pearson's r

$$r = \frac{155.77}{(18.61)(12.55)} = \frac{155.77}{233.56} = .67$$

Exercise Answer 7–4   Coefficient of Determination

$r = .67$; $r^2 = .45$; Based on Pearson's r, 45% of the variation in sexual assaults is explained by the variation in burglaries.

Exercise Answer 7–5   Statistical Significance

$r = .67$; $df = (12 - 2) = 10$; statistically significant at the .05 level ($>.57$).

Computer Applications for Selected Exercises

Exercise Answer 7–1   Scattergrams

For this exercise, you need to enter the (x,y) pairs as separate columns in the Data Editor. Each row holds one pair. Include a month column to label the rows (Figure 7.4).

Construct the scattergram or scatterplot by first opening the Graphs menu. Choose Scatter, which is a little more than halfway down the list (Figure 7.5).

There is more than one kind of scatterplot. You are making a simple scatter for this exercise (Figure 7.6).

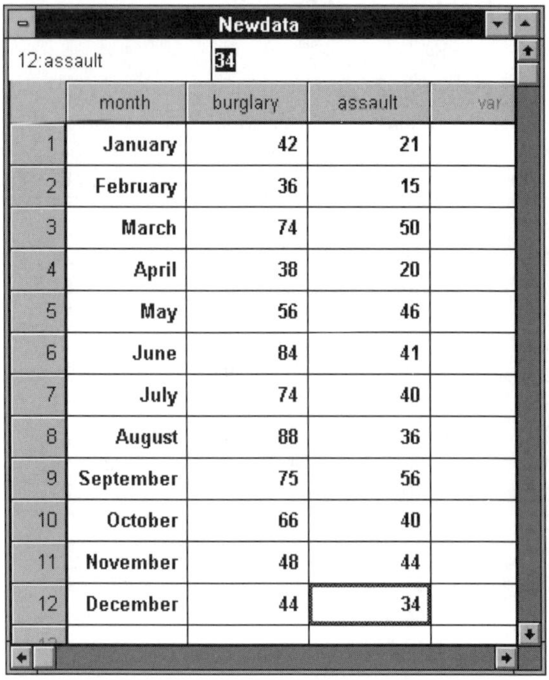

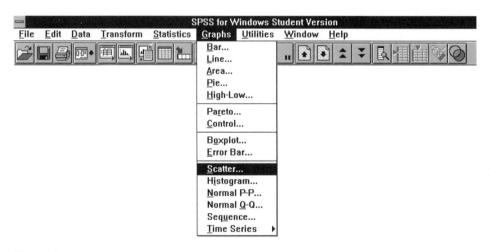

Figure 7.4

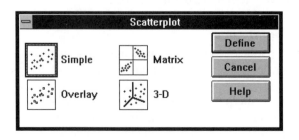

Figure 7.5

Figure 7.6

Click once in the box next to Simple. Choose Define to go to the Simple Scatterplot dialog box (Figure 7.7). Type burglary in the X Axis box and assault in the Y Axis box. Type month in the Label Cases by: box. Choose OK to run the graph.

The chart first comes up in the Chart Carousel (Figure 7.8). This is a holding place for charts. At this point, you decide whether you want to edit and keep the chart or discard it. To edit the chart click on Edit on the Chart Carousel. The

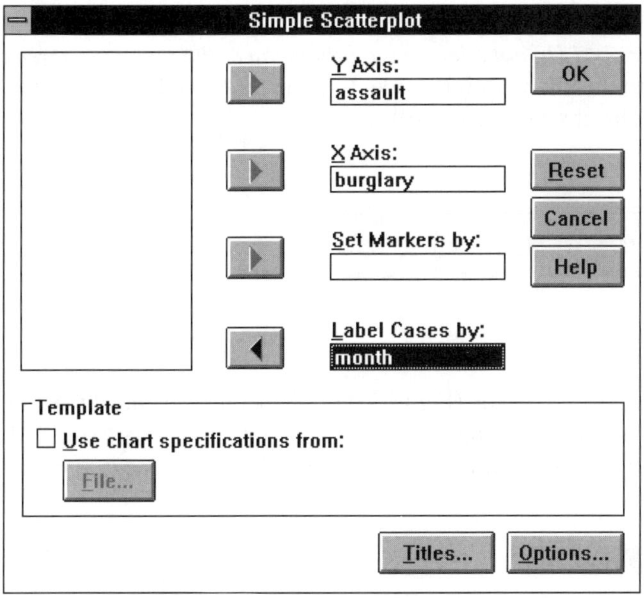

Figure 7.7

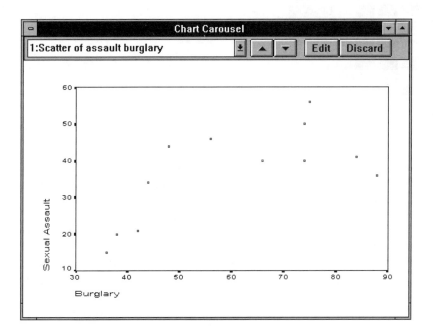

Figure 7.8

button is immediately below the Chart Carousel title bar to the left of the `Discard` button (Figure 7.9).

Edit | Discard

Figure 7.9

Do not click on `Discard`*! Do not click on the Edit menu at the top of the screen either!* Now you are in the chart editing mode. Use the tools on the right half of the toolbar to modify the chart (Figure 7.10).

Figure 7.10

The Colors icon looks like a crayon (Figure 7.11). Click once on one of the dots in the scatterplot. Black "handles" appear, indicating that the points are selected. Click on the crayon and choose a new color. Click on `Apply`. Choose `Close`.

Colors

Color
● Fill
○ Border

Apply
Close
Reset
Help

Save as Default   Edit...

Figure 7.11

The Markers icon looks like an asterisk (*) (Figure 7.12). You can use it to change the shape and size of the points in the chart. If the points in the chart have not been selected, click on one of the points in the chart. Click once on `Markers`. Choose a new shape and then choose `Apply All`. Choose `Close`.

The Point Identification tool provides information about the points on the graph. Click once on the icon (Figure 7.13).

Your mouse pointer becomes a set of cross hairs. Zoom in on the highest point on the graph and click once. The label for that point appears in the graph (Figure 7.14). Click on the Point Identification icon to turn off the tool.

Does this graph show a relationship between burglary and sexual assault? Is there anything important to know about September?

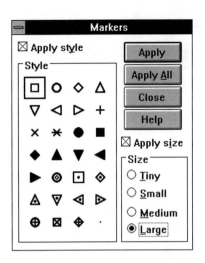

Figure 7.12

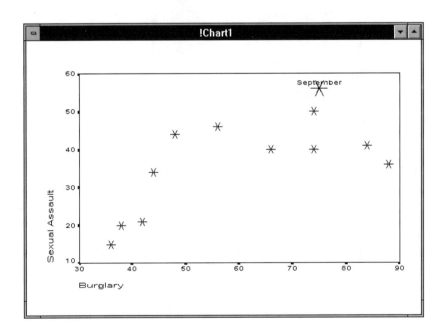

Figure 7.13

Figure 7.14

Exercise Answer 7–3 Pearson's r and
Exercise Answer 7–5 Strength of Pearson's r

Pearson's *r*, or the Pearson correlation coefficient, is calculated with the Correlate procedure. Go to the Statistics menu and choose `Correlate` (Figure 7.15)

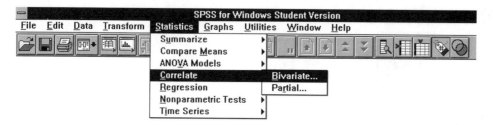

Figure 7.15

Use `Bivariate` for this exercise. Bivariate correlations measure the association between two variables.

Move the burglary and assault variables into the center of the box. The `Display actual significance level` box in the lower left of this dialog box gives the option to display the exact or actual significance (Figure 7.16). You do not need it for this exercise, so uncheck it. Choose `OK`.

```
┌────────────────────────────────────────────────────────────┐
│ ▬                    Bivariate Correlations                  │
├────────────────────────────────────────────────────────────┤
│ ┌─────────────┐        Variables:          ┌──────────┐      │
│ │ month       │        burglary            │    OK    │      │
│ │             │        assault             └──────────┘      │
│ │             │                                              │
│ │             │   ┌───┐                     ┌──────────┐     │
│ │             │   │ ◄ │                     │  Reset   │     │
│ │             │   └───┘                     └──────────┘     │
│ │             │                             ┌──────────┐     │
│ │             │                             │  Cancel  │     │
│ │             │                             └──────────┘     │
│ │             │                             ┌──────────┐     │
│ └─────────────┘                             │   Help   │     │
│ ┌─Correlation Coefficients──────────────────────────────┐   │
│ │ ☒ Pearson  □ Kendall's tau-b  □ Spearman             │   │
│ └───────────────────────────────────────────────────────┘   │
│ ┌─Test of Significance──────────────────────────────────┐   │
│ │  ● Two-tailed          ○ One-tailed                   │   │
│ └───────────────────────────────────────────────────────┘   │
│ □ Display actual significance level        ┌───────────┐    │
│                                            │ Options... │    │
│                                            └───────────┘    │
└────────────────────────────────────────────────────────────┘
```

Figure 7.16

The output shows a correlation coefficient of .6667 (Figure 7.17). The single asterisk next to the coefficient indicates that it is significant at least at the .05 level. You would have to turn on the "exact" box if you needed a better estimate.

```
                        - -  Correlation Coefficients  - -

                 BURGLARY    ASSAULT

BURGLARY    1.0000        .6667*
ASSAULT      .6667*      1.0000

* - Signif. LE .05      ** - Signif. LE .01      (2-tailed)

" . " is printed if a coefficient cannot be computed
```

Figure 7.17

The value of 1.0000 for BURGLARY against BURGLARY indicates perfect correlation. This is because burglary correlates perfectly with itself. There is no variation to measure when a variable is correlated with itself.

Notes

1. Karl Pearson (1857–1936) was a famous psychologist and statistician. He derived the formula for the correlation coefficient, which provides an index of the strength (magnitude) and direction (nature) of the relationship between two variables, both of which are measured on an interval or ratio scale.

2. One measures variation by computing the difference of scores from the mean. A measure of covariation is based on the same concept.

3. We made a similar statement in chapter 4 about the computation of variance and standard deviation. In general, equations that include deviation terms such as $(X - \overline{X})$ are more tedious to compute than equations that do not include these terms.

4. Pearson's r is formed by division of the observed covariance that could maximally be found if the relationship were perfect. Hence, r is a percentage of maximum covariance. As such, r cannot range beyond 1.00.

5. The term $|r|$ is read *the absolute value of r*. The absolute value of a number is its positive value, irrespective of its algebraic sign. For example, $|-3| = 3$ and $|3| = 3$. Thus, $|r| = r$, whether r is positive or negative.

6. See chapter 6 for a review of hypothesis testing.

7. If one were to use statistical techniques to measure curvilinear relationships, one would find a correlation coefficient of .85 for the data in Figure 7.3.

8. Linear Regression and Prediction

Transferred to Training

Your foot has finally healed and it's time to leave research and development (R & D) and go back to patrol. After several months in R & D, however, you really don't want to go back to patrol. You've found working in R & D interesting, and the experience has given you more of a chance to make use of your college education. When your current supervisor advises you that you must transfer out, you decide to see if there is somewhere else you can go. As it so happens, a position in the training academy is available. You apply for transfer and, thanks to a strong recommendation from your current supervisor, your transfer is approved.

On your first day at the academy, the captain, who is your new supervisor, tells you that the chief is considering changing the entry-level educational requirements from a high school diploma to some level of college education. However, the chief is not sure what the best level is or whether a change is really necessary. Therefore, R & D has been asked to gather data on education and policing.

You find this topic interesting, but because you are no longer with R & D, you begin to wonder what this has to do with you. Before you can ask, the captain informs you that R & D has requested your assistance. It seems that research conducted in the early 1970s examined how well college-educated officers performed in the academy. R & D wants you to examine whether educational level, specifically years of college, can predict the performance of recruits at the police academy. It has been suggested that you measure education as the number of years of college a recruit has completed and performance as the number of examinations on which a recruit had scored 90 or more by the end of the academy. (Each recruit takes ten examinations during the academy.) The question is: How are you going to do this?

Linear Regression and Prediction

This chapter discusses a bivariate statistical problem known as *linear regression*. The topics of correlation and regression are interrelated. Both deal with the relationship between two variables. In an important respect, regression problems depend on correlation. However, regression analysis takes correlation a step further; it involves using information about one variable (X) to make predictions about another variable (Y).

Concept of Prediction

We make predictions every day, often without even being aware of it. For example, you may look out the window each morning to see if it is cloudy to decide whether you should take an umbrella. In a basic sense, you are performing a regression analysis, which involves gathering information about X (the number of clouds in the sky) to predict Y (the likelihood of rain). You base your prediction on your prior knowledge about the relationship between X (cloudy skies) and Y (rain). That is, in the past, you have noticed that many times when it is cloudy outside, it rains, but this does not happen on every occasion. Sometimes when it is not very cloudy, it rains; other times, when it is cloudy, it does not rain. The relationship between X and Y is not perfect (i.e., the correlation is not 1). Nonetheless, clouds and rain occur together often enough that you can remain fairly confident that your prediction is correct more often than it is wrong.

Prediction is a central component of many decisions in criminal justice. For example, probation officers gather information about offenders at intake to predict their risk of committing crimes while on supervision. Those who score high on risk (X) are assumed to be more prone to subsequent arrests (Y). On the basis of this prediction, probation officers develop supervision plans that specify the nature and extent of their contacts with offenders. Offenders who score high on risk at intake are supervised more closely; those who score low are supervised less closely. These decisions are not useful or effective if there is no relationship between risk scores and behavior on probation.

Basic Assumptions and Terminology

This chapter discusses a particular type of regression problem that requires specific assumptions and is limited to certain types of variables. These problems are called simple linear or bivariate regression problems. *Bivariate regression*, as its name implies, deals with two variables. As noted in chapter 7, these variables are commonly labeled X and Y. The variable X serves as the basis for prediction and is called the *predictor variable*. Y is the variable that is being predicted from X; it is called the *criterion* or *outcome variable*. We gather information on the X variable to make predictions about the Y variable.

To use the regression techniques discussed in this chapter, X and Y have to be measured at least on an interval scale. They also have to be related to each other; that is, X and Y must have a *linear relationship*. If these assumptions are violated, the solutions are not valid.

What do we mean by a linear relationship? As discussed in chapter 7, linear relationships between X and Y appear as a straight line in a scatterplot. The X variable is plotted on the horizontal axis, and the Y variable is plotted on the vertical axis. The values of these two variables go together as *ordered pairs*, which provide the points that form the line plotted on the graph.

Linear Regression Problem

To illustrate how linear regression techniques are used in criminal justice, we return to the probation example. Hare (1993), a clinical psychologist, studied a psychiatric disorder called *psychopathy*. Hare found that offenders who score higher on this condition are more likely to break rules and to continue to commit crimes in spite of the threat of future punishment. Psychopathy is characterized by a lack of conscience and empathy for other people, a need for excitement and instant gratification, and an inability to control impulses. Psychopaths believe they are exempt from the norms and laws that govern human behavior. They have inflated ideas about themselves and their own importance.

A probation administrator wants to determine if psychopathy scores derived from Hare's psychopathy assessment tool can be used to predict which offenders are likely to ignore the conditions of their probation. To ascertain whether predictions about violations can be made on the basis of psychopathy levels, the probation administrator scores 10 closed probation cases on X (psychopathy) and Y (number of rule infractions while on probation supervision). These data are presented in Table 8.1. As you can see, each case has a score on both the X and Y variables, which was the same situation with correlation problems. Every X score is paired with a Y score for every case in the study. We took the data in Table 8.1 and plotted them in Figure 8.1 to form a scatterplot or scatter diagram.

The scatterplot in Figure 8.1 shows that X and Y have a positive relationship, that is, as X (psychopathy scores) increases, Y (number of rule infractions) increases and vice versa. The relationship between X and Y, however, is not perfect. How do we know that? We arrive at this conclusion in two ways. First, we can look at the scatter diagram and see that all the points do not fall exactly on a straight line, which happens only when X and Y are perfectly related. Second, we can calculate the correlation between X and Y (see chapter 7). From the information in Table 8.1, we find in the following way that $r = .66$:

$$r = \frac{N\Sigma(xy) - \Sigma(x)\Sigma(y)}{\sqrt{[N\Sigma x^2 - (\Sigma x)^2][N\Sigma y^2 - (\Sigma y)^2]}}$$

$$r = \frac{10(451) - (68)(58)}{\sqrt{[10(652) - 4,624][10(379) - 2,809]}}$$

$$r = \frac{4,510 - 3,604}{\sqrt{(1,896)(981)}} = \frac{906}{1,364} = .66$$

Table C in the Appendix shows that the value for r with 8 degrees of freedom is statistically significant at the .05 level.

Can we use X values to make predictions or guesses about Y values? We are on the right track. Earlier in this chapter we indicated that certain assumptions must be met before we can use regression techniques. By choosing variables (psychopathy scores and rule violations) that are measured on at least an interval scale, we meet one of these assumptions. By finding that X and Y are significantly correlated, we meet another. The last assumption is that X and Y have a linear relationship. A quick look at the data shows that a straight line can adequately depict the relationship between X and Y.

Table 8.1   Probationers' Psychopathy Scores and Rule Violations

Probationer	Psychopathy Score (X)	No. of Rule Violations (Y)
1. Ellis	14	10
2. Reed	3	2
3. Moore	12	4
4. Samuels	2	8
5. Johnson	10	8
6. Bollini	4	3
7. Manfredi	1	0
8. White	6	5
9. Smith	11	9
10. Gilbert	5	4
Mean	6.80	5.30
s	4.59	3.30

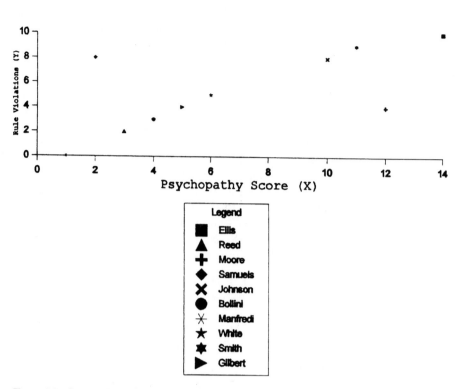

Figure 8.1   Scatterplot of Scores and Violations

The only time that all (X, Y) points fall precisely on a straight line (i.e., when X and Y have a linear relationship) is when $r = \pm 1.00$. The larger r is, the closer the plotted points of the ordered pairs of X and Y approximate a straight line.

When $r = \pm 1.00$, there is only one possible Y value for any given X value, and prediction is perfect. In other words, if we were to use X to make predictions about Y, we would never make a mistake. After all, when $r = \pm 1$, then $r^2 = 1$, and 100 percent of the variance in Y is explained by Y's relationship to X. In the social sciences, including criminal justice, perfect relationships never occur because researchers are dealing with people and their complex behaviors. Although psychopathy and rule breaking are closely associated (i.e., as one goes up so does the other in most cases), there are two probationers in the sample who deviate from the pattern. Moore (Case 3) scored high on psychopathy but broke few rules. Samuels (Case 4) scored low on psychopathy and broke many rules.

In a prediction problem, we want to arrive at a particular value for Y that is based on a particular value for X. This is a simple task when all the X and Y values fall exactly on a straight line. However, as we have already conceded, this hardly happens with real data about real people. Our task is to find a line that best fits the actual points and then to use that line for prediction purposes. Before we do so, we need to review some basic material about straight lines.

Exercise 8–1   Linear Regression

To address the problem R & D wants you to research, that is, predicting whether education affects examination scores in the academy, the results of ten academy graduates are examined. Education, the X variable, is measured as number of years of college. The number of examinations with a score of 90 or greater is the Y variable. Plot the following pairs of scores. What type of correlation is observable? Calculate the correlation. Does it support your observation?

Recruit	No. of Years of College (X)	No. of Exams (Y)
Adams	6	9
Baker	3	8
Charles	2	6
Daniels	1	5
Edwards	4	9
Frank	1	7
Graham	5	10
Henry	2	4
Innez	4	10
Jones	3	8

Formula for a Straight Line

When there is one X variable (predictor) and one Y variable (outcome) and their relationship is expressed as a straight line, the procedure for predicting Y from X is called *simple linear regression.* Any straight line can be represented by the equation

$$Y = bx + a \qquad\qquad \text{Equation 8.1}$$

What do the components of this formula mean? We are already familiar with X and Y. These variables are plotted on the X and Y axis, respectively. The constant *a* is where the line crosses the Y axis when X = 0 and is called the Y intercept. The constant *b* is the slope of the line, which is the slant of the line (see chapter 7). *Slope* also is defined as the amount of change in Y associated with one unit of change in X. Slope is how steeply the line inclines or goes up when the relationship between X and Y is positive or how sharply it declines or goes down when the relationship is negative. The slope and Y intercept are called *regression constants* because for any given data set with X and Y variables there is only one value for the slope and only one value for the Y intercept. Slope is also commonly referred to as the *regression coefficient.*

Figure 8.2 provides an example of a line defined by the equation Y = 2X + 3. We can plot this line by making up values for X and computing Y. For example, when X = 0, Y = 2(0) + 3 = 3. When X = 1, Y = 2(1) + 3 = 5. The line crosses the Y axis at + 3, which means that the Y intercept (*a*) = + 3. When we start anywhere on the line and move one unit over horizontally, we have to go up two units to touch the line again. That is, when we move across one unit on X, we go up two units on Y, which is the value of *b*, the slope of the line.

Finding the Regression Line

Our basic task in linear regression is to find values that form the equation for the straight line. With that equation, we can take any value on X (the predictor), plug it into the equation, and solve algebraically for Y (the criterion). For example, with the linear equation, Y = 2X + 3 , if X equals 4, our best guess about Y is that it equals 11. However, when we create a scatterplot with real data, we are not likely to find that the actual points for X and Y form a straight line. How can we apply regression procedures to make predictions?

Statisticians have found a way to use regression techniques for prediction even when the data do not form a straight line. They have derived formulas for finding *a* and *b* that minimize error in prediction. Of course, the accuracy of prediction depends on the strength of the relationship between X and Y. When X and Y have

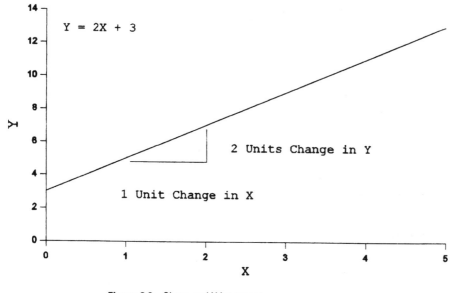

Figure 8.2 Slope and Y Intercept

a significant correlation, the variance in Y is explained by Y's relationship to X. If $r = 0$, none of the variance in Y is explained by X and predictions are not useful. In fact, when $r = 0$, the best we can do is to predict $\overline{Y}$ for every value of X.

You may be asking, "Why are you presenting a problem that involves predicting probationers' rule breaking from their psychopathy levels when the rule-breaking behavior of the 10 offenders in the sample is already known?" When we have real measures of both variables, it is unnecessary to forecast one from the other. However, at the beginning of probation we do not know exactly how a probationer is going to behave. Closed cases were chosen for the purpose of relating X and Y in situations in which an offender's performance on the criterion variable had already been documented. From this information, we can calculate the correlation between X and Y and find a regression line that can be used with subsequent cases in which only X values are known and Y values represent a future behavior or outcome.

We want to use the data in Table 8.1 to find an equation for a straight line that allows us to predict or forecast a probationer's risk given his or her psychopathy level at intake. This prediction helps a probation officer to decide how closely probationers are to be monitored. Specifically, the more rule breaking that is predicted about a certain probationer, the more stringently the officer supervises that offender through reports, field visits, arrest checks, contacts with employers, drug tests, or other surveillance mechanisms that are available in that jurisdiction. In short, prediction tools are a way for officers to develop effective supervision plans that take into account differences in offender risk for future criminality. The officer is taking information he or she gathers in the present to guess about behaviors that may occur in the future.

With the data in Table 8.1, we can derive values for the slope and Y intercept using the following equations:

$$b = \frac{N\Sigma xy - (\Sigma x)(\Sigma y)}{N\Sigma x^2 - (\Sigma x)^2}$$ Equation 8.2

$$a = \overline{Y} - b\overline{X}$$ Equation 8.3

Table 8.2 Formulas for Slope and Y Intercept

Probationer	Psychopathy Score (X)	No. of Rule Violations (Y)	(X^2)	(XY)
1. Ellis	14	10	196	140
2. Reed	3	2	9	6
3. Moore	12	4	144	48
4. Samuels	2	8	4	16
5. Johnson	10	8	100	80
6. Bollini	4	3	16	12
7. Manfredi	1	0	1	0
8. White	6	5	36	30
9. Smith	11	9	121	99
10. Gilbert	5	4	25	20
Sum	68	53	652	451
Mean	6.8	5.3		

The terms for computing a and b are shown in Table 8.2. Several steps are required to derive b. We have to find the sum of X (Σx), the sum of Y (Σy), the sum of X^2 (Σx^2), and the sum of X quantity squared ($\Sigma x)^2$, and the sum of the cross products of X and Y (Σxy). Inserting these quantities in the formula yields a value for b, which in the example equals .478. Now we can find a by plugging in b, multiplying it by $\overline{X}$ and subtracting that result from $\overline{Y}$. We can see that $a = 2.036$. The resultant regression formula is

$$b = \frac{N(\Sigma xy) - (\Sigma x)(\Sigma y)}{N\Sigma x^2 - (\Sigma x)^2} = \frac{10(451) - (68)(53)}{10(652) - 4{,}624}$$

$$b = \frac{N(\Sigma xy) - (\Sigma x)(\Sigma y)}{N\Sigma x^2 - (\Sigma x)^2} = \frac{906}{1{,}896} = .478$$

$$a = \overline{Y} - b\overline{X} = 5.3 - (.478)(6.8) = 2.036$$

$$Y = .478X + 2.036$$

Exercise 8–2   Equation for a Straight Line

Using the data from Exercise 8–1, derive the values for the slope and Y intercept. What is the final regression formula?

Now we can insert values for X to predict values on Y. The predicted values are called *Y predicted* or *Y estimate* and are symbolized as $\tilde{y}$. The symbol over Y is called a *tilde*. *Y predicted* reminds us that $\tilde{y}$ values may not always equal actual values of Y. In Table 8.3, inserted into the regression formula, are the same values for X that were in the initial data set to find predicted Y values. For example, when X = 14, $\tilde{y} = 8.76$, when X = 3, $\tilde{y} = 3.48$. Because our values for X were from our initial data set, we can compare each Y-predicted value with each actual Y value for each X value we inserted in the formula. By doing so, we have found a way to examine the accuracy of our predictions.

Exercise 8–3   Predicted Values of Y

Using the data from the previous exercises, calculate the predicted values of Y using the regression formula. How do these values compare with the actual values of Y?

Table 8.3   Differences Between Actual Y Values and Predicted Y Values: Standard Error of the Estimate

Probationer	Psychopathy Score (X)	No. of Actual Rule Violations (Y)	No. of Predicted Rule Violations ($\tilde{y}$)	Differences, Actual and Predicted $(Y - \tilde{y})$	Differences Squared $(Y - \tilde{y})^2$
1. Ellis	14	10	8.76	+ 1.24	1.54
2. Reed	3	2	3.48	− 1.14	1.30
3. Moore	12	4	7.80	− 3.80	14.44
4. Samuels	2	8	3.00	+ 5.00	25.00
5. Johnson	10	8	6.84	+ 1.16	1.35
6. Bollini	4	3	3.96	− .96	.92
7. Manfredi	1	0	2.52	− 2.52	6.35
8. White	6	5	4.92	+ .08	.00
9. Smith	11	9	7.32	+ 1.68	2.82
10. Gilbert	5	4	4.44	− .44	.19
Sum				.00	53.92

Σ (positive differences) = 9.2 Σ (negative differences) = −9.2

Accuracy of Prediction

If $r = \pm 1.00$, all the Y predicted values and all the actual values of Y fall exactly on a straight line. With our data, prediction is not perfect because predicted Y values and actual Y values are not the same. However, predicted Y values and actual Y values are very close, so our prediction is fairly accurate.

Figure 8.3 shows the regression line formed from our regression equation. The slope equals .478 and the Y intercept equals 2.036. We can take any two of the ordered pairs consisting of x and $\tilde{y}$ data points and form this straight line. Also shown are differences between predicted Y values and actual Y values. These differences are called *residuals*, which is another way of saying that the actual Y values do not lie on the regression line. The residuals are the differences between actual and predicted values of Y. The predicted values fall on the regression line, but the actual values typically do not.

In Table 8.3, we subtracted each predicted Y value from each actual Y value and added the differences. The sum of these differences equals zero because the residuals above the line cancel out the residuals below the line. This happens for any set of X and Y data, that is, $\Sigma(Y - \tilde{y})$ always equals 0. Therefore, this quantity cannot be used as an index of the accuracy of predictions because even when the prediction is highly accurate or only somewhat accurate, it always equals zero.

A useful formula for assessing the accuracy of prediction can be derived by first squaring each $(Y - \tilde{y})$ and then adding the squared differences to eliminate the zero result, which always occurs if the differences are summed without first being squared.

The sum of the squared differences between actual Y scores and predicted Y scores is an important value in linear regression. When statisticians developed formulas for a and b, they used this value as the basis for their equations. Their formulas for the regression constants satisfied what is known as the *least-squares criterion*. The regression constants for any given set of data on X and Y are calculated to minimize error in prediction. The error that they minimize is $\Sigma(Y - \tilde{y})^2$. In other words, the line that is fit to the data in a scatterplot minimizes the sum of the squares of the distances between the actual Y points and the regression line (i.e., the predicted Y points). That is why a regression line is some-

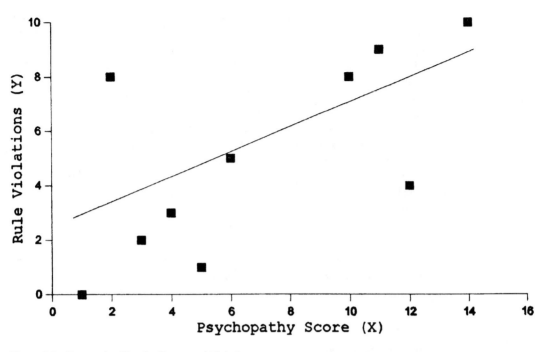

Figure 8.3 Regression Line for Score and Violations

times referred to as the *best fitting* line. It provides a line that makes predictions as accurate as they can be given the data.

Stopping with the sum of the squared differences as the measure of prediction error leaves another problem. That is, the sum of the squared differences almost always is large for large data sets simply because large sets have more numbers. To eliminate this size factor, we divide by $N - 2$, which statisticians have found gives a better result for sample data than simply dividing by N. The last problem with this formula is that it results in a quantity with squared units. So we simply take the square root of the value. Now we have an equation that we can use to measure prediction accuracy.

Equation 8.4 is called the *standard error of estimate* ($S_{y \cdot x}$). It looks like the equation for standard deviation, and it has properties similar to those of the standard deviation. Like standard deviation, standard error is a measure of variability—the variability of actual Y values around predicted Y values. The more actual data points vary around predicted data points, the more inaccurate the predictions. The less variability there is, the less inaccuracy there is. As standard error decreases, accuracy in prediction improves.

$$S_{y \cdot x} = \sqrt{\frac{\Sigma(Y - \tilde{y})^2}{N - 2}}$$ Equation 8.4

The computations for the standard error of estimate for our data are found in Table 8.3. We took the sum of the squared differences between actual Y values and predicted Y values, divided by $N - 2$, and then found the square root.

$$S_{y \cdot x} = \sqrt{\frac{\Sigma(Y - \tilde{y})^2}{N - 2}} = \sqrt{\frac{53.92}{8}} = \sqrt{6.74} = 2.60$$

The result is 2.60 rule violations. The standard error of the estimate is the average of the squared errors in prediction. How do we interpret this value? The standard error indicates how much, on average, predicted Y values deviate from actual Y values. In the example, $S_{y \cdot x}$ equals 2.60 rule violations. This means that, on average, our predictions of Y deviate ± 2.60 units. The value of $S_{y \cdot x}$ is comparable to the standard deviation, which tells how much scores typically deviate from their mean.

What if $r = \pm 1$? This means that $Y = \tilde{y}$ for every value of X. Our predictions are perfectly accurate and the numerator in Equation 8.4 equals zero, thus the standard error also equals zero. A standard error of the estimate with a value of zero indicates that there is no error in prediction (i.e., our predictions are flawless). What if $r = 0$? If that is the case, using X values to predict Y values is a waste of time because our predictions do not have a foundation or basis in the relationship between X and Y, and they are not precise. For every value of X, we might just as well guess $\overline{Y}$. We can gain a clearer understanding of this concept when instead of using raw scores to compute the regression equation, we use z scores, which are discussed in chapter 4.

Exercise 8–4   Standard Error of Estimate

According to the data in the previous exercises, what is the standard error of estimate?

Linear Regression with z Scores

Making predictions with z scores is simple once we understand the basic regression formula. In the formula $\tilde{y} = bx + a$, we insert a value for X, multiply it by b, and add a to find the value for $\tilde{y}$. The regression formula using z scores is about the same. The bivariate prediction formula for z scores only changes some of the terminology and reflects the properties of standard scores. The b in the standard score formula is called a *standardized regression coefficient* because it involves a standard score and it is symbolized by the lower case Greek letter beta (β). Beta is sometimes referred to as a *beta weight*. In bivariate regression with standard scores, β is always equal to r, the correlation between X and Y. The equation is as follows:

$$z_{\tilde{y}} = \beta(z_x) \qquad \text{Equation 8.5}$$

Equation 8.5 requires that we find the z score equivalent for any raw score X and multiply it by β. The product $\beta(z_x)$ gives the predicted value of the standard score on Y that corresponds to a particular standard score on X.

We can use Equation 8.5 to predict z_y from z_x with data from Table 8.1. Johnson (subject 5) has a raw score on the psychopathy scale of 10. To use the z score formula, we have to convert Johnson's score to a z score. The formula for a standard score is

$$z_x = \frac{X - \overline{X}}{S_x}$$

The average of the psychopathy scores is 6.8 and the standard deviation is 4.59. The z score that corresponds to a raw score of 10 is found by subtracting 6.8 from 10 and dividing the difference by 4.59. The resultant z score is .70 and the correlation between psychopathy and rule violations is .66. The z score for Johnson's predicted number of rule violations equals .70(.66) or .46 standard deviation units above the mean of rule violations. We can convert $z_{\tilde{y}} = .46$ to a raw score to see if it yields the same result we found using the raw score formula by solving algebraically for Y in the formula

$$.46 = (Y - 5.3) \div 3.30$$

where

$$z_{\bar{y}} = .46, \bar{y} = 5.3, \text{ and } S_y = 3.30$$

When we solve for Y

$$.46(3.30) = Y - 5.3$$

$$1.52 = Y - 5.3$$

$$Y = 6.8$$

The value 6.8 is the same Y-predicted score for Johnson, which we found using the raw score formula to predict rule violations.

We want to return to our earlier point regarding the values of Y when $r = 0$. When $r = 0$, knowing a person's score on the predictor variable X is not helpful or informative, that is, it does not help us to make an accurate guess about the value of Y that corresponds to any particular value of X. In that case, we guess $\bar{y}$ for every value of X. With standard scores, the mean of z is 0. When $r = 0$, $z_{\bar{y}} = \beta(z_x) = 0(z_x) = 0$; therefore, $z_{\bar{y}} = 0$. Therefore, our prediction of $z_{\bar{y}}$ is always 0, which corresponds to the mean of Y.

At the other extreme, when $r = 1$, there is a perfect relationship between X and Y, and our predictions are always correct. The values of $z_{\bar{y}}$ correspond exactly to z_x values. Scores of $z_{\bar{y}}$ greater than and less than $\bar{y}$ are in exactly the same position as z_x scores greater than and less than $\bar{x}$. When $r = 1$, $z_{\bar{y}} = \beta(z_x) = 1(z_x) = z_x$; therefore, $z_{\bar{y}} = Z_x$.

The same logic can be seen in an alternative equation for $S_{y \cdot x}$. Equation 8-4 can be time consuming for computing the standard error of the estimate. An equation that is more convenient to use is as follows:

$$S_{y \cdot x} = S_y \sqrt{1 - r^2} \qquad \text{Equation 8.6}$$

The maximum and minimum values for $S_{y \cdot x}$ can be easily seen from this formula. When $r = 0$, $S_{y \cdot x} = S_y$. In this case, the dispersion of Y scores around the regression line is as large as the standard deviation of Y, which is the dispersion of Y scores around their mean. Therefore, knowing X does not reduce error in prediction. When $r = 1$, $S_{y \cdot x} = 0$. In this case, there is no dispersion of actual Y scores around the regression line and no error in predicting Y from X. With our data and Equation 8.6, we calculate the following:

$$S_{y \cdot x} = 3.30 \sqrt{1 - .66^2} = 3.30 \sqrt{.5644} = 3.30(.7513) = 2.479$$

This is close to the result obtained with Equation 8.4.

Another Look at Prediction Error

Another way to evaluate the usefulness of the prediction equation is to assess how much better we do making predictions of rule violations (Y) with psychopathy scores (X) than we do making predictions of Y without information about X or any other predictor variable. Three steps are involved in this strategy. First, we have to compute the amount of squared error that we make in prediction when using X. We computed this number in Table 8.3 when we obtained the standard error of the estimate. This number is the sum of the squared differences between actual Y values and predicted Y values (i.e., the least-squares criterion) and is found at the bottom of the last column of Table 8.3. It is 53.92. The $\Sigma(Y - \bar{y})^2$ is called the *sum of the squared errors* (SS_E).

Second, we compute the amount of squared error that results if we make our predictions about Y without knowing anything about the variables that predict rule violations, including psychopathy scores. In this case, the best guess we can make about a probationer's rule violations is to predict the average number of rule violations for all probationers. As discussed in chapter 2, the average is the only measure of central tendency that takes into account all the scores in a distribution by summarizing or capturing the location of those scores. We also saw in the section on linear regression and z scores that when $r = 0$, $z_{\bar{y}}$ equals zero, which is the mean of z_y. Without information on which to base our predictions, our most reliable estimate of Y comes from using $\bar{y}$ for every X score. Calculation of the amount of squared error without using X (the predictor variable) or any other predictor variable involves computing the amount of squared error from the mean of y for every value of X. This is found by subtracting $\overline{Y}$ from every value of Y, squaring the differences, and then summing them, which is called the *total squared error* for predictions from the mean (SS_T). This is the numerator of the formula for variance, which is the average of the squared deviations of scores around their mean (see chapter 4).

Third, we then subtract SS_E from SS_T and divide by SS_T. This is the formula for determining the *proportionate reduction in prediction error* that results if we use X scores to predict Y scores instead of simply guessing the average rule breaking for every probationer at intake.

$$\text{Proportionate reduction in prediction error} = \frac{SS_T - SS_E}{SS_T} \qquad \text{Equation 8.7}$$

Table 8.4 shows the calculation of this value, which is equal to .45.

For Table 8.4, proportionate reduction in error is calculated as follows:

$$\frac{SS_T - SS_E}{SS_T} = \frac{98.1 - 53.92}{98.1} = \frac{44.18}{98.1} = .45$$

What if $r = 0$? The reduction in error also is 0 because SS_T equals SS_E (i.e., using X to predict Y has no advantage over simply guessing $\bar{y}$ for every X value). When predictions are perfect and $r = \pm 1.00$, SS_E equals 0 and the proportionate reduction in prediction error is 100 percent. In the example, the proportionate reduction in error (.45) is close to the middle of the range in terms of its advantage over using the mean of Y to predict every individual value of X.

Proportionate reduction in error equals r^2, which is the proportion of variance in Y that is explained by Y's relationship to X. In the example, r for psychopathy scores and rule violations is equal to .66, and the square of .66 is approximately .45. Nearly half of the variability in Y scores can be attributed to psychopathy.

Table 8.4   Computation of the Proportionate Reduction in Error

Case No.	Y	$(y - \bar{y})^2$	
1	10	$(10 - 5.3)^2$	22.09
2	2	$(2 - 5.3)^2$	10.89
3	4	$(4 - 5.3)^2$	1.69
4	8	$(8 - 5.3)^2$	7.29
5	8	$(8 - 5.3)^2$	7.29
6	3	$(3 - 5.3)^2$	5.29
7	0	$(0 - 5.3)^2$	28.09
8	5	$(5 - 5.3)^2$	.09
9	9	$(9 - 5.3)^2$	13.69
10	4	$(4 - 5.3)^2$	1.69

$\Sigma Y = 53$; $\bar{y} = 5.3$; $SS_T = 98.1$

Psychopathy does not account for the other influences over probationers' rule-breaking behaviors. However, when we know a probationer's psychopathy score, we reduce our error in prediction by 45 percent.

We can divide SS_T and SS_E by their appropriate denominators to find the total variance of Y (S^2_y) and the variance of the errors of estimate ($S^2_{y \cdot x}$). The total variance of Y can be partitioned (divided) into two components:

$$S^2_y = S^2_{\bar{y}} + S^2_{y \cdot x} \qquad \text{Equation 8.8}$$

where

S^2_y = total variance of Y
$S^2_{\bar{y}}$ = variance of the predicted Y scores
$S^2_{y \cdot x}$ = variance of the errors of estimate

If we divide each term by S^2_y we find that

$$\frac{S^2_y}{S^2_y} = \frac{S^2_{\bar{y}}}{S^2_y} + \frac{S^2_{y \cdot x}}{S^2_y}$$

The following expression is the ratio of the variance of predicted scores to total variance.

$$\frac{S^2_{\bar{y}}}{S^2_y}$$

It is the proportion of the total variance of Y that is explained by knowledge of X (in the prediction of Y from X). This equals r^2, the coefficient of determination, which was discussed in chapter 7. Therefore,

$$1 = r^2 + \frac{S^2_{y \cdot x}}{S^2_y}$$

The following term is sometimes called the *coefficient of alienation:*

$$\frac{S^2_{y \cdot x}}{S^2_y}$$

It is the proportion of Y that is *not* explained by Y's relationship to X. It is symbolized k^2. Therefore,

$$1 = r^2 + k^2$$

That is, the total variance (100%) in Y (rule breaking) is found by adding the proportion of the variance in Y (.45) that is explained by X (psychopathy scores) and the total variance in Y that is not explained by X, which is $1 - r^2$ or .55 and is the value for k^2. In chapter 9, we add a second predictor variable to try to explain more of the variance in Y (i.e., to reduce the variance in Y that is unexplained).

Exercise 8–5   Proportionate Reduction in Error

Continuing with the data from previous exercises, calculate the proportionate reduction of error coefficient. How much of the variance in Y (recruit success) is explained by the variance in X (years of college)?

Summary

Linear regression is a bivariate statistical technique, which like correlation, involves two variables (X and Y) that are related to each other as a straight line. In *regression analysis*, X is called the *predictor variable* and Y the *outcome variable*.

We use data on both the X axis and the Y axis (after outcomes have been obtained) to find a regression line with a slope (*b*) and Y intercept (*a*) that minimize the sum of the squared errors in prediction (i.e., that satisfies the *least-squares criterion*). The regression line allows us to use a score on X (a current assessment or measure) to make a prediction about a score on Y (a future behavior or performance). The equation for predicting Y from X can be found with raw scores or standard scores. When $r < 1$, errors are made in prediction; that is, actual Y values deviate from predicted Y values.

Overall, error is measured with the *standard error of estimate*, which is the average deviation of actual Y values from predicted Y values. When $r = 1$ and prediction is perfect, the standard error is 0 because the predicted values of Y equal the actual values of Y. At the other extreme, when $r = 0$, the standard error equals the standard deviation of Y values, and knowing X does not improve prediction of Y.

The *total variance* of Y can be partitioned into two additive components: r^2, which is the proportion of variance in Y explained by X, and k^2, which is the proportion of variance in Y *not* explained by X. The values r^2 and k^2 are called the *coefficient of determination* and the *coefficient of alienation*, respectively. The sum of r^2 and k^2 always equals 1, or 100 percent of the variance in Y.

Using the information described in this chapter, one can attempt to make predictions. In the vignette, you are in a position that requires you to predict whether education is related to the academy success of recruits. Education is measured as years of college, and success is viewed as the number of examination scores greater than 90. The exercises throughout this chapter provide you with an answer.

Answers to Exercises

Exercise Answer 8–1   Linear Regression
Observation: Positive correlation, as years of college increases so do the number of examinations with scores greater than 90.

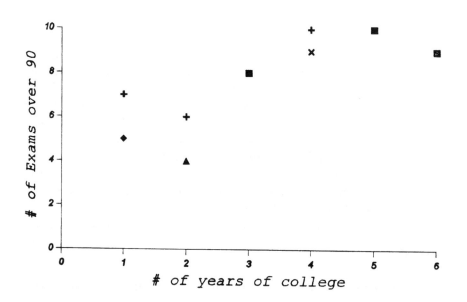

Figure 8.4   Scatter Diagram

$$r = \frac{N\Sigma xy - \Sigma x \Sigma y}{\sqrt{[N\Sigma x^2 - (\Sigma x)^2][N\Sigma y^2 - (\Sigma y)^2]}}$$

$$= \frac{10(260) - (31)(76)}{\sqrt{[10(121) - (961)][10(616) - (5{,}776)]}}$$

$$= \frac{2{,}600 - 2{,}356}{\sqrt{[1{,}210 - 961][6{,}160 - 5{,}776]}}$$

$$= \frac{244}{\sqrt{(249)(384)}} = \frac{244}{\sqrt{95{,}616}} = \frac{244}{309} = .79$$

Note: Exercise Table 8.2 also applies to Exercise 8–1.

Exercise Answer 8–2 Equation for a Straight Line

Recruit	No. of Years of College (x)	No. of Exams with Scores over 90 (y)	(x²)	(xy)
Adams	6	9	36	54
Baker	3	8	9	24
Charles	2	6	4	12
Daniels	1	5	1	5
Edwards	4	9	16	36
Frank	1	7	1	7
Graham	5	10	25	50
Henry	2	4	4	8
Innez	4	10	16	40
Jones	3	8	9	24
Sum	31	76	121	260
Mean	3.1	7.6		

$$b = \frac{N(\Sigma xy) - (\Sigma x)(\Sigma y)}{N\Sigma x^2 - (\Sigma x)^2} = \frac{10(260) - (31)(76)}{10(121) - 961}$$

$$b = \frac{2{,}600 - 2{,}356}{1{,}210 - 961} = \frac{244}{249} = .979$$

$$a = \overline{Y} - b\overline{X} = 7.6 - (.98)(3.1) = 4.56$$

The regression formula is as follows:

$$\tilde{y} = .979X + 4.56$$

Exercise Answer 8–3 Predicted Values of Y

The regression formula is as follows:

$$\tilde{y} = .979X + 4.56$$

Recruit	X	Y	$\tilde{Y}$
Adams	6	9	10.43
Baker	3	8	7.50
Charles	2	6	6.52
Daniels	1	5	5.54
Edwards	4	9	8.48
Frank	1	7	5.54
Graham	5	10	9.46
Henry	2	4	6.52
Innez	4	10	8.48
Jones	3	8	7.50

Exercise Answer 8–4   Standard Error of Estimate

Recruit	x	y	$\tilde{y}$	$(y - \tilde{y})$	$(y - \tilde{y})^2$
Adams	6	9	10.43	−1.43	2.04
Baker	3	8	7.50	.50	.25
Charles	2	6	6.52	− .52	.27
Daniels	1	5	5.54	− .54	.29
Edwards	4	9	8.48	.52	.27
Frank	1	7	5.54	1.46	2.13
Graham	5	10	9.46	.54	.29
Henry	2	4	6.52	−2.52	6.35
Innez	4	10	8.48	1.52	2.31
Jones	3	8	7.50	.50	.25
Sum				.00	14.45

$$S_{y \cdot x} = \sqrt{\frac{\Sigma(Y - \tilde{y})^2}{N - 2}} = \sqrt{\frac{14.45}{8}} = \sqrt{1.81} = 1.35$$

The standard error of estimate is ±1.35 examinations.

Exercise Answer 8–5   Proportionate Reduction in Error

Recruit	Y	$(Y - \bar{Y})^2$	
Adams	9	$(9 - 7.6)^2$	1.96
Baker	8	$(8 - 7.6)^2$	.16
Charles	6	$(6 - 7.6)^2$	2.56
Daniels	5	$(5 - 7.6)^2$	6.76
Edwards	9	$(9 - 7.6)^2$	1.96
Frank	7	$(7 - 7.6)^2$	.36
Graham	10	$(10 - 7.6)^2$	5.76
Henry	4	$(4 - 7.6)^2$	12.96
Innez	10	$(10 - 7.6)^2$	5.76
Jones	8	$(8 - 7.6)^2$	.16
Sum	76		SS_T 38.40
Mean	7.6		SS_E 14.45

$$\frac{SS_T - SS_E}{SS_T} = \frac{38.40 - 14.45}{38.40} = \frac{23.95}{38.40} = .62$$

Sixty-two percent of the variance in academy success can be explained by years of college, leaving 38 percent attributable to other factors.

Computer Applications for Selected Exercises

Exercise Answer 8–1   Linear Regression
The data for this exercise are in the raw form in which they were collected. They were not summarized before you received them. Compare these data with what you had at the beginning of Exercise 2–1.

The recruit column is used only as a label, so you can set it up as you did the label column in Exercise 5–2. When you set up columns for number of years in

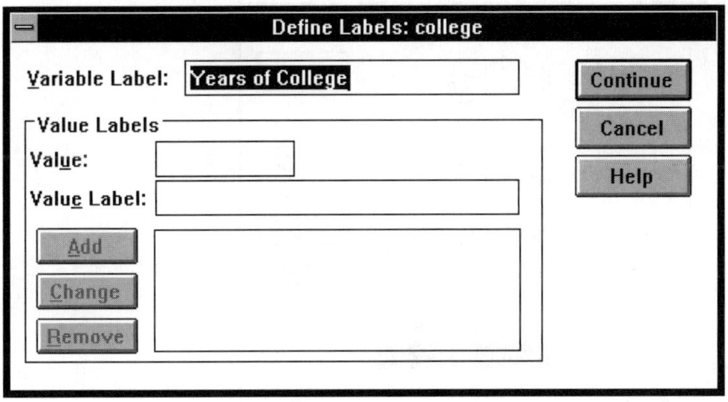

Figure 8.5

college and number of examination scores greater than 90, make sure to include descriptive variable labels (Figure 8.5). These variable labels become the titles for the axes in any charts you draw.

The final data set is illustrated in Figure 8.6.

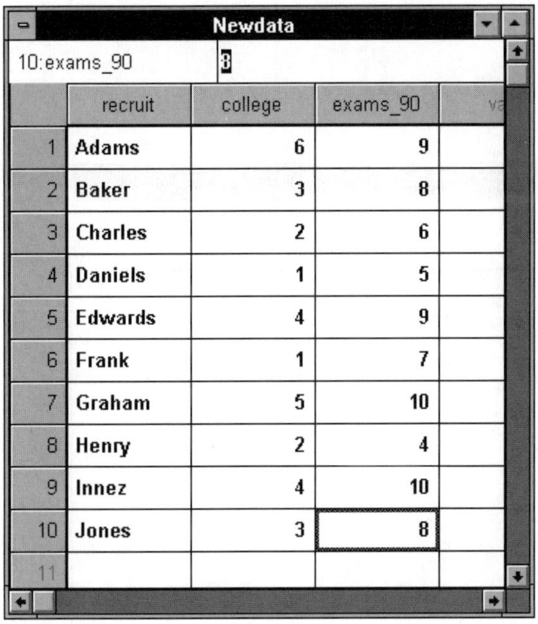

	recruit	college	exams_90
1	Adams	6	9
2	Baker	3	8
3	Charles	2	6
4	Daniels	1	5
5	Edwards	4	9
6	Frank	1	7
7	Graham	5	10
8	Henry	2	4
9	Innez	4	10
10	Jones	3	8
11			

Figure 8.6

To plot the information, use the Simple Scatterplot procedure from Exercise 7–1. Most of the time, the independent variable (the variable that is used to make predictions) is on the X axis and the dependent variable (the variable you are trying to predict) is on the Y axis. The X variable for this graph is `college`, the Y variable is number of examination scores greater than 90 (`exams_90`). Include `recruit` as a label variable so you can use the point identification feature (Figure 8.7).

Choose `OK` to draw the plot (Figure 8.8).

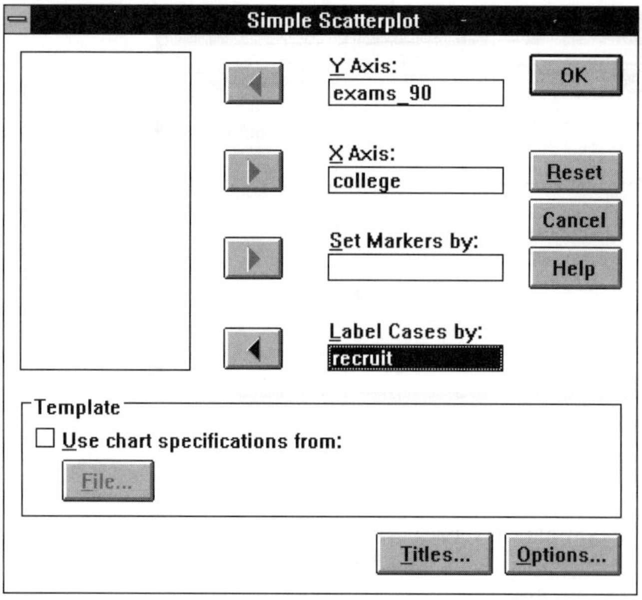

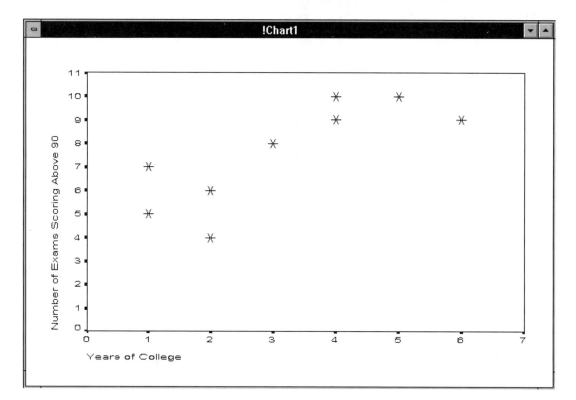

Figure 8.7

Figure 8.8

It looks as if there may be a relationship between years of college and ability to score greater than 90 on an examination. If there is no relationship, you see a cloud with points scattered everywhere on the graph. In this chart, however, it looks as if the points hover on a line that slopes gradually up toward the upper-right corner of the graph. Further supporting that conclusion, there are no points in the lower-right corner or in the upper-left corner. The chart suggests a positive correlation between years in college and exam-taking ability.

You can test the conclusion by using the correlations procedure, as you did for Exercise 7–3. For this exercise, put the two variables in the center of the dialog box and choose OK (Figure 8.9).

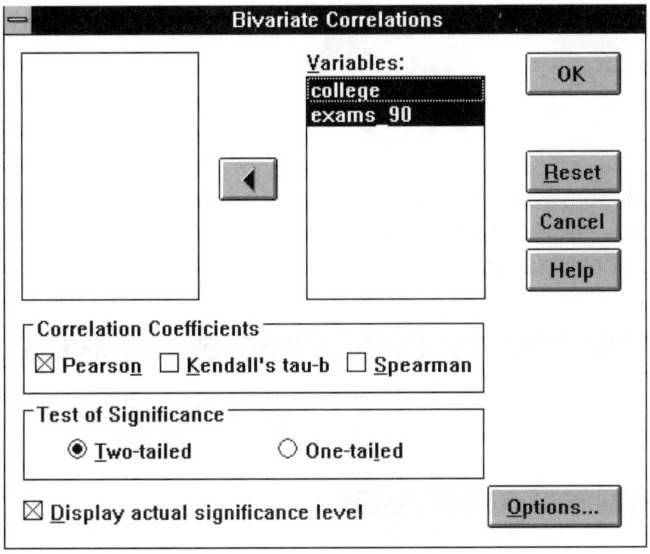

Figure 8.9

Leave the default or automatic settings in place. This means that you see the exact significance levels displayed (Figure 8.10).

```
            - -  Correlation Coefficients   - -

              COLLEGE      EXAMS_90

COLLEGE       1.0000         .7891
              (    10)     (    10)
              P= .         P= .007

EXAMS_90        .7891       1.0000
              (    10)     (    10)
              P= .007      P= .

(Coefficient / (Cases) / 2-tailed Significance)

" . " is printed if a coefficient cannot be computed
```

Figure 8.10

The correlation between `college` and `exam_90` is positive and has a value of .7891. This value is fairly close to 1, indicating a strong correlation. Moreover, the exact significance is .007. This value is much less than .05; it is unlikely this result occurred by chance. In fact, the result indicates that you see a correlation this high by chance in only seven samples out of 1,000.

Exercise Answer 8–2   Equation for a Straight Line

To calculate the slope and Y intercept using *SPSS for Windows*, you need to run the Regression procedure. First click on the Go to the Data Editor icon on the toolbar to bring the focus back to the data (Figure 8.11).

Figure 8.11

The data menus and toolbar are back in place. Go to the Statistics menu and choose `Regression`. You need to calculate the equation for a straight line, so choose `Linear` on the submenu (Figure 8.12).

SPSS for Windows Student Version
File Edit Data Transform **Statistics** Graphs Utilities Window Help

Summarize ▸	
Compare Means ▸	
ANOVA Models ▸	
Correlate ▸	
Regression	Linear...
Nonparametric Tests	Curve Estimation...
Time Series ▸	

Figure 8.12

Enter the data as you did in the scatterplot. The dependent variable is number of examinations on which the recruit scored greater than 90. The independent variable is number of years the recruit attended college. To find the regression constants, you can accept all the default settings for the dialog, so choose OK to see the results (Figure 8.13).

There is a great deal of information here. At the top of the listing, *SPSS* tells you exactly which analysis you requested (Figure 8.14).

You asked for a regression with EXAMS_90 as the dependent variable and COLLEGE as the independent variable.

After the title, the correlation statistics are presented (Figure 8.15). You could have run Regression to obtain the Pearson *r*. This is the multiple *r*, however. It gives the same value only if you restrict Regression to one dependent and one independent variable. You do not see the significance displayed. If you round the multiple *r* to four places, you see the same value you obtained for the Correlate procedure.

The next section of the output is the analysis of variance summary (Figure 8.16). You obtain the basic parts of the regression formula displayed as totals.

Finally, you receive the information needed to write the equation for the line. *SPSS* reminds you that you can use this information in an equation (Figure 8.17).

```
Listwise Deletion of Missing Data

Equation Number 1    Dependent Variable..    EXAMS_90    Number of Exams Scoring A

Block Number  1.  Method:  Enter       COLLEGE


Variable(s) Entered on Step Number
   1..    COLLEGE   Years of College


Multiple R              .78909
R Square                .62266
Adjusted R Square       .57549
Standard Error         1.34583

Analysis of Variance
                        DF       Sum of Squares       Mean Square
Regression               1            23.91004          23.91004
Residual                 8            14.48996           1.81124

F =      13.20089        Signif F =   .0067


------------------ Variables in the Equation ------------------

Variable             B          SE B         Beta         T    Sig T

COLLEGE          .979920      .269705      .789086      3.633   .0067
(Constant)      4.562249      .938170                   4.863   .0013


End Block Number    1   All requested variables entered.
```

Figure 8.13

```
Equation Number 1    Dependent Variable..    EXAMS_90    Number of Exams Scoring A

Block Number  1.  Method:  Enter       COLLEGE


Variable(s) Entered on Step Number
   1..    COLLEGE   Years of College
```

Figure 8.14

```
Multiple R              .78909
R Square                .62266
Adjusted R Square       .57549
Standard Error         1.34583
```

Figure 8.15

```
Analysis of Variance
                        DF       Sum of Squares       Mean Square
Regression               1            23.91004          23.91004
Residual                 8            14.48996           1.81124

F =      13.20089        Signif F =   .0067
```

Figure 8.16

```
----------------- Variables in the Equation -----------------

Variable              B          SE B        Beta        T   Sig T

COLLEGE          .979920      .269705      .789086     3.633   .0067
(Constant)      4.562249      .938170                  4.863   .0013
```

Figure 8.17

Each line gives information about the contribution of that element to the final equation. The slope for college is given in years as the B value and in standardized units (i.e., standard deviation units) as the Beta. The constant is the Y intercept.

The final regression formula is as follows:

$$exam\_90 = (0.98 * college) + 4.56$$

You can use this equation to predict the number of examinations on which a recruit scores more than 90.

If a new recruit had two years of college, on how many examinations can you predict that she would score more than 90?

You can answer the question as follows using the regression formula:

$$exam\_90 = (0.98 * college) + 4.56$$

$$exam\_90 = (0.98 * 2) + 4.56$$

$$exam\_90 = 1.96 + 4.56$$

$$exam\_90 = 6.52$$

If a new recruit had four years of college, on how many examinations do you expect him to score 90 or better? The answer is 8.48. Does your answer agree with this?

SPSS can draw the regression line on the scatterplot. Go to the Chart menu and choose Options, or double-click in any clear area inside the chart. The Scatterplot Options dialog box appears (Figure 8.18).

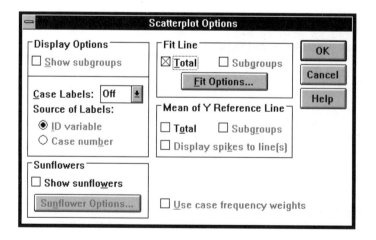

Figure 8.18

Check the Total box in the Fit Line section. Choose OK to view the new chart with a linear fit line (Figure 8.19).

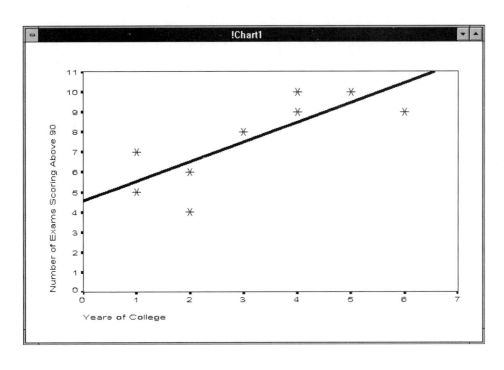

Figure 8.19

Check the values you calculated for two and four years of college. Do they match the points on the line? Look at where the linear regression line crosses the Y axis. Is this the same place the value of the constant indicates the line crosses?

Exercise Answer 8–4   Standard Error of Estimate

The standard error of the estimate's value is printed in the statistics section at the beginning of the Regression output (Figure 8.20).

```
Multiple R              .78909
R Square                .62266
Adjusted R Square       .57549
Standard Error         1.34583
```

Figure 8.20

The standard error of the estimate is the last line of this summary section. It is 1.35 for this equation.

Reference

Hare, R. D. 1993. *Without Conscience: The Disturbing World of Psychopaths Among Us.* New York: Pocket Books.

9. Multiple Regression

Understanding the Variation in Drug Case Sentencing

For the past ten years, drug cases have inundated criminal courts throughout the United States. To handle the influx of drug defendants, many criminal justice systems have instituted specialized drug courts that hear only drug cases. You are a graduating senior in criminology in a large midwestern city with aspirations for attending graduate school. Because you have been interested in the topic of drugs and crime, for the past few years you have worked as a volunteer in a court specializing in drug cases. You have made such an impression on the chief judge that he has offered you a full-time job when you graduate from college and are accepted into a graduate program. Before you can graduate, however, you must complete a senior project.

During your four years in the criminology program, many of your papers focused on the response of the criminal justice system to drug cases. You want to do your thesis on the same topic. Through your volunteer work, you have stayed abreast of the changes that the local courts have made to keep up with the tremendous volume of drug cases. Specialized night narcotics courts hear only drug cases. These courts were designed to relieve the burden that such cases impose on the day courts and to free the day courts to concentrate on more serious violent crimes. The founders of the night drug court believed that the judges and attorneys working there would develop great expertise in processing drug cases.

You have already observed several sessions of drug court and are beginning to understand its culture, operations, and dispositions. To study the sentencing patterns in the court, you are using a 15-point scale to rate the severity of the sentences that night court judges impose on defendants. The higher the rating, the more severe is the sentence. Most of the offenses heard in night drug court are felony class 4 drug possessions. You soon notice that defendants charged with this crime receive a variety of sentences.

In your view, the disparity in sentencing is an interesting phenomenon worthy of further investigation. At least it seems to be a viable topic for your senior project. You are particularly curious about the factors that influence sentencing decisions in these cases. It cannot be the seriousness of the crimes because seriousness is basically the same for all cases of felony class 4 drug possession. Therefore, the question you want to answer in your project is: What accounts for the disparity?

You have approached several night court judges and attorneys and have told them about your observations and interests. They seem excited about your research and pledge their cooperation and assistance. They explain that sentencing differences for the same offense are probably due to defendants' criminal records (i.e., number of prior convictions in their criminal histories) and employment records (i.e., the number of months they have been legally employed in the past year). That is, judges are more willing to give defendants a lighter sentence if they have shorter records and if they demonstrate the capability of maintaining gainful employment. These persons are considered better risks in the community, more amenable to change, and less worthy of punishment.

In a preliminary first step toward completion of your project, you randomly select five defendants sentenced during one week in night drug court. All of them were convicted of class 4 drug possessions. You rated the five cases on the severity of their sentences on a scale of 1 to 15, from least severe to most severe. In addition, you obtain permission to go through the case files to gather information about criminal record (i.e., number of prior convictions) and recent employment history (i.e., number of months employed in the last year). Having recently completed an elementary course in statistics, you understand the concepts of correlation and prediction. You conclude that differences in sentencing severity for drug possession cases is variance that needs to be explained. You remember how to work bivariate regression problems, but that technique is not appropriate for what you want to do because two variables are presumed to explain and predict sentencing severity. You realize that your data analysis requires a slightly more advanced form of analysis—multiple regression—for which you must refresh yourself.

Multiple Regression Analysis

In chapter 8, bivariate linear regression was introduced and used to make predictions about the behavior of probationers. In the example, probation officers scored offenders at intake on psychopathy and used a regression equation to predict rule breaking. Psychopathy and rule breaking had a significant positive relationship ($r = .66$). The higher the psychopathy score, the higher the predicted number of rule infractions and the more strenuous the level of supervision. Using the prediction scale made more operational sense than monitoring every probationer at the average supervision level, which would have been required had there been no data available on the factors predictive of probation performance. In fact, we improved prediction accuracy considerably over simply guessing that every probationer posed average probation risk.

Can we make even better predictions? Certainly there is room for improvement. More than half (55%) of the variance in rule breaking is not explained. There are probably other factors related to probation performance. If we identify these other factors, we can include them in the regression equation to make our predictions more accurate, that is, to explain even more of the variance in Y. In bivariate linear regression, there is room for only one predictor and one criterion variable. We want to include more predictors, which is the purpose of the technique in this chapter, which is called *multiple regression analysis*.

Identical to its counterpart in bivariate statistics (simple linear regression), multiple regression involves *predictor variables* that are used to forecast a *criterion variable*. It does not, however, restrict the number of predictor variables to one. It adds one or more predictor variables (X) to improve predictions. Multiple regression basically is an extension of bivariate linear regression. We add only one additional variable to the bivariate regression model to expand it into a multiple regression model. Including more than one predictor demands mathematical procedures that are beyond the scope of this book.

If you understand bivariate regression, then you have the basic knowledge required for understanding multiple regression. Multiple regression is particularly useful when the two independent variables are related to each other (i.e., *interrelated*), which occurs frequently in social science research.

Basics and Assumptions

As with bivariate regression, multiple regression requires the following basic assumptions. Assumption 1 is that X_1 (the first predictor variable) and X_2 (the second predictor variable) both are related to Y (the criterion variable). We are simply adding more information to improve our guesses about rule infractions. It is comparable to adding humidity to cloudiness to predict rain. We assume that this additional piece of data improves our forecasting ability or at least does not make it worse. For example, it might be the case that when we predict rain from cloudiness alone, we are correct 60% of the time but when we also use humidity, we are correct 75% of the time. In other words, we improve our ability to forecast by 15%. But this happens only if humidity is actually related to the likelihood of rain. If it is not, then we do not improve prediction accuracy, and adding humidity to the equation is not useful. Therefore, X_2 has to be related to Y and it must bear a linear relationship to Y (Assumption 2). In addition, X_1, X_2, and Y all must be measured on at least an interval scale (Assumption 3). More assumptions exist but are not discussed in this text because of their complexity.

In multiple regression analysis, weights are assigned to each of the predictors in an equation to derive a weighted linear combination of variables that minimizes error in prediction. Multiple regression applies the least-squares criterion or solution to obtain the values of the weights or regression coefficients that minimize, overall, the squared differences between the predicted and actual scores on the criterion. The basic formula for multiple regression is as follows:

$$\tilde{y} = b_1 x_1 + b_2 x_2 + a \qquad \text{Equation 9.1}$$

As in the bivariate regression formula, there are two constants, *a* and *b*. The *a* constant is the intercept, which is the predicted value for *y* when x_1 and x_2 equal zero. The slopes b_1 and b_2 are the weights attached to the variables in the linear combination that gives us predicted values for *y* on the basis of different scores or values on X_1 and X_2.

When several variables are included in a multiple regression model, we can use a variety of procedures for selecting the best predictors. For example, if we believe that twelve variables are potentially related to (i.e., are predictive of) a criterion variable, we can use a variety of techniques to select from that set only the predictor variables that are statistically related to the criterion. In this chapter, we discuss only situations that involve two predictors; therefore, sophisticated techniques are unnecessary.

Example of Multiple Regression

Research suggests that age is a prime predictor of criminal behavior. In the probation field, numerous studies have shown that age predicts arrests and other violations of probation conditions. Younger offenders are poorer risks during probation than are older offenders. Armed with this information, we can try to improve our prediction model by adding age to the equation along with psychopathy scores. Using the prediction scale, officers score offenders at intake on psychopathy and age. They then incorporate age and psychopathy into a prediction equation designed to take into account the influence of both variables. The regression equation consists of two predictor variables instead of just one, a situation that requires multiple regression instead of simple or bivariate regression. Adding another variable to the model only slightly changes the logic or strategy of the procedures.

Partial Correlation

When we add another variable to our bivariate prediction model to form a multiple regression equation, we will probably find that the new factor (X_2) is related to the first variable (X_1) in the regression equation. This is easy to understand because both X_1 and X_2 are related to Y so they are also usually related to each other. In fact, X_2 may explain some of the same variance in Y that X_1 explains. However, you do not want X_2 to explain too much of the same variance that X_1 explains; otherwise, you will be inserting an overlapping or redundant variable into your equation. You want to include a second variable that not only is related to Y but also explains variance in Y that is not explained by X_1. If X_2 explains the same variance that X_1 explains, then X_2 does not contribute to the predictive power of the equation. Simply put, X_2 adds more work (i.e., officers have to collect information on another variable) without a payoff (i.e., X_2 does not explain additional variance).

By adding another variable to the equation, we add two more correlations. With one predictor variable, we have only the correlation between X and Y. With two predictor variables, we have the correlation between X_1 and Y, X_2 and Y, and X_1 and X_2. Table 9.1 presents data on the age of each of the ten probationers introduced in chapter 8. It also shows the correlation between age (X_2) and rule infractions (Y), which as you can see, equals $-.930$, and is significant at the .05 level. Age is strongly related to rule violations but, unlike psychopathy, it is related in an inverse or negative direction. That is, as offenders age, they are less likely to break rules. Table 9.1 shows that age is related to psychopathy. Here, $r_{x_1x_2} = -.719$. As psychopathy increases, rule breaking increases; as age decreases, rule breaking increases; and as age decreases, psychopathy increases.

The fact that X_1 and X_2 are related to each other cannot be ignored in our multiple regression problem. Because they are related to each other, they explain some of the same variance in Y. To account for the overlap in the explanatory powers of X_1 and X_2, we have to calculate what is known as a *partial correlation*. A partial correlation is the correlation between a specific predictor and the criterion after the influence of other predictor variables have been removed (i.e., partialed out of both the specific predictor and the criterion). A partial correlation tells us the unique contribution that each predictor makes toward explaining the criterion.

Because we have two predictor variables, we can compute two partial correlations. The first is the partial correlation between rule violations (Y) and psychopathy (X_1), removing from both Y and X_1 any variance that is explained by age (X_2). Equation 9.2 shows how to compute $r_{yx_1 \cdot x_2}$ (the correlation between rule violations and psychopathy without the influence of age).

$$r_{yx_1 \cdot x_2} = \frac{r_{yx_1} - r_{yx_2} r_{x_1x_2}}{\sqrt{1 - r_{yx_2}^2} \sqrt{1 - r_{x_1x_2}^2}} \qquad \text{Equation 9.2}$$

Table 9.1 Descriptive Statistics and Intercorrelations for Rule Violations, Psychopathy Scores, and Age

Probationer	Psychopathy Score (X_1)	Age in Years (X_2)	No. of Rule Violations (Y)
1. Ellis	14	17	10
2. Reed	3	32	2
3. Moore	12	22	4
4. Samuel	2	19	8
5. Johnson	10	20	8
6. Bollini	4	34	3
7. Manfredi	1	35	0
8. White	6	25	5
9. Smith	11	18	9
10. Gilbert	5	26	4
Mean	6.800	24.800	5.300
S	4.590	6.779	3.302

Correlations

Psychopathy score (X_1)	1.000		
Age (X_2)	−.719	1.000	
Rule violations (Y)	.664	−.930	1.000

To find a partial r, we have to first determine the bivariate correlations between each of the pairs of variables. These are shown in Table 9.1. Thus,

$$r_{yx_1 \cdot x_2} = \frac{.664 - (-.930)(-.719)}{\sqrt{1 - (-.930)^2} \sqrt{1 - (-.719)^2}} = \frac{-0.005}{0.255} = -0.020$$

The second partial correlation is between rule violations (Y) and age (X_2), removing from both Y and X_2 any variance that is explained by psychopathy (X_1). The equation is as follows:

$$r_{yx_2 \cdot x_1} = \frac{r_{yx_2} - r_{yx_1} r_{x_1 x_2}}{\sqrt{1 - r_{yx_1}^2} \sqrt{1 - r_{x_1 x_2}^2}} \qquad \text{Equation 9.3}$$

Therefore, we have the following:

$$r_{yx_2 \cdot x_1} = \frac{-.930 - (.664)(-.719)}{\sqrt{1 - (-.664)^2} \sqrt{1 - (-.719)^2}} = \frac{-0.453}{0.520} = -0.871$$

The result of the first partial correlation is surprising. It tells us that the bivariate correlation between rule violations and psychopathy, which was .664, becomes trivial when we remove the influence of age. In other words, if we look within age categories (i.e., we control for age), the correlation between psychopathy and rule breaking is −.020, which is not significant. Specifically, young probationers with high psychopathy scores are no more likely to break rules than are young probationers with low psychopathy scores. The same applies within groups of older probationers. There, too, psychopathy score cannot be used to predict rule breaking when age is held constant.

The second partial correlation tells a different story. When we compute the partial correlation between rule violations and age while holding constant the effects of psychopathy scores, we find that the correlation between age and rule violations remains strong and significant ($-.871$), albeit slightly reduced. Therefore, holding constant psychopathy scores does not appreciably change the relationship between these two variables. Specifically, among probationers with high psychopathy scores, younger offenders are still significantly more likely to break rules compared to older offenders. Among probationers with low psychopathy scores, younger offenders are still more likely to break rules than are older offenders.

Exercise 9–1   Partial Correlations

Using the following data collected for the five defendants during the preliminary step of your project, calculate the partial correlations. What do the correlations indicate? Which is more important to predicting sentencing severity, prior convictions or months employed?

Defendant	No. of Prior Convictions (X_1)	No. of Months Employed (X_2)	Sentencing Severity (Y)
Allen	3	4	10
Balboa	1	10	8
Carson	2	6	6
Dent	6	3	13
Elton	4	9	9
Mean	3.20	6.40	9.20
S	1.92	3.05	2.59

Correlations

Prior convictions (X_1)	1.00		
Months employed (X_2)	$-.61$	1.00	
Sentence severity (Y)	.84	$-.58$	1.00

Finding Regression Constants

Because X_1 (psychopathy) and Y (rule breaking) are correlated, we can predict Y from X_1 (see chapter 8). The bivariate regression equation for these two variables is $\hat{y} = .478x_1 + 2.036$. We can insert a value for X_1 to find the predicted value of Y. We can do the same for the second independent variable X_2. We find that the prediction equation is $\hat{y} = -0.453x_2 + 16.537$.

The problem is combining information from X_1 and X_2 to make predictions about Y. In multiple regression, we have to find the influence of one variable while holding constant or partialing out the effects of the other. We did this when we found the partial correlations $r_{yx_1 \cdot x_2}$ and $r_{yx_2 \cdot x_1}$. Now the task is to find values for the regression constants b_1 and b_2 that hold constant the effects of one predictor variable on both the criterion variable and the other predictor variable. The regression constants b_1 and b_2 are called *partial regression slopes*.

The concept of partial regression slope is related to the concept of partial correlation. Let us revisit Equation 9.1, which is the basic multiple regression for two independent variables.

$$\tilde{y} = b_1x_1 + b_2x_2 + a \qquad \text{Equation 9.1}$$

The equation predicts Y (rule breaking) from both X_1 and X_2, which are the two independent variables, psychopathy scores and age, respectively. Attached to X_1 and X_2 are b_1 and b_2, which are the partial regression slopes for each of the variables. The term b_1 is the slope of the straight regression line that relates Y to X_1 when the other independent variable X_2 is controlled or held constant. It is the change in Y associated with a unit increase in X_1 while X_2 is controlled. To be particular about the notation we can write b_1 as $b_{yx_1 \cdot x_2}$, but this becomes burdensome, especially when there are more than two predictors in the equation. The coefficient b_2 is the slope of the straight regression line that relates Y to X_2 with X_1 controlled or held constant. It is the change in Y associated with a unit increase in X_2 while X_1 is controlled.

Equations 9.4, 9.5, and 9.6 show how to compute b_1, b_2, and a, respectively.

$$b_1 = \frac{s_y(r_{yx_1} - r_{yx_2}r_{x_1x_2})}{s_{x_1}(1 - r^2_{x_1x_2})} \qquad \text{Equation 9.4}$$

$$b_2 = \frac{s_y(r_{yx_2} - r_{yx_1}r_{x_1x_2})}{s_{x_2}(1 - r^2_{x_1x_2})} \qquad \text{Equation 9.5}$$

$$a = \bar{y} - b_1\bar{x}_1 - b_2\bar{x}_2 \qquad \text{Equation 9.6}$$

Using the means, standard deviations, and correlation coefficients from Table 9.1 we have the following:

$$b_1 = \frac{3.302(.664 - (-.930)(-.719))}{4.590(1 - (-.719)^2)} = \frac{-0.015}{2.217} = -0.007$$

$$b_2 = \frac{3.302\,(-.930 - (.664)(-.719))}{6.779(1 - (-.719)^2)} = \frac{-1.494}{3.275} = -0.456$$

and

$$a = 5.300 - (-0.007)(6.800) - (-0.456)(24.800) = 16.656$$

Thus the regression equation for predicting rule breaking from both psychopathy and age is

$$\tilde{y} = -0.007x_1 - 0.456x_2 + 16.656 \qquad \text{Equation 9.7}$$

Equation 9.7 shows that both partial regression slopes are negative, which reflects the negative partial correlations we found earlier. When we control for age, psychopathy scores explain a minuscule amount of rule breaking, which is why the partial regression slope is so close to zero. The real predictive power of this equation comes from age, after we control for psychopathy.

Exercise 9–2 Regression Constants

With the means, standard deviations, and correlation coefficients from Exercise 9.1, calculate the regression constants. What is the regression equation for predicting sentencing severity from number of prior convictions and number of months employed?

Making Predictions

To find a predicted value for Y, we perform the calculations in exactly the same way we did for bivariate regression. We simply insert values for X_1 and X_2 and solve the equation. For example, if $X_1 = 6$ and $X_2 = 19$, then $\bar{y} = -0.007(6) - 0.456$th $(19) + 16.656 = 7.950$. This means that we predict about eight rule violations for a probationer who is 19 years of age and who has a psychopathy score of 6.

Exercise 9–3   Making Predictions

While working with the preliminary data you decide to try to predict the sentence severity for five more defendants. Using the following data, and the regression equation from Exercise 9–2, predict the sentence severity for the five defendants.

Defendant	No. of Prior Convictions (X_1)	No. of Months Employed (X_2)
Jones	3	9
Dantzker	1	11
Sinacore	6	2
Seng	4	4
Lurigio	8	6

Multicollinearity

The correlation between X_1 and X_2, or the intercorrelations among independent variables in a multiple regression equation, is called *multicollinearity*. The greater the multicollinearity, the more difficult it is to arrive at a mathematical solution to a multiple regression problem. In fact, if X_1 and X_2 in the example were perfectly correlated (i.e., $r_{x_1 x_2} = 1.00$), we would not be able to achieve a multiple regression solution. Correlations of .80 or higher between predictors are usually considered high. In those situations, one of the two highly correlated variables is dropped from the equation, or the two variables are combined if possible. From a practical standpoint, low multicollinearity results in more efficient prediction because redundancy is eliminated. The best case occurs when each predictor variable is correlated with the criterion but not correlated with the other predictor variables. In the example, the high correlation between age and psychopathy results in attenuation of the correlation between psychopathy and rule breaking.

Multiple Correlation Coefficient

The relationship between the combination of predictors and the criterion is found by means of calculation of R, which is called the *multiple correlation coefficient*. R ranges from 0 to 1 and is, in essence, the bivariate correlation between the predicted scores and the actual scores on the criterion variable. When there are two predictors, R can be computed from Equation 9.8:

$$R = \sqrt{\frac{r_{yx_1}^2 + r_{yx_2}^2 - 2r_{yx_1}r_{yx_2}r_{x_1x_2}}{1 - r_{x_1x_2}^2}}$$

Equation 9.8

Using the bivariate correlation coefficients from Table 9.1, we see that

$$R = \sqrt{\frac{.664^2 + (-.930)^2 - 2(.664)(-.930)(-.719)}{1 - (-.719)^2}} = .930$$

which indicates that there is a very high correlation between rule violation and the optimal combination of psychopathy and age.

Exercise 9–4   Multiple Correlation Coefficient

What is the multiple correlation coefficient for the data from Exercise 9–1?

Prediction Accuracy
Multiple Coefficient of Determination

How much does the weighted linear combination of variables help with prediction of the criterion? To answer that question, we can compute an index of prediction accuracy called the *multiple coefficient of determination* (R^2). The multiple coefficient of determination is analogous to r^2. That is, R^2 is the proportion of variance in the criterion variable Y that is explained by Y's relationship to the combination of the predictor variables. Another way of putting it is that the coefficient of multiple determination indicates the proportion of variance in Y that is explained by the weighted linear combination of predictor variables X_1 and X_2. That is, it tells us how much of the difference in rule breaking among probationers is predictable from age and psychopathy as specified in the multiple regression equation. In the case of the example $R^2 = .930^2 = .865$, it means that psychopathy and age account for 86.5 percent of the variance in rule violation.

By subtracting R^2 from 1, we obtain the proportion of variance in Y that is not explained by the weighted linear combination of X_1 and X_2. Therefore, $1 - R^2 = 1 - .930^2 = .135$, which means that psychopathy and age do not account for 13.5% of the variance in rule violation.

Exercise 9–5   Multiple Coefficient of Determination

With respect to sentencing severity (as shown in Exercise 9–1), what is the multiple coefficient of determination? What does it explain about the variance with regard to prior convictions and months employed?

Standard Error of Estimate

Another method for calculating the accuracy of prediction is to find the *standard error of estimate* (SE_{est}). The standard error of estimate in multiple regression has the same meaning it does in bivariate regression. It is calculated with Equation 9.9,

$$SE_{est} = \sqrt{\frac{\Sigma(y - \tilde{y})^2}{N - k - 1}} \qquad \text{Equation 9.9}$$

where k is the number of predictor variables. Differences between actual or observed scores on a criterion are called *errors* or *residuals*. SE_{est} is the standard deviation of the distribution of error scores. It also can be defined as the average error in prediction. The smaller the standard error, the more accurate is the prediction.

Table 9.2   Terms for Computing the Standard Error of Estimate

Probationer	Psychopathy Score (X_1)	Age in Years (X_2)	No. of Rule Violations (Y)	(y)	($Y - y)^2$
1. Ellis	14	17	10	8.810	1.416
2. Reed	3	32	2	2.040	0.002
3. Moore	12	22	4	6.541	6.458
4. Samuel	2	19	8	7.982	0.000
5. Johnson	10	20	8	7.469	0.282
6. Bollini	4	34	3	1.120	3.536
7. Manfredi	1	35	0	0.684	0.468
8. White	6	25	5	5.214	0.046
9. Smith	11	18	9	8.375	0.391
10. Gilbert	5	26	4	4.765	0.585
Sum					13.184

Table 9.2 shows the squared residuals needed to compute SE_{est}. From this we have

$$SE_{est} = \sqrt{\frac{13.184}{10 - 2 - 1}} = 1.372$$

which indicates that the prediction of rule violations will be off, on average, ± 1.372 units. In the previous section, we predicted that a 19-year-old probationer with a psychopathy score of 6 would have 7.950 rule violations. The standard error of estimate tells us that the real number of rule violations will be somewhere between 7.950 ± 1.372, or 6.578 to 9.322. Rounding the estimate informs us that we should expect seven to nine rule violations. The standard error of estimate indicates that the predictions will not be too far off from real values.

Shrinkage

The multiple regression shown in Equation 9.1 is based on data gathered on the ten probationers in the study. We cannot use this equation to make predictions about another sample of probationers that differs in any way from the original sample and still expect to find the same degree of prediction accuracy. Prediction accuracy in multiple regression is expected to decrease, or shrink, when we transfer the equation for use with a different sample drawn from the same population (Cohen and Cohen 1983). Equation 9.10 shows how to compute shrinkage, which is denoted $\tilde{R}$.

$$\tilde{R}^2 = 1 - (1 - R^2)\frac{N - 1}{N - k - 1} \qquad \text{Equation 9.10}$$

Applying this equation to the example renders

$$\tilde{R}^2 = 1 - (1 - .930^2)\frac{10 - 1}{10 - 2 - 1} = .826$$

which tells us to expect in general that psychopathy and age explain 82.6% of the variance in rule violations rather than 86.5%, as previously calculated.

Summary

Bivariate linear regression analysis is used to make predictions about a *criterion variable* (Y) by using information on an *independent variable* (X) that is related to the criterion. *Multiple regression* extends linear regression with one independent variable to linear regression with two or more independent variables. The purpose of multiple regression is to include additional information (i.e., more independent variables) to make predictions more accurately (i.e., to explain more variance in Y).

Multiple regression involves a weighted linear combination of variables that minimizes error in prediction. When more than two independent variables are included, more sophisticated mathematical procedures are needed to solve multiple regression problems. With two independent variables, however, solutions are possible with simpler calculations.

Multiple regression uses two independent variables (X_1 and X_2). Three correlations must be considered: the correlation between X_1 and Y, between X_2 and Y, and between X_1 and X_2. Because X_1 and X_2 are related to each other and each is related to Y, special techniques have to be employed to identify the unique contributions that X_1 and X_2 make to explaining Y after one removes the influence of each variable on the other and on the criterion.

Partial correlations are measures of the relationship between each predictor variable and the criterion while one holds constant the effects of the other predictor variable. *Partial regression slopes* reflect the change in Y with a unit change in one of the predictor variables, after the influence of the other predictor variable is controlled.

The relationship between the set of predictors and the criterion is measured by means of *multiple correlation* (R). The square of the multiple correlation (R^2) is called the *multiple coefficient of determination*, which indicates the proportion of variance in Y that is explained by Y's relationship to the combination of predictor variables. Use of a multiple regression equation developed from one sample to make predictions on another may result in *shrinkage* of the size of R^2.

Answers to Exercises

Exercise 9–1 Partial Correlation
Prior convictions and sentencing severity with months employed controlled

$$r_{yx_1 \cdot x_2} = \frac{.84 - (-.58)(-.61)}{\sqrt{1 - (-.58)^2} \sqrt{1 - (-.61)^2}} = \frac{.84 - (.35)}{\sqrt{1 - .34} \sqrt{1 - .37}}$$

$$= \frac{.84 - .35}{\sqrt{.66} \sqrt{.63}} = \frac{.49}{(.81)(.79)} = \frac{.49}{.64} = .77$$

Months employed and sentencing severity with prior convictions controlled

$$r_{yx_2 \cdot x_1} = \frac{-.58 - (.84)(-.61)}{\sqrt{1 - (.84)^2} \sqrt{1 - (-.61)^2}} = \frac{-.58 - (-.51)}{\sqrt{1 - .71} \sqrt{1 - .37}}$$

$$= \frac{-.58 + .51}{\sqrt{.29} \sqrt{.63}} = \frac{-.07}{(.54)(.79)} = \frac{-.07}{.43} = -.16$$

When months employed is controlled, a strong positive correlation exists. This indicates that the more prior convictions, the higher is the sentence severity. When prior convictions is controlled, there is a weak negative correlation between sentence severity and months employed.

Exercise 9–2   Regression Constants and Equation

Prior convictions

$$b_1 = \frac{2.59[.84 - (-.58)(-.61)]}{1.92(1 - (.61)^2)} = \frac{2.59(.84 - .35)}{1.92(1 - .37)}$$

$$= \frac{2.59(.49)}{1.92(.63)} = \frac{1.27}{1.21} = 1.05$$

Months employed

$$b_2 = \frac{2.59[(-.58) - (.84)(-.61)]}{3.05(1 - (.61)^2)} = \frac{2.59(-.58) - (-.51)}{3.05(1 - .37)}$$

$$= \frac{2.59(-.07)}{3.05(.63)} = \frac{-0.18}{1.92} = -0.09$$

$$a = 9.20 - (1.05)(3.20) - (-.09)(6.40)$$

$$= 9.20 - (3.36) - (-.58) = 6.42$$

Regression equation

$$\tilde{y} = 1.05X_1 - 0.09X_2 + 6.42$$

Exercise 9–3   Making Predictions

The sentencing severity prediction for Jones is as follows:

$$\tilde{y} = 1.05(3) - 0.09(9) + 6.42 = 8.76$$

The sentencing severity prediction for Dantzker is as follows:

$$\tilde{y} = 1.05(1) - 0.09(11) + 6.42 = 6.48$$

The sentencing severity prediction for Sinacore is as follows:

$$\tilde{y} = 1.05(6) - 0.09(2) + 6.42 = 12.54$$

The sentencing severity prediction for Seng is as follows:

$$\tilde{y} = 1.05(4) - 0.09(4) + 6.42 = 10.26$$

The sentencing severity prediction for Lurigio is as follows:

$$\tilde{y} = 1.05(8) - 0.09(6) + 6.42 = 14.28$$

With the data provided, we predict that Sinacore and Lurigio receive the most severe sentences and Dantzker receives the least severe sentence.

Exercise 9–4   Multiple Correlation Coefficient

$$R = \sqrt{\frac{(.84)^2 + (-.58)^2 - 2(.84)(-.58)(-.61)}{1 - (-.61)^2}}$$

$$= \sqrt{\frac{.71 + (.34) - 2(.30)}{1 - .37}} = \sqrt{\frac{1.05 - .60}{.63}}$$

$$= \sqrt{\frac{.45}{.63}} = \sqrt{.71} = .85$$

The coefficient .85 indicates a high correlation between sentence severity and the optimal combination of prior convictions and months employed.

Exercise 9–5   Multiple Coefficient of Determination

$$R^2 = (.85)^2 = .72$$

This result indicates that prior convictions and months employed account for 72% of variance in sentence severity.

Computer Applications for Selected Exercises

Exercise Answer 9–1   Partial Correlations

The data are provided in raw form, so you need to set up a column for each variable. The first column (`defendnt`) is for labeling the rows, so you can set it up as a string column. The other columns are numeric (Figure 9.1).

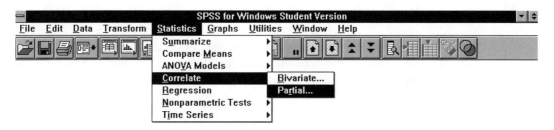

Newdata

5: severe   9

	defendnt	priors	months	severe	var
1	Allen	3	4	10	
2	Balboa	1	10	8	
3	Carson	2	6	6	
4	Dent	6	3	13	
5	Elton	4	9	9	

Figure 9.1

To calculate the partial correlations using *SPSS for Windows*, go to the Statistics menu and use `Correlate`. You used `Bivariate` in Exercise 7–3. Use `Partial` for this exercise (Figure 9.2).

SPSS for Windows Student Version

File   Edit   Data   Transform   Statistics   Graphs   Utilities   Window   Help

Summarize ▸
Compare Means ▸
ANOVA Models ▸
Correlate ▸   Bivariate...
Regression   Partial...
Nonparametric Tests ▸
Time Series ▸

Figure 9.2

You need to derive two partial correlations—one for each of the independent variables. The dependent variable stays the same for both calculations. First, find the partial correlation between months employed and severity of sentence, controlling for prior convictions (Figure 9.3).

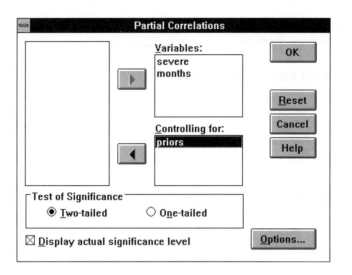

Figure 9.3

When the dialog box is set up, choose OK to run the analysis. The output shows the partial correlations for the pair you requested (Figure 9.4).

```
- - -   P A R T I A L     C O R R E L A T I O N     C O E F F I C I E N T S   - - -

Controlling for..      PRIORS

                SEVERE      MONTHS

SEVERE          1.0000        -.1534
                (    0)       (    2)
                P= .          P= .847

MONTHS           -.1534       1.0000
                (    2)       (    0)
                P= .847       P= .

(Coefficient / (D.F.) / 2-tailed Significance)

" . " is printed if a coefficient cannot be computed
```
Figure 9.4

Sentencing severity is negatively correlated with months employed, and the absolute value of the correlation is close to zero. It is negative because of the sign. This means that the two are inversely related. When one goes up, the other goes down. In other words, when time employed goes up, sentencing severity goes down.

Now determine the partial correlation between sentencing severity and prior convictions, controlling for months employed (Figure 9.5).

The output shows a stronger positive correlation between sentencing severity and number of prior convictions (Figure 9.6). That is, according to these data, you expect a more severe sentence for those who had more prior offenses when the number of months employed is held constant.

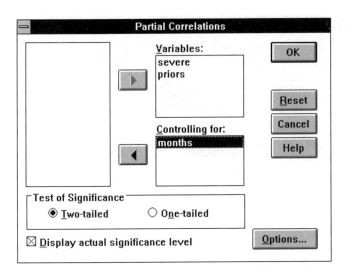

Figure 9.5

```
- - -  P A R T I A L   C O R R E L A T I O N   C O E F F I C I E N T S  - - -

Controlling for..    MONTHS

                SEVERE       PRIORS

SEVERE         1.0000         .7573
               (     0)      (     2)
               P= .          P= .243

PRIORS          .7573        1.0000
               (     2)      (     0)
               P= .243       P= .

(Coefficient / (D.F.) / 2-tailed Significance)

" . " is printed if a coefficient cannot be computed
```

Figure 9.6

Exercise Answer 9–2 Regression Constants

Use the data from Exercise 9–1 in the Regression procedure to have *SPSS* calculate the regression constants. Use the same dialog box that you used in Exercise 8–2. Sentencing severity is the dependent variable. The independent variables are priors and months. Put those into position and choose OK to run the analysis (Figure 9.7).

The full output from the procedure is shown in Figure 9.8. To construct the regression equation, you need only look at the last section, Variables in the Equation.

With the B values, you can define the regression equation, as you did in Exercise 8–2. The final regression equation is as follows:

Sentencing severity = (1.05 * number of prior convictions)

+ (−.09 * number of months employed) + 6.41

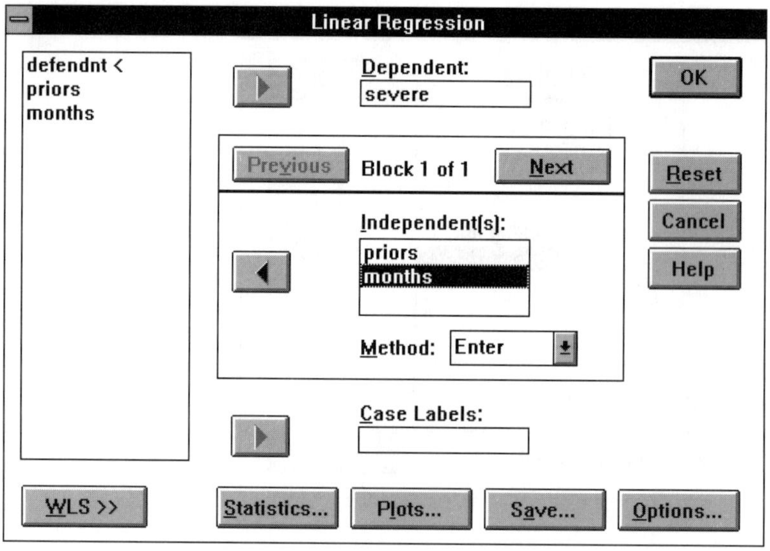

Figure 9.7

```
Equation Number 1    Dependent Variable..   SEVERE   Sentencing Severity

Block Number  1.  Method:  Enter      PRIORS   MONTHS


Variable(s) Entered on Step Number
   1..    MONTHS    Months Employed
   2..    PRIORS    Prior Convictions


Multiple R            .84756
R Square              .71837
Adjusted R Square     .43673
Standard Error       1.94265

Analysis of Variance
                  DF      Sum of Squares      Mean Square
Regression         2          19.25221          9.62611
Residual           2           7.54779          3.77389

F =        2.55071       Signif F =   .2816


----------------- Variables in the Equation -----------------

Variable           B           SE B         Beta          T    Sig T

PRIORS         1.048951      .639577      .779505      1.640   .2427
MONTHS         -.088578      .403415     -.104359      -.220   .8466
(Constant)     6.410256     4.253861                   1.507   .2708


End Block Number   1   All requested variables entered.
```

Figure 9.8

Exercise Answer 9–3 Making Predictions

Following the model in Exercise 8–2, you can write the equation, substitute in the values for priors and months, and then figure out the prediction for each new defendant. For situations in which you have only a few cases, it is often easy to do this with a calculator. When you want to predict more values, it is useful to enter the formula into the computer to find the predicted values.

Set up the raw data in the Data Editor following the format you used for Exercise 9–1 for the defendant, prior conviction, and months employed columns (Figure 9.9).

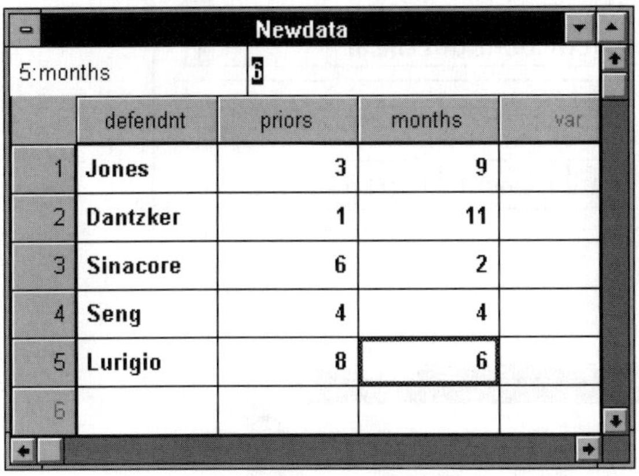

	defendnt	priors	months	var
1	Jones	3	9	
2	Dantzker	1	11	
3	Sinacore	6	2	
4	Seng	4	4	
5	Lurigio	8	6	
6				

Figure 9.9

You used a formula to calculate values in Exercise 5–2. Now use the Compute function found in the Transform menu (Figure 9.10).

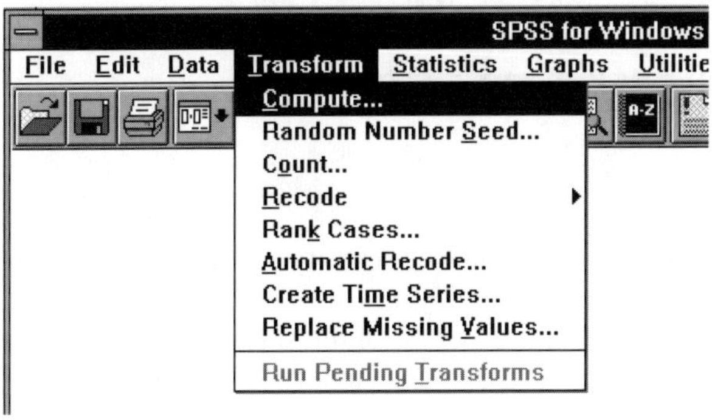

Figure 9.10

Set up the Target Variable: as severe. Enter the regression formula in the Numeric Expression: box (Figure 9.11). Use the variable names from your data set.

Choose OK to run the computation. The answer appears in the rightmost column in the Data Editor (Figure 9.12).

Even with six months of employment, Lurigio had the most severe sentence.

Return to Equation 1 (see Figure 9.8) to find the values for R, the multiple correlation coefficient, and R^2, the multiple coefficient of determination. $R = .85$.

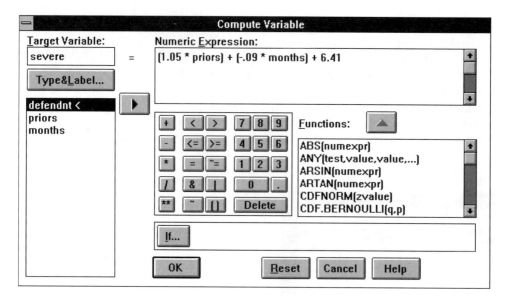

Figure 9.11

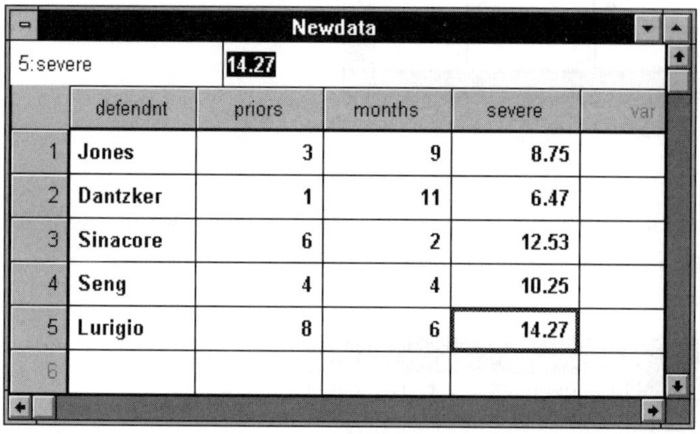

Figure 9.12

This indicates a high correlation between sentence severity and the optimal combination of prior convictions and months employed.

The value for R^2 is 0.72. This indicates that 72% of the variance in sentencing severity is explained by number of prior convictions and months employed.

Reference

Cohen, J., and Cohen, P. 1983. *Applied Multiple Regression/Correlation Analysis for the Behavioral Sciences*. Hillsdale, N.J.: Lawrence Erlbaum.

10. Student's *t* Test

Senior Project

It's senior year and to receive honors recognition in criminal justice at graduation, you must first complete a senior project. Because you want that distinction, you contact your advisor for assistance. The advisor tells you that you must write a brief proposal explaining your plan for the project. The proposal is evaluated by a department committee that decides whether to approve it. Once you have received approval from the committee, you may proceed with your project. The advisor also informs you that the deadline for proposals is in a few weeks. You realize that you had better get busy. You are not sure what to do, so you begin to talk with various graduate students and faculty members in an effort to get some ideas.

After a couple of days of discussions and topic searching you've narrowed your choices to two: (1) comparing knowledge of the criminal justice system between students who major in criminal justice and those who do not, and (2) whether students' perceptions about policing change after students complete their introductory police-related course. Both topics present interesting possibilities and allow you to put into practice what you learned in your research methods and statistics courses. In particular, you realize that Student's *t* test, which initially exasperated you, is probably the statistical technique you need to use. It's time to make a decision on your topic and start writing your proposal. You say to yourself, "I'd better review the Student *t* test."

Student's *t* Test for Independent and Related Samples

In analyzing criminal justice data, people often find themselves making comparisons in terms of averages. For example, the faculty at a police academy might be interested in seeing whether the graduating class of 1994 performed better or worse than the graduating class of 1993 on a standardized examination. To do this, the faculty can compute the mean of the examination scores for each of the two classes and see which one is higher.

Although a simple comparison of means is easy, one is faced with an important question because the means rarely are equal. A discrepancy of some degree typically exists. Does the discrepancy in the means reflect a fundamental distinction in the groups from which the means were computed, or can the difference be explained in terms of chance? To gain an appreciation of this issue, assume that the academy faculty finds that the mean examination scores are 105.7 for the class of 1993 and 110.3 for the class of 1994. The means are numerically different. However, the difference indicates one of two possibilities. The higher mean may indicate that the 1994 cadets were better prepared than those in the 1993 class. If this is the case, the discrepancy in the means reflects a real difference in knowledge. On the other hand, the higher mean may simply be a chance happening, which occurs if the cadets in the two classes really perform at the same level. In that case, the difference in the means is considered unimportant or trivial.[1]

To help decide whether there is a real or statistically meaningful difference between two groups, we can turn to the statistical tools of *hypothesis testing*. In hypothesis testing, the null hypothesis (H_0) is that an observed difference between two means is trivial. The rival hypothesis (H_1) is that the observed difference is real. We need to determine the probability that H_0 is true. If the probability is small, say 5 percent or less, we can reject H_0 in favor of H_1. This is accomplished with *Student's t test*.

Conceptual groundwork needs to be laid before we discuss the application of the *t* test to the difference between two groups. We reconsider the *z* distribution (the standard normal curve) to see how it is useful for determining the probability that a difference exists between an individual and a population. Next we discuss the *z* distribution as a sampling distribution and learn how this distribution is useful for comparing a sample with a population. We then see how the *t* distribution is a special type of sampling distribution. It is similar to *z* but is used when sample sizes are small. It is the *t* distribution on which we rely for analysis of the difference between two samples.

Standard Normal Curve Revisited

In chapters 2 and 4, we presented the standard normal curve, or *z* distribution, as a special type of frequency distribution that helps to determine the percentage of scores. The curve is used to determine the percentage of scores that lie between two score values in a population of a normally distributed variable.[2] For example, the *z* distribution in the Appendix (Table A) shows that about 34 percent of the scores in a population are between the mean and a score that is 1 standard deviation above the mean, that is, a *z* score of $+1.00$. Because of the symmetry of the normal distribution, we know that an additional 34 percent of the scores are between the mean and a score that is one standard deviation below the mean, a *z* score of -1.00. About 68 percent of the scores in the population are between *z* scores of $+1.00$ and -1.00.

The relationship of score value ranges and the percentage of scores in the population can be viewed from a different perspective. For example, one can ask, "If I randomly sample one raw score from a population, what is the chance that it has a value between one standard deviation above and one standard deviation below the mean?" One also can ask, "What is the chance that the *z* score that corresponds to the raw score is between $+1.00$ and -1.00?" The answer to both questions is 68 percent.

Our knowledge of the standard normal curve indicates that the farther is a score from its mean, the lower is its probability of occurring. Because a randomly drawn score from a population has a 68 percent likelihood of having a value between one standard deviation above and one standard deviation below the mean, it makes sense that a score has a 32 percent likelihood of being beyond those limits. This is shown in Table A in the Appendix. For a *z* score of 1.00, the third column shows that 15.87 percent of the scores are beyond that point. Multiplying 15.87 percent by 2 (to account for both sides of the distribution) gives 31.74 percent, which can be rounded to 32 percent. One also can see that *z* scores at or beyond the value of ± 1.5 have a 13 percent chance of being picked at random. Scores of z at or beyond the value of ± 1.96 have only a 5 percent chance of being picked at random.

Using the Standard Normal Curve in Hypothesis Testing

The standard normal curve can be used to test the null hypothesis that a person who is measured on some characteristic is not different from a population of persons measured on that same characteristic. For example, assume that all police academies in the United States pooled test scores of graduating cadets on the standardized examination mentioned earlier. Also assume that the mean test score is 107.4 and the standard deviation is 10.6. Remember that the mean is denoted μ (lower case Greek mu) and the standard deviation is denoted σ (lower case Greek sigma) because these figures refer to a population.

Police cadet Gerald Anderson graduates in a later year and achieves a score of 116 on the standardized examination. Is Gerald's performance similar to that of the cadets whose population mean is 107.4, or does his score indicate that he has performed better than the members of that population? To answer this question, we need to develop an analytic strategy.

If the population distribution of test scores is normal, we know that the highest frequency of scores is at the mean and that the frequency decreases away from the mean in either direction. If the normal distribution of scores accounts for all cadets in the population, there is a cutoff score that is equally distant above and below the mean that accounts for scores of most individuals, say 95 percent. We are interested in this score because it is difficult to find a score that includes 100 percent of the population.[3] If cadet Anderson's examination score falls within the 95 percent cutoff scores, there is no reason to believe that his performance is different from that of the population. If, however, his score goes beyond the upper cutoff or below the lower cutoff, there is reason to believe that his performance is better or worse than that of the individuals in the population. After all, the probability that one will achieve a score beyond the 95 percent cutoff is 5 percent. This probability is too small to suggest the likelihood of the truth of H_0.

We can generalize this logic with z scores. Table A in the appendix shows that a z score of ± 1.96 is the 95 percent cutoff for the standard normal curve. Thus if an individual's score is similar to the scores of a population, there is a 95 percent likelihood that his or her corresponding z score falls within ± 1.96. There is only a 5 percent likelihood that the score equals or exceeds those limits. This means that if Gerald Anderson's test performance is similar to the population of graduate cadets, there is a 95 percent likelihood that the z score for his performance falls between ± 1.96. If Gerald's score is fundamentally different from that of the population (either better or worse), his z score probably equals or exceeds ± 1.96.

Table 10.1 displays this logic in five steps of a hypothesis testing process. First, the null and rival hypotheses are specified. The null hypothesis is a statement that asserts no systematic process or effect has occurred (see chapter 6). In this case, H_0 is that the performance of the cadet in question is not different from that of the population to which he is being compared. The logical alternative is expressed in H_1, which is that the cadet's performance is different. The hypotheses are written in terms of μ. Either the cadet's performance is not different from that of the population whose $\mu = 107.4$, or his performance is different from that of the population.[4] Logic dictates no other alternatives.

Next we specify *level of significance*. H_0 is tested in the hypothesis testing process (see chapter 6). As such, we are inclined to reject H_0 if the probability of

Table 10.1   Steps in Testing a Hypothesis

An individual's performance on a standardized examination is not different from that of a population of graduating cadets.

---

1. H_0: An individual whose examination score is 116 is not different from the population where $\mu = 107.4$.

   H_1: An individual whose examination score is 116 is different from the population where $\mu \neq 107.4$.

2. Level of significance, $\alpha = .05$
3. Decision rule: If z falls within ± 1.96, do not reject H_0.
                    If z equals or exceeds ± 1.96, reject H_0 in favor of H_1.

4. $z = \dfrac{116 - 107.4}{10.6} = 0.81$

5. Conclusion: Do not reject H_0.

---

its likelihood is small, say 5 percent. The level of significance is often abbreviated α (lower case Greek alpha).

Because we are using the standard normal curve, the level of significance (also called alpha level) refers to the cutoff scores discussed earlier. Therefore, if H_0 is true, there is a 95 percent likelihood that the computed z score falls within ± 1.96. There is only a 5 percent likelihood that it equals or exceeds these limits. Table 10.1 shows the decision rule that states we cannot reject H_0 if the z score falls within ± 1.96 and that we can reject H_0 in favor of H_1 if the z score equals or exceeds ± 1.96.

We compute the z score for cadet Anderson's raw test score of 116 by using the equation presented in chapter 4 (see Equation 10.1). This gives a z score of 0.81 and leads us to not reject H_0 (see Table 10.1). From the available information, there is no reason to believe that Gerald Anderson's performance on the standardized examination is different from the known population of cadets.

$$z = \frac{X - \mu}{\sigma}$$

Equation 10.1

Sampling Distributions

The hypothesis testing steps displayed in Table 10.1 provide a method to compare an individual's performance with that of a known population. Although this is useful, it does not readily help in the comparison of the two samples, which is our interest. We need to build on the hypothesis testing process with statistical tools that help us work with samples. The first step in this direction is to understand sampling distributions.

Up to this point, the frequency distributions in this book have comprised individual scores. It is important to know, however, that distributions can be constructed of summary statistics such as mean, median, and standard deviation. Frequency distributions of summary statistics are called *sampling distributions*.

Figure 10.1 shows how a sampling distribution of the mean is constructed. The figure shows that a sampling distribution originates from a population.

Given any population with a mean of μ and a standard deviation of σ, a very large number of equally sized random samples can be drawn, and the mean

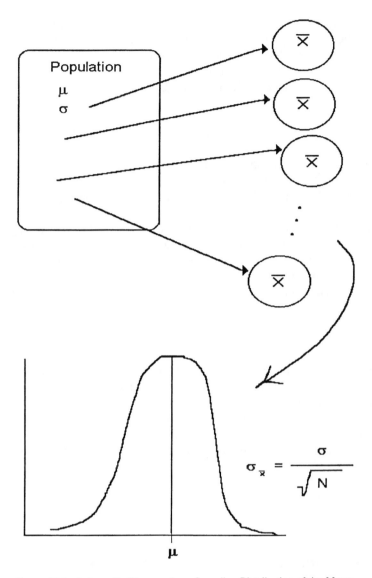

Figure 10.1   Schematic Diagram for a Sampling Distribution of the Mean

($\overline{X}$) computed on each. This is done with a procedure known as *sampling with replacement*. In this procedure, the first sample of size *N* is randomly drawn. The mean is computed ($\overline{X}$), and the scores are returned to the population. The second sample of size *N* is randomly drawn, the mean is computed ($\overline{X}$), and the scores are again returned to the population. If this procedure is performed a very large number of times, one has an array of sample means that can be made into a frequency distribution like raw scores. The resulting frequency distribution composed of sample means is called a *sampling distribution of the mean*.[5]

Like all other frequency distributions, a sampling distribution of the mean has central tendency and variability. Statisticians have found that the arithmetic average of a sampling distribution of the mean is μ, the mean of the population. This finding is quite intuitive because one might naturally assume that the average of random samples taken from a population equals μ.

Although the arithmetic average of a sampling distribution of the mean is μ, the standard deviation is not σ. The standard deviation is related to σ and to N, the size of the samples drawn from the population. The standard deviation of a sampling distribution of the mean is called the *standard error of the mean*, abbreviated as $\sigma_{\bar{x}}$. This is presented in Equation 10.2.

$$\sigma_{\bar{x}} = \frac{\sigma}{\sqrt{N}}$$

Equation 10.2

If the size of N is large enough, about 30 or more, and the variable in the population is normal, the sampling distribution of the mean also is normal. This indicates that we can apply the logic of Table 10.1 to the comparison of a sample with a population.

If the sampling distribution of the mean is normal, we can identify two sample mean values that are equally distant above and below μ that account for 95 percent of the sample means drawn from the population. We do not know those mean values, but their corresponding z score values are going to be ± 1.96. The z score for a sample mean is given in Equation 10.3.

$$z = \frac{\bar{x} - \mu}{\sigma_{\bar{x}}}$$

Equation 10.3

The structure of the equation is identical to that of the original z score formula, only the terms are different. Equation 10.3 is used to compute the difference between a sample mean and μ and then divides by the standard deviation of the sampling distribution (i.e., the standard error of the mean). When the formula for the standard error of the mean is incorporated into Equation 10.3, we have an equation that can easily be used for hypothesis testing. This equation is as follows:

$$z = \frac{\bar{x} - \mu}{\dfrac{\sigma}{\sqrt{N}}}$$

Equation 10.4

Using the Sampling Distribution of the Mean in Hypothesis Testing

The sampling distribution of the mean can be used to test the null hypothesis that a sample of individuals measured on a characteristic is not different from a particular population. For example, let's assume that 37 graduating cadets from the Larson County Police Academy have taken the standardized examination mentioned earlier. Remember that there is a known population of cadets who took this examination whose $\mu = 107.4$ and $\sigma = 10.6$. Assume further that the mean test score for the Larson County cadets is $\overline{X} = 111.7$. Is this sample of cadets similar to the population whose $\mu = 107.4$, or does the mean score indicate that the individuals in the sample have performed better than the cadets in the population?

Table 10.2 displays the five steps of the hypothesis testing process that relate to this question. The z score for the sample mean of 111.7 is 2.47. Because the z score exceeds 1.96, there is less than a 5 percent probability of obtaining a score of this size (or higher) by chance if H_0 is true. Thus we are led to reject H_0 in favor of H_1. Because the sample mean is greater than the population mean, one can infer that the group of cadets at Larson County Police Academy probably performed better than the cadets in the population.

Table 10.2 Steps in Testing a Hypothesis

The hypothesis is that the performance of a sample of cadets on a standardized examination is not different from that of a population of graduating cadets.

1. H_0: The sample of cadets whose mean is 111.7 is not different from the population where $\mu = 107.4$.

   H_1: The sample of cadets whose mean is 111.7 is different from the population where $\mu \neq 107.4$.

2. Level of significance, $\alpha = .05$
3. Decision rule:

   If z falls within ± 1.96, do not reject H_0.
   If z equals or exceeds ± 1.96, reject H_0 in favor of H_1.

4. $z = \dfrac{111.7 - 107.4}{\dfrac{10.6}{\sqrt{37}}} = \dfrac{4.30}{\dfrac{10.6}{6.08}} = \dfrac{4.30}{1.74} = 2.47$

5. Conclusion: Reject H_0 in favor of H_1.

Exercise 10–1 Sampling Distribution of the Mean—Hypothesis Testing

Using the steps in Table 10.2, determine whether the mean scores on the academy examination of the following cadet classes are or are not different from the population, $\mu = 107.4$ and $\sigma = 10.6$.

Cadet Class 1, $N = 57$; $\overline{X} = 113.3$
Cadet Class 2, $N = 41$; $\overline{X} = 106.5$
Cadet Class 3, $N = 33$; $\overline{X} = 110.2$

Central Limit Theorem

A sampling distribution of the mean is normal if the population variable is normal and if the size of the samples is large enough, about 30 or more. This seems quite intuitive. What is more important to realize, however, is that a sampling distribution of the mean is approximately normal even if the population distribution departs considerably from normality (provided the sample size is large enough). The statistical principle that supports this is called the *central limit theorem*. The mathematical foundation of the central limit theorem is beyond the scope of this text. However, the theorem can be demonstrated quite easily (Figure 10.2).

The left hand side of Figure 10.2 presents frequency histograms of scores in three populations that we designed.[6] Each comprises 500 scores. The top graph shows a population for which the scores are normally distributed. The middle graph shows a population for which the scores are nearly equal in frequency of occurrence, thus the rectangular shape of the distribution. Graphs with this shape are often referred to as being *square*. The bottom graph shows a population from which the scores are highly skewed. In this population, low scores are numerous and the frequency of higher scores decreases rapidly.

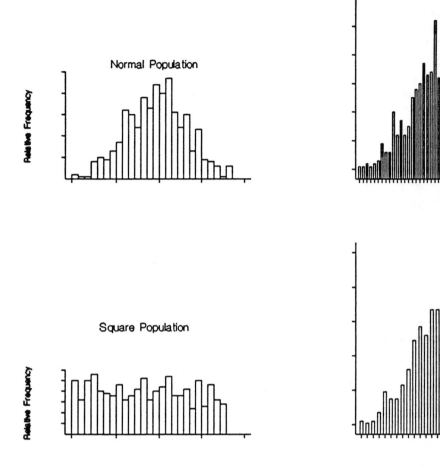

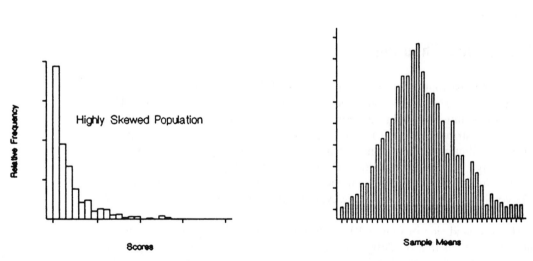

Figure 10.2   Distribution of Scores for Three Populations and for the Sampling Distributions Created from Those Populations

Table 10.3   Central Tendency and Variability for Three Populations and for Sampling Distributions Created from Those Populations

Type	Population μ	Population σ	Sampling Distribution (1000 samples, N = 30) Mean	Sampling Distribution (1000 samples, N = 30) SD	Standard Error of the Mean $\left(\dfrac{\sigma}{\sqrt{30}}\right)$
Normal	49.609	4.853	49.646	0.890	0.886
Square	52.391	1.430	52.386	0.292	0.261
Skewed	51.336	1.621	51.328	0.311	0.296

SD, standard deviation.

Using a special computer program, we constructed a sampling distribution of the mean from each of the three populations. In each case, 1,000 random samples of 30 scores were drawn (with replacement) from the population. The mean of each sample was recorded and a frequency distribution of the sample means was made. The sampling distributions of the mean are displayed on the right hand side of Figure 10.2. The sampling distributions are normal, despite the shape of the distributions from which the samples were drawn.[7]

Table 10.3 presents the numerical information for the graphs in Figure 10.2. The table shows the means and standard deviations for the scores in the population and the means and standard deviations of the 1,000 sample means drawn to create the sampling distributions. For example, the table shows that the mean and standard deviation of the scores in the normal population are 49.609 and 4.853, respectively. The average of the 1,000 sample means drawn from the normal population is 49.646, which (as expected) is very close to μ. The standard deviation of the 1,000 sample means from the normal population is 0.890, which (as expected) is very close to the computation of $\sigma/\sqrt{30}$ (the standard error of the mean).

As one might expect, complex mathematical principles account for what is displayed in Figure 10.2. However, we do not need to understand those principles to see why the theorem works.

If sampling from the population is conducted in a random manner with a large enough sample, one tends to capture a full range of score values: high, medium, and low. The average of such a range neutralizes the effect of high and low scores, and the sample mean takes on an intermediate value. As sampling continues, however, there are instances in which the full spectrum of scores is not acquired. In these instances, high values or low values occur in unusually large numbers, and the sample mean takes on a nonintermediate value. In the long run, more samples have a mean with an intermediate value, and fewer samples have a mean with a high or low value. A frequency histogram of the means reveals the bell-shaped curve that is characteristic of a normal distribution.

Student's *t* Distribution

The central limit theorem dictates how a sampling distribution of the mean has a normal shape as long as the sample size is large enough. This is true even if the population from which the samples are drawn deviates markedly from normality. What happens if sample sizes are small? After all, criminal justice practitioners do not always have data that come from samples that comprise 30 or more individuals.

The construction of sampling distributions with small samples was studied by a statistician named William Sealy Gossett, who was a long-standing employee of the Guinness Beer Company.[8] Because of his concern for anonymity, Gossett wrote under the pseudonym *Student*. As a result of his work, Student discovered that small-sample sampling distributions from normal populations are bell shaped in nature but the overall shape is related to sample size. Statisticians refer to sample size as degrees of freedom (*df*) (see chapter 6). These sampling distributions are labeled with the letter *t* to differentiate them from the normal distribution (*z*).

Figure 10.3 shows the shape of a *t* distribution for different degrees of freedom. Each distribution is bell shaped, but the shape becomes more stable as the degrees of freedom increase. The figure shows that when the degrees of freedom are infinitely large (*df* = ∞), the *t* distribution becomes normal.

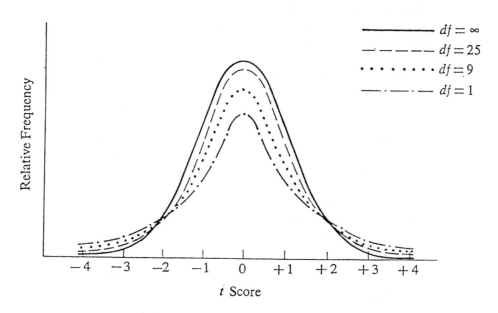

Figure 10.3   Shape of Student's _t_ Distribution for Different Degrees of Freedom

_t_ Distribution in Hypothesis Testing

When conducting an analysis with small samples, one needs to refer to Student's *t* distribution for hypothesis testing. Equation 10.5 shows the *t* equation for which $df = N - 1$.

$$t = \frac{\bar{x} - \mu}{\frac{\sigma}{\sqrt{N}}}$$

                                                                 Equation 10.5

The equation is the same as that for computing *z*. What is different is that we must refer to a table of *t* to find the cutoff scores necessary for the decision rule part of the hypothesis testing process.

In addition to analyses with small samples, Student's *t* distribution is used when the population standard deviation, σ, is unknown and must be estimated from a sample, regardless of sample size. Equation 10.6 shows the *t* formula, which contains *s*, the sample standard deviation, in place of σ.

$$t = \frac{\bar{x} - \mu}{\frac{s}{\sqrt{N}}}$$ Equation 10.6

At this point, let us consider an example. Assume that a suburban police chief has learned about a general job satisfaction survey that recently has been administered to state police officers as part of the governor's new quality of work life program. The chief is concerned about job satisfaction in his own department and therefore decides to ask a small group of his police officers to complete the survey. Twelve individuals are randomly chosen from the total group of suburban police officers and are given the opportunity to answer the survey. When completed, the surveys are scored, and the following satisfaction scores are obtained: 37, 28, 22, 41, 33, 22, 39, 29, 26, 28, 24, and 30. The mean and standard deviation of these scores are 29.92 and 6.39, respectively. If the mean satisfaction score of the state police officers is 31.5, does the chief have reason to believe that his sample of 12 suburban officers is less satisfied than officers who work for the state?

Before answering this question, we need to evaluate the details of our statistical problem so that the correct equation is chosen. First, we can see that a sample is being compared with a population. The sample comprises 12 suburban police officers. The population is all police officers who work for the state. The only information we have about the population is that the mean satisfaction score is 31.5. Sigma is not known and we have to estimate it with the standard deviation of the sample. Given these details, Equation 10.6 is the best one to use.

Table 10.4 presents the steps in testing the hypothesis that the sample of suburban officers is not different from the population of state police in terms of job satisfaction. It is similar to Table 10.2, except that we now have to rely on t distribution to provide the cutoff scores needed to reject or not reject H_0.

Critical t values are presented in Table D of the Appendix. To find the critical t for the test in Table 10.4 we need the level of significance (i.e., the α level) and degrees of freedom. For Equation 10.6, the degrees of freedom are $N - 1$. Thus for this example, $df = 12 - 1 = 11$. If we set α at the usual level, we need to find the critical t for $\alpha = .05$ and 11 degrees of freedom.

Table 10.4   Steps in Testing a Hypothesis
The hypothesis is that the job satisfaction of a sample of local police is not different from that of the population of state police.

1. H_0: The sample of officers whose mean is 29.92 is not different from the population where $\mu = 31.5$.

   H_1: The sample of officers whose mean is 29.92 is different from the population where $\mu \neq 31.5$.

2. Level of significance, $\alpha = .05$; $df = 12 - 1 = 11$
3. Decision rule:

   If t falls within ± 2.201, do not reject H_0.
   If t equals or exceeds ± 2.201, reject H_0 in favor of H_1.

4. $t = \dfrac{29.92 - 31.5}{\frac{6.39}{\sqrt{12}}} = \dfrac{-1.58}{\frac{6.39}{3.46}} = \dfrac{-1.58}{1.85} = -0.86$

5. Conclusion: Do not reject H_0.

The top of Table D has two headings—one that shows the level of significance for a one-tailed (directional) test, and one that shows the same for a two-tailed (nondirectional) test. For now, we use the latter. An explanation is given in the next section.

To find critical t, we identify the column labeled with the α level and then search the left side of the table for the row that corresponds to the *df*. The critical t is at the intersection of that row and column. When $\alpha = .05$ and $df = 11$, the critical t is 2.201.

The computations in Table 10.4 indicate that $t = -0.86$, which is within the range of ± 2.201; we are unable to reject H_0. Given the available data, the police chief has no reason to believe that the sample of 12 suburban officers is any more or less satisfied on the job than the population of state police officers.

Exercise 10–2   Student's *t* and Hypothesis Testing

Using the steps and data for the state police in Table 10.4, determine whether the job satisfaction scores from samples of three other city police agencies are not different from that of the state police population.

City A, $\overline{X} = 36.23$; $N = 25$; $s = 7.67$

City B, $\overline{X} = 28.71$; $N = 19$; $s = 5.22$

City C, $\overline{X} = 33.44$; $N = 31$; $s = 6.08$

Directional and Nondirectional Tests

Up to this point, we have been stating research hypotheses in a nondirectional way. For example, H_1 for the test in Table 10.4 was stated as "The sample of officers whose mean is 29.92 is different from the population whose $\mu = 31.5$." Stating the research hypothesis this way implies that one is interested in the results of the analysis no matter how the sample is different from the population. The chief probably is interested in knowing if his sample of police officers is more satisfied or less satisfied than the population to which it is being compared. This type of situation requires a *nondirectional* or *two-tailed test*. The test is said to be two-tailed because the cutoff scores are equally spaced above and below the mean in both ends of the z or t distribution.

There are times, however, when statistical results are expected in a particular direction and one has no scientific or practical interest in an outcome that is to the contrary. For example, consider a university criminal justice department that has redesigned a course entitled *Law and Society*. The faculty believes that students learn more in the course taught with the new design than with the old one. During a trial semester, the newly designed course is offered to criminal justice students. To examine the effect of the new design, scores on a standardized final examination are compared with those of all students who have taken the course with the old design in previous semesters.

Given that the new course design is believed to enhance learning, the faculty expects that students in the new course not only perform differently from the population of previous students but also perform better. If, in fact, the students do perform better, the faculty can continue with the new course design and perhaps write an article for a teaching journal to promote the design for use at other colleges and universities. If it turns out that the new course design is not effective, the faculty can simply revert to the old design. This type of situation can be analyzed with a *directional* or *one-tailed* test. The test is said to be one-tailed because a cutoff score from only one tail of the z or t distribution is needed for hypothesis testing.

The choice between performing a one-tailed test and conducting a two-tailed test is made by the person conducting the study. There are, however, a number of technical and philosophical factors to consider (Fleiss 1981; Goldfried 1959; Kimmel 1957). Investigators can use this distinction to act unethically in the statistical analysis of their data. For example, the critical *t* value for the analysis in Table 10.4 is 2.201. This is for a two-tailed, or nondirectional, test. Table D in the Appendix, however, shows that the critical *t* value for a one-tailed test with $\alpha = .05$ and 11 degrees of freedom is 1.796. An unscrupulous person might be inclined to conduct a one-tailed test, simply because he or she wants to make it easier to reject the null hypothesis.[9]

The various aspects of one-tailed and two-tailed tests are beyond the scope of this text. However, you should routinely conduct a two-tailed test, even though you have an expectation about the outcome of your results. If you conduct a two-tailed test, you must interpret and report your results, even if the outcome is contrary to your prediction.[10] Consider conducting a one-tailed test only in the rare situations in which you expect the outcome to be in one direction and you do not want to or are not ethically bound to report your work if results are opposite that expectation.

Student's *t* Test Applied to Independent and Related Samples

This chapter begins with a discussion of the comparison of two samples. So far, we have not developed a statistical method for dealing with this situation, but we do so in this section.

The logic for comparing two samples is similar to that discussed in the previous sections. To create a test of statistical significance for the difference between two samples, a new sampling distribution must be defined.

Figure 10.4 provides a conceptual diagram for what is called the *sampling distribution for the difference in means*. There are two samples, each drawn from its own population. One constructs the sampling distribution by drawing a random sample of size N_1 from population 1 and a random sample of size N_2 from population 2.[11] The mean of each sample is computed, and the difference is calculated (i.e., $\overline{X}_1 - \overline{X}_2$). The scores are then returned to their respective populations. Sampling continues in a like manner until there are a very large number of mean differences. (The distribution is of the differences between means, not of the means themselves.)

If sample sizes are large enough, the frequency distribution of mean differences is normal. The mean of this distribution is $\mu_1 - \mu_2$.[12] The standard deviation of this distribution, called the *standard error of mean differences*, is obtained with Equation 10.7.

$$\sigma_{\bar{x}_1 - \bar{x}_2} = \sqrt{\frac{\sigma_1^2}{N_1} + \frac{\sigma_2^2}{N_2}} \qquad \text{Equation 10.7}$$

As with other normal distributions, there are upper and lower cutoffs that enclose 95 percent of the mean differences. Although we do not know what those cutoffs are, we know that their corresponding z scores are ± 1.96. The z score for a mean difference is computed in the following way:

$$z = \frac{(\overline{X}_1 - \overline{X}_2)(\mu_1 - \mu_2)}{\sqrt{\frac{\sigma_1^2}{N_1} + \frac{\sigma_2^2}{N_2}}} \qquad \text{Equation 10.8}$$

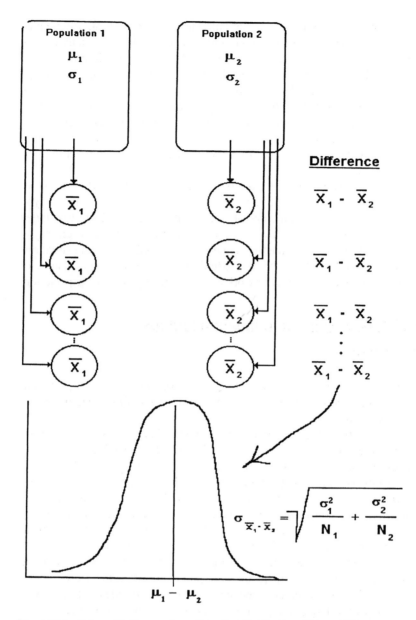

Figure 10.4   Schematic Diagram for a Sampling Distribution of Mean Differences

Equation 10.8 looks more complex than other z score equations, but the underlying structure is a familiar one. Simply stated, the z score is found by subtracting the average of the mean differences from a particular mean difference. The result is divided by the standard deviation of mean differences. This is the general formula for finding any type of z score.

Student's *t* Test for Independent Samples

Equation 10.8 can be modified to reflect certain assumptions and conditions. For example, the equation is often used to test the null hypothesis that the difference in sample means is zero. This implies that each sample has been drawn from a population with the same mean, thus $\mu_1 - \mu_2 = 0$. This causes the right-hand term of the numerator to drop out, as follows:

$$z = \frac{\overline{X}_1 - \overline{X}_2}{\sqrt{\dfrac{\sigma_1^2}{N_1} + \dfrac{\sigma_2^2}{N_2}}}$$ Equation 10.9

If we make the assumption that the variability of both populations is the same, then $\sigma_1^2 = \sigma_2^2 = \sigma^2$. This is called the *homogeneity of variance assumption*. If σ^2 is placed in Equation 10.9, it can be factored, making the equation look like the following:

$$z = \frac{\overline{X}_1 - \overline{X}_2}{\sqrt{\left[\dfrac{1}{N_1} + \dfrac{1}{N_2}\right]\sigma^2}}$$ Equation 10.10

It is normally the case that one does not know σ^2 and must estimate it from the variability of scores in the samples. Doing this, of course, means that we now have to refer the computation to the t distribution instead of z, regardless of the sample sizes. Therefore, the statistical equation to use in the comparison of two samples is given by Equation 10.11, for which $df = N_1 + N_2 - 2$.

$$t = \frac{\overline{X}_1 - \overline{X}_2}{\sqrt{\left[\dfrac{1}{N_1} + \dfrac{1}{N_2}\right]\left[\dfrac{s_1^2(N_1 - 1) + s_2^2(N_2 - 1)}{N_1 + N_2 - 2}\right]}}$$ Equation 10.11

Although the term on the right-hand side of the denominator looks ominous, one can see that it is an approximation of σ^2. In essence, the term averages the variances of both samples, which are assumed to be similar or homogeneous. Note how s^2 appears for each sample.

Assumptions

There are four basic assumptions or conditions that must be met when one uses Student's t test for independent samples (Equation 10.11). First, it is assumed that the two samples are formed by selecting random and independent samples of individuals. Second, the two samples are mutually exclusive. This means that an individual is in one and only one sample. Third, the population variances from which the samples are formed are homogeneous. Fourth, the sampling distribution of $\overline{X}_1 - \overline{X}_2$ is normal in form.

Example

Imagine that a state department of corrections wants to train prison health care personnel in new procedures for documenting, filing, and managing medical records. Also assume there are two methods for teaching this material. For the sake of simplicity, we call them method A and method B.

To help state officials decide which of the two teaching methods to use, a pilot project is conducted in which 20 health care personnel are randomly selected from across the state. On a designated day, these individuals are flown to the state capitol and are then randomly assigned to participate in a session that is taught with teaching method A or teaching method B. Ten individuals are assigned to each group. At the conclusion of each session, participants complete a test that measures how much they have learned.

The mean and standard deviation of the test scores for the participants taught with method A are 73.8 and 8.5, respectively. The mean and standard deviation of the test scores for the participants taught with method B are 87.4 and 7.9,

Table 10.5 Steps in Testing a Hypothesis

The hypothesis is that two teaching methods do not differ in effectiveness.

1. H_0: Methods A and B do not differ in their effectiveness to instruct participants, $\mu_1 - \mu_2 = 0$.

   H_1: Methods A and B do differ in their effectiveness to instruct participants, $\mu_1 - \mu_2 \neq 0$.

2. Level of significance, $\alpha = .05$; $df = 10 + 10 - 2 = 18$
3. Decision Rule:

   If t falls within ± 2.101, do not reject H_0.
   If t equals or exceeds ± 2.101, reject H_0 in favor of H_1.

4. $$t = \frac{73.8 - 87.4}{\sqrt{\left[\dfrac{1}{10} + \dfrac{1}{10}\right]\left[\dfrac{8.5^2(10-1) + 7.9^2(10-1)}{10 + 10 - 2}\right]}} = -3.71$$

5. Conclusion: Reject H_0 in favor of H_1.

respectively. The means for the groups differ, but we are left with a basic question. Does this difference reflect a trivial discrepancy that might naturally occur if the teaching methods have an equal influence, or does the difference indicate a real distinction in the knowledge of participants? The test of significance that helps answer this question is displayed in Table 10.5.

The null hypothesis being tested here is that the teaching methods do not differ in effectiveness in instruction of participants. As always, the hypothesis is stated in terms of the population means. If H_0 is true, the $\overline{X}_1$ and $\overline{X}_2$ both reflect population means of the same value; $\mu_1 = \mu_2$, which means that $\mu_1 - \mu_2 = 0$.

The rival hypothesis is the logical alternative to H_0. If H_0 is that the two teaching methods do not differ in effect, then H_1 is that they do. The rival hypothesis is two-tailed. This is a clear application of a two-tailed test because there is no prior belief regarding the efficacy of either teaching method. From the state's perspective, method A or method B is to be used to train health care personnel, whichever is shown to work better. If H_1 is true, then $\overline{X}_1$ and $\overline{X}_2$ reflect different population means; $\mu_1 \neq \mu_2$, which means that $\mu_1 - \mu_2 \neq 0$.

For a .05 α level with 18 degrees of freedom ($df = N_1 + N_2 - 2 = 10 + 10 - 2 = 18$), Table D in the Appendix shows that the critical two-tailed t value is ± 2.101. The computed t value is -3.71, which is beyond -2.101. We therefore reject H_0 in favor of H_1. Given the mean scores, it appears as if participants learned more when taught with method B.

Exercise 10–3 Testing a Hypothesis

The hypothesis is that the academy's final examination scores for cadets with a college degree do not differ from scores of cadets without college degrees. Following the steps in Table 10.5, test the hypothesis by using the following data.

1. Both groups, $N = 13$
2. College degree: Mean examination score, 93.7; $s = 4.2$
   No degree: Mean examination score, 89.3; $s = 5.6$

Student's *t* Test for Related Samples

The use of independent samples is only one way in which group means can be compared. There are projects in which information is acquired from the same group of individuals at two periods in time. For example, a police chief might be interested in comparing the average number of moving violation citations that were issued by patrol officers during January with those issued during June in a particular year. In this situation, the means are computed on correlated or related samples, because the citations for each month are issued by the same set of officers.

In addition to conducting projects that measure the same group at two times, investigators conduct projects in which there are two separate groups of individuals who are matched in some way. This also constitutes correlated or related samples. For example, an insurance company might be interested in measuring the attitudes of court personnel and their spouses toward a new plan for retirement benefits. Even though the employees and their spouses are two separate groups of individuals, each pair has a common experience from living with each other. This implies that the attitude scores of the employees probably correlate with those of their spouses (whether or not there is a difference between them).

Data from correlated groups requires a special formulation of the *t* test. Given that scores come in pairs, the analysis focuses on d, the difference between the scores. We need to compute $d = X_1 - X_2$ for each pair of scores. The difference in the means of two related groups is reflected in $\bar{d}$, the mean of the score differences.[13]

The characteristics of the sampling distribution of $\bar{d}$ is similar to the distribution depicted in Figure 10.1. We can construct a *t* equation in the following way:

$$t = \frac{\bar{d} - \mu_{\bar{d}}}{s_{\bar{d}}} \qquad \text{Equation 10.12}$$

If H_0 is true, $\mu_{\bar{d}}$ equals 0. We can substitute this into equation 10.12 along with a formula for the standard error of $\bar{d}$. This gives the following:

$$t = \frac{\bar{d}}{\dfrac{s_d}{\sqrt{N}}} \qquad \text{Equation 10.13}$$

A computational form is as follows:

$$t = \frac{\Sigma d}{\sqrt{\dfrac{N\Sigma d^2 - (\Sigma d)^2}{N - 1}}} \qquad \text{Equation 10.14}$$

which has $N - 1$ degrees of freedom. In this equation, Σd is the sum of the difference scores; Σd^2 is the sum of the squared difference scores; and $(\Sigma d)^2$ is the sum of the difference scores, quantity squared. N is the number of persons or pairs of scores.

Assumptions

There are three basic assumptions that must be met when one uses Student's *t* test for related samples (Equation 10.14). First, there is random and independent sampling of individuals. Second, the scores of the two groups are correlated. This means that each individual contributes two scores or that one score is furnished from each of two people who are matched in some way. Third, the population distribution of d is normal.

Example

To develop a new stress reduction program in a metropolitan police department, a police psychologist needs to know if patrol officers and their partners have different perceptions of on-the-job danger. Because of financial and time constraints, only a sample of the police force can be evaluated on this topic. One patrol team (composed of two officers each) is randomly selected from each of ten precincts. All of the sampled individuals receive a comprehensive survey and are asked to describe perceptions of occupational stress and danger. One of the questions is "How much danger do you think you experience in the day-to-day work as a patrol officer in your precinct?" Everyone is asked to respond on a 10-point scale in which *1* indicates "Not much danger" and *10* indicates "A high degree of danger."

The two groups of officers in this project are matched because they are partners. It is reasonable to assume that partners have a common work experience that leads to correlation in their perceptions. The psychologist needs to use Student's *t* test for related samples for a statistical comparison of perceived ratings of danger.

Table 10.6 displays the information needed to compute Student's *t* test for related samples. The data are arranged as if we were going to compute a correlation coefficient. The ratings are indeed correlated. The Pearson coefficient for these data is 0.62. This table also shows that the mean perceived danger rating for one group of patrol officers is 5.30. The same mean rating is 4.50 for their partners. Does this difference reflect a trivial discrepancy that might naturally occur if patrol partners have an equal perception of danger, or does the difference indicate a real distinction in the perception of danger? The test of significance that helps answer this question is displayed in Table 10.7.

The null hypothesis being tested here is that the patrol partners do not differ in their perception of occupational danger. If H_0 is true, both sample means reflect population means of the same value; thus $\mu_1 - \mu_2 = 0$. However, if H_1 is true, the patrol partners do have different perceptions of danger. This indicates that the sample means reflect different population means; $\mu_1 - \mu_2 \neq 0$.

For a .05 α level with 9 degrees of freedom ($df = N - 1 = 10 - 1 = 9$), Table D in the appendix shows that the critical two-tailed *t* value is ± 2.262. The com-

Table 10.6   Computations for Student's *t* Test in Which Perceived Danger Is Compared Among Ten Pairs of Patrol Officers

Patrol Pair	Officer 1	Officer 2	d	d²
A	6	4	2	4
B	5	5	0	0
C	6	2	4	16
D	5	6	−1	1
E	6	5	1	1
F	9	8	1	1
G	3	2	1	1
H	4	2	2	4
I	4	5	−1	1
J	5	6	−1	1
Sum	53	45	8	30
Mean	5.30	4.50		
SD	1.64	2.01		

SD, standard deviation.

Table 10.7   Steps in Testing a Hypothesis

The hypothesis is that perceptions of danger do not differ among patrol partners.

1. H_0: Patrol partners do not differ in their perception of occupational danger, $\mu_1 - \mu_2 = 0$.

   H_1: Patrol partners do differ in their perception of occupational danger, $\mu_1 - \mu_2 \neq 0$.

2. Level of significance, $\alpha = .05$; $df = 10 - 1 = 9$
3. Decision rule:

   If t falls within ± 2.262, do not reject H_0.
   If t equals or exceeds ± 2.262, reject H_0 in favor of H_1.

4. $t = \dfrac{8}{\sqrt{\dfrac{10(30) - (8)^2}{9}}} = \dfrac{8}{5.12} = 1.56$

5. Conclusion: Do not reject H_0.

puted t value is 1.56, which is within the critical cutoff. We therefore cannot reject H_0. The data do not suggest that perceptions of danger differ between patrol partners.[14]

Exercise 10–4   Testing a Hypothesis

The null hypothesis is that perceptions about correctional officers among students do not change after the students complete a course in introduction to corrections. Using the steps in Table 10.7 and the following data, test the hypothesis. The data are from a sample of 12 students who were part of a class in policing who were given a pre-class and a post-class perceptions test. The test consisted of 25 negative perceptions about correctional officers. Respondents checked each perception they had about correctional officers. The higher the score, the more negative was the student's perception.

	Score on Pre-class Test	Score on Post-class Test	d	d^2
Student 1	17	13	4	16
Student 2	15	13	2	4
Student 3	16	10	6	36
Student 4	19	15	4	16
Student 5	12	8	4	16
Student 6	10	6	4	16
Student 7	10	9	1	1
Student 8	14	11	3	9
Student 9	18	10	8	64
Student 10	13	13	0	0
Student 11	14	7	7	49
Student 12	15	12	3	9
Sum	173	127	46	236
Mean	14.42	10.58		
SD	2.87	2.75		

SD, standard deviation.

Summary

Criminal justice practitioners often make comparisons between groups of individuals by way of averages. Although it is easy to see that one mean is higher or lower than another, we have learned that such discrepancies may or may not be indicative of an important finding. On one hand, the means for two groups can be different because there is a fundamental distinction between the groups on the variable that was measured. On the other hand, the difference in means can be simply a function of chance. We use *hypothesis testing* to differentiate these two situations.

Sampling distributions make statistical work with means possible. An empirical sampling distribution of the mean is created by making a frequency distribution of a large number of sample means that are drawn from a population. The *central limit theorem* specifies that the sampling distribution of the mean is normal even if the population distribution departs considerably from normality, provided that the sample size is large enough.

To evaluate two sample means, we need a *sampling distribution of mean differences*. This sampling distribution helps determine if the difference between two means is attributable to chance or to a systematic influence. If sample sizes are large enough, we can refer to the *z* distribution for a particular mean difference. If sample sizes are small or we have to estimate population variances from the sample scores, then we need to refer to Student's *t* distribution.

One formula for *Student's t test* is used for analyzing data from independent groups. Another formula is used for related groups. Projects with independent groups involve data that are collected from individuals who are in one and only one group. Projects with related groups involve data that are collected from (1) the same individuals measured at two points in time or (2) two different groups of individuals who are matched in some way.

Tests of significance are conducted as either one-tailed or two-tailed tests. A *one-tailed test* uses a cutoff score that is located in either the upper tail or the lower tail of the *z* or *t* distribution. *Two-tailed tests* use cutoff scores that are located in both the upper tail and the lower tail. We recommend two-tailed tests of significance even if there is a strong expectation about the results. A one-tailed test should be conducted only in rare situations in which results are expected to be in one direction and the investigator does not want to or is not ethically bound to report results opposite the expectation.

Answers to Exercises

Exercise Answer 10–1   Sampling Distribution of the Mean— Hypothesis Testing

Cadet Class 1, $N = 57$; $\bar{x} = 113.3$

1. H_0: The sample of cadets whose mean is 113.3 is not different from the population whose $\mu = 107.4$.

   H_1: The sample of cadets whose mean is 113.3 is different from the population whose $\mu \neq 107.4$.

2. Level of significance, $\alpha = .05$; $\sigma = 10.6$
3. Decision rule:

If z falls within ± 1.96, do not reject H_0.
If z equals or exceeds ± 1.96, reject H_0 in favor of H_1.

4.

$$z = \frac{113.3 - 107.4}{\dfrac{10.6}{\sqrt{57}}} = \frac{5.90}{\dfrac{10.6}{7.55}} = \frac{5.90}{1.40} = 4.21$$

5. Conclusion: Reject H_0 in favor of H_1.

Cadet Class 2, $N = 41$; $\bar{x} = 106.5$

1. H_0: The sample of cadets whose mean is 106.5 is not different from the population whose $\mu = 107.4$.

   H_1: The sample of cadets whose mean is 106.5 is different from the population whose $\mu \neq 107.4$.

2. Level of significance, $\alpha = .05$; $\sigma = 10.6$
3. Decision rule:

   If z falls within ± 1.96, do not reject H_0.
   If z equals or exceeds ± 1.96, reject H_0 in favor of H_1.

4.

$$z = \frac{106.5 - 107.4}{\dfrac{10.6}{\sqrt{41}}} = \frac{-.99}{\dfrac{10.6}{6.40}} = \frac{-.99}{1.66} = -.60$$

5. Conclusion: Do not reject H_0 in favor of H_1.

Cadet Class 3, $N = 33$; $\bar{x} = 110.2$

1. H_0: The sample of cadets whose mean is 110.2 is not different from the population whose $\mu = 107.4$.

   H_1: The sample of cadets whose mean is 110.2 is different from the population whose $\mu \neq 107.4$.

2. Level of significance, $\alpha = .05$; $\sigma = 10.6$
3. Decision rule:

   If z falls within ± 1.96, do not reject H_0.
   If z equals or exceeds ± 1.96, reject H_0 in favor of H_1.

4.

$$z = \frac{110.2 - 107.4}{\dfrac{10.6}{\sqrt{33}}} = \frac{2.80}{\dfrac{10.6}{5.74}} = \frac{2.80}{1.85} = 1.51$$

5. Conclusion: Do not reject H_0 in favor of H_1.

Exercise Answer 10–2   Student's t and Hypothesis Testing

City A, $N = 25$; $\bar{x} = 36.23$; $s = 7.67$

1. H_0: The sample of officers whose mean is 36.23 is not different from the population whose $\mu = 31.5$.

H_1: The sample of officers whose mean is 36.23 is different from the population whose $\mu \neq 31.5$.

2. Level of significance, $\alpha = .05$; $df = 25 - 1 = 24$
3. Decision rule:

If t falls within ± 2.064, do not reject H_0.
If t equals or exceeds ± 2.064, reject H_0 in favor of H_1.

4.

$$t = \frac{36.23 - 31.5}{\dfrac{7.67}{\sqrt{25}}} = \frac{4.73}{\dfrac{7.67}{5.00}} = \frac{4.73}{1.53} = 3.09$$

5. Conclusion: Reject H_0 in favor of H_1.

City B, $N = 19$; $\bar{x} = 28.71$; $s = 5.22$

1. H_0: The sample of officers whose mean is 28.71 is not different from the population whose $\mu = 31.5$.

   H_1: The sample of officers whose mean is 28.71 is different from the population whose $\mu \neq 31.5$.

2. Level of significance, $\alpha = .05$; $df = 19 - 1 = 18$
3. Decision rule:

If t falls within ± 2.101, do not reject H_0.
If t equals or exceeds ± 2.101, reject H_0 in favor of H_1.

4.

$$t = \frac{28.71 - 31.5}{\dfrac{5.22}{\sqrt{19}}} = \frac{-2.79}{\dfrac{5.22}{4.36}} = \frac{-2.79}{1.20} = -2.33$$

5. Conclusion: Reject H_0 in favor of H_1.

City C, $N = 31$; $\bar{x} = 33.44$; $s = 6.08$

1. H_0: The sample of officers whose mean is 33.44 is not different from the population whose $\mu = 31.5$.

   H_1: The sample of officers whose mean is 33.44 is different from the population whose $\mu \neq 31.5$.

2. Level of significance, $\alpha = .05$; $df = 31 - 1 = 30$
3. Decision rule:

If t falls within ± 2.045, do not reject H_0.
If t equals or exceeds ± 2.045, reject H_0 in favor of H_1.

4.

$$t = \frac{33.44 - 31.5}{\dfrac{6.08}{\sqrt{31}}} = \frac{1.94}{\dfrac{6.08}{5.57}} = \frac{1.94}{1.09} = 1.77$$

5. Conclusion: Do not reject H_0.

Exercise Answer 10–3 *Testing a Hypothesis*

The hypothesis is that the academy's final examination scores for cadets with college degrees do not differ from scores of cadets without college degrees.

Both groups, $N = 13$

College degree: Mean examination score, 93.7; $s = 4.2$

No degree: Mean examination score, 89.3; $s = 5.6$

1. H_0: Examination scores for officers with a degree and those for officers without a degree do not differ, $\mu_1 - \mu_2 = 0$.

   H_1: Examination scores for officers with a degree and those for officers without a degree do differ, $\mu_1 - \mu_2 \neq 0$.

2. Level of significance, $\alpha = .05$; $df = 13 + 13 - 2 = 24$
3. Decision rule:

   If t falls within ± 2.064, do not reject H_0.
   If t equals or exceeds ± 2.064, reject H_0 in favor of H_1.

4.
$$t = \frac{93.7 - 89.3}{\sqrt{\left[\frac{1}{13} + \frac{1}{13}\right]\left[\frac{4.2^2(13 - 1) + 5.6^2(13 - 1)}{13 + 13 - 2}\right]}} = 2.27$$

5. Conclusion: Reject H_0 in favor of H_1.

Exercise Answer 10–4 *Testing a Hypothesis*

The hypothesis is that perceptions about correctional officers among students do not change after the students complete a course in introduction to corrections.

1. H_0: Students do not differ in their perception of correctional officers after completing an introductory course, $\mu_1 - \mu_2 = 0$.

   H_1: Students do differ in their perception of correctional officers after completing an introductory course, $\mu_1 - \mu_2 \neq 0$.

2. Level of significance, $\alpha = .05$; $df = 12 - 1 = 11$
3. Decision rule:

   If t falls within ± 2.201, do not reject H_0.
   If t equals or exceeds ± 2.201, reject H_0 in favor of H_1.

4.
$$t = \frac{46}{\sqrt{\frac{12(236) - (46)^2}{11}}} = \frac{46}{\sqrt{\frac{716}{11}}} = \frac{46}{8.07} = 5.70$$

5. Conclusion: Reject H_0 in favor of H_1.

Computer Applications for Selected Exercises

Exercise Answer 10–4 *t test for Related Samples*

Unlike the data in Exercises 10–1, 10–2, and 10–3, the data in Exercise 10–4 are given in raw form for each student. You need it in this format to perform the *t* test in *SPSS for Windows*. You need one column for each variable. The sum, mean, and standard deviation information at the bottom of the table in the exercise are automatically generated by *SPSS,* so you do not have to enter it in the Data Editor (Figure 10.5).

	student#	pretest	posttest	var
1	1	17	13	
2	2	15	13	
3	3	16	10	
4	4	19	15	
5	5	12	8	
6	6	10	6	
7	7	10	9	
8	8	14	11	
9	9	18	10	
10	10	13	13	
11	11	14	7	
12	12	15	12	
13				

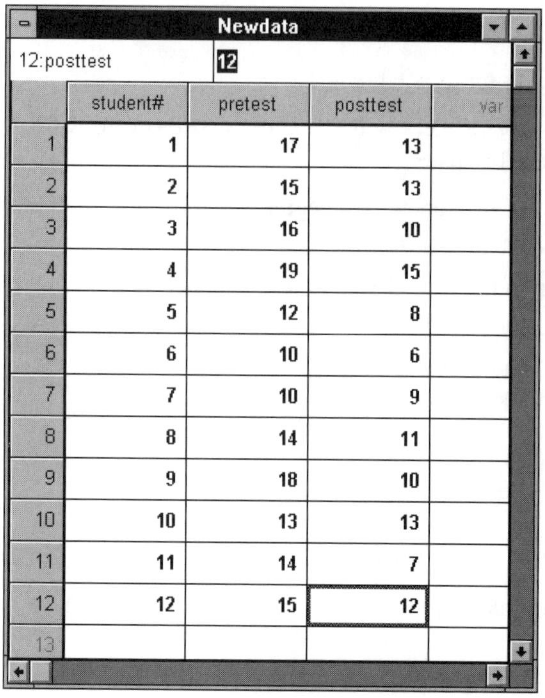

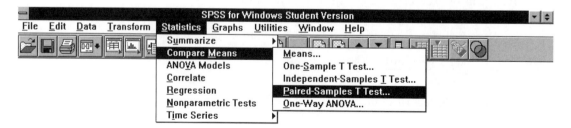

Figure 10.5

The student numbers are just that: numbers. By labeling the column `student#`, you eliminate the need to type *student* in every row of the data set.

The two-sample *t* test for related samples is called a paired *t* test in *SPSS for Windows*. The term *paired* is easy to remember if you know that the test is calculated on a pair of values for each row in the data set.

Go to the Statistics menu and choose `Compare Means` and `Paired-Samples T Test` (Figure 10.6).

Figure 10.6

In all the dialog boxes with which you have worked so far, you selected one variable at a time from the list on the left and moved it to the list in the middle using the large arrow. For the paired test, however, you need to tell *SPSS* exactly which pairs to use. Click once on the first variable in the pair, `pretest`. Now click once on the second variable, `posttest`. Look in the lower-left corner of the dialog box at the `Current Selections` section. *SPSS* shows which variables compose the pair (Figure 10.7).

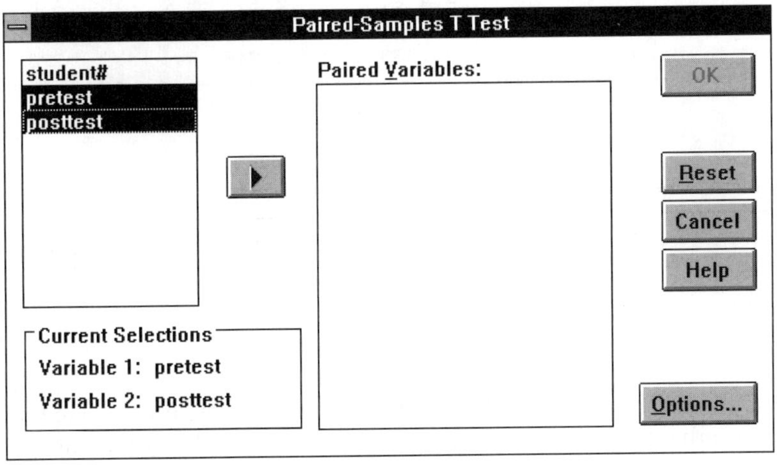

Figure 10.7

Click once on the large arrow in the center of the dialog box to move the pair into the analysis position (Figure 10.8).

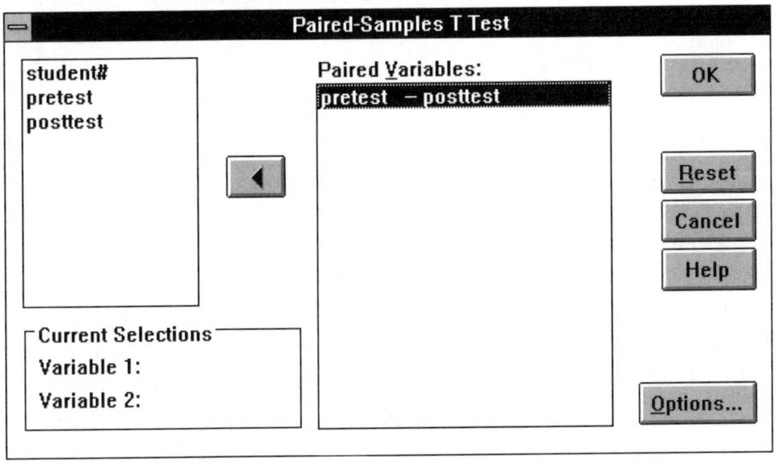

Figure 10.8

The paired variables are listed as pairs, separated by a dash (—) in the `Paired Variables:` list in the center of the dialog box. You can specify as many pairs as you want. Choose `OK` to run the analysis.

The results are shown in Figure 10.9. The output is displayed in two tables. The top table provides the summary information about the variables. Check to see that the values for mean and standard deviation match those provided in the exercise.

The second table gives the *t*-test statistics. The mean difference between the pretest and posttest is 3.83. The two-tailed significance is 0.000. This means that

t-tests for Paired Samples

Variable	Number of pairs	Corr	2-tail Sig	Mean	SD	SE of Mean
PRETEST				14.4167	2.875	.830
	12	.657	.020			
POSTTEST				10.5833	2.746	.793

Paired Differences Mean	SD	SE of Mean	t-value	df	2-tail Sig
3.8333	2.329	.672	5.70	11	.000
95% CI (2.354, 5.313)					

Figure 10.9

the actual significance value is less than 0.0005, the highest value after rounding that makes the printed value non-zero. You conclude that the policing training had an effect on students' perceptions of officers.

Higher scores on the test indicate more negative perceptions of correctional officers. The pretest is listed first, then the posttest. The mean paired difference is positive. This means that pretest scores are higher on average than posttest scores. A look at the actual data shows that pretest scores are the same or higher in all cases. A higher score indicates a more negative perception at the pretest. The paired *t* test shows that students' perceptions of correctional officers are less negative after the policing class.

Notes

1. One can understand how numbers are different by chance by considering the roll of dice. Although each die contains the numbers 1 through 6, it is typically the case that the toss of two dice yields different numbers. If the dice are fair, this numerical difference is due to chance, not to any fundamental distinction in the dice themselves.

2. Review chapters 2 and 4 to refresh your knowledge of *z* scores and the normal curve.

3. It is statistically impossible to identify upper and lower scores in a normal distribution that includes 100 percent of the population. This is because the tails of a normal distribution (as defined by a mathematical equation) are asymptotic to the abscissa. In other words, as values on the abscissa (i.e., scores) become farther from the mean, the tails of the normal distribution become closer and closer to the abscissa but never touch it.

4. Given the example so far, only one population has been defined. If the cadet in question (Gerald Anderson) is not similar to the people in the defined population, you assume that he is similar to people in another population, even though such a population is not currently defined. If, for example, Mr. Anderson's performance on the standardized examination is indicative of an outstanding (rather than typical) cadet, you assume that his score is similar to the scores in the population of outstanding cadets, even though such a population has not yet been identified.

5. A sampling distribution can be constructed from any statistic. For example, if you measure the median of random samples, the resulting frequency distribution is called a *sampling distribution of the median*. A frequency distribution of sample standard deviations is a *sampling distribution of the standard deviation*.

6. The scales on all of the distributions in Figure 10.2 have been deleted to aid visualization.

7. At close inspection, one sees that the sampling distribution from the skewed population is not symmetric like that from the square population. This is because the scores for the skewed population deviate more from normal distribution than do the scores for the square population. To achieve a better sampling distribution for the skewed population, one needs a sample size larger than 30.

8. The life of William Gossett is an interesting one. Some refer to him as a statistician who was an advisor to the Guinness Beer Company. Others view him as a brewer who devoted his free time to the development of statistics. In either case, a colleague and friend (McMullen 1939) saw that Gossett's greatest strength was his connection between mathematical statistics and the practical problems that he sought to solve. Indeed, the *t* test has become one of the most useful statistical tools for addressing practical problems.

9. For any α level, the critical *z* value for a one-tailed test is smaller than that for a two-tailed test. The same is true for critical *t* values given any α level and degrees of freedom. The reason is directly related to the way in which the area in the tails is allocated. If $\alpha = .05$, the cutoff scores for a two-tailed test are those that isolate 2.5 percent of the distribution in the upper tail (i.e., the upper cutoff) and 2.5 percent in the lower tail (the lower cutoff). In a one-tailed test, the single cutoff score is that which isolates 5 percent of the distribution in either the upper tail or the lower tail.

10. For example, assume that you conduct a one-tailed *t* test in which you expect that group A performs better than group B. Given that you are conducting a one-tailed test, you can reject H_0 only if group A performs significantly better than group B. However, if you conduct a two-tailed test, you can reject H_0 if group A performs significantly better than group B *or* if group B performs significantly better than group A.

11. N_1 does not have to equal N_2, but each has to be constant for all samples that are drawn.

12. We are not providing mathematical proof, but if the mean of a sampling distribution of $\overline{X}$ is μ, it is reasonable to assume that the mean of the sampling distribution of $\overline{X}_1 - \overline{X}_2$ is $\mu_1 - \mu_2$.

13. We encourage readers to check the validity of the statements made in this book. To show that $\overline{d} = \overline{X}_1 - \overline{X}_2$, create a set of number pairs, as if you were going to compute a correlation coefficient. Calculate the mean of X_1 and X_2 and take the difference. Next, compute *d* for each number pair and then take the average. If there are no computational errors, $\overline{d} = \overline{X}_1 - \overline{X}_2$.

14. Use of Student's *t* test for independent samples (Equation 10.11) to analyze the data from patrol partners results in $t = 0.98$ instead of $t = 1.56$ as shown in Table 10.7. The discrepancy between the *t* values exists because the former does not take into account the correlation between the two sets of ratings. This demonstrates the importance of using the correct *t* equation for a particular situation.

References

Fleiss, J. L. 1981. *Statistical Methods for Rates and Proportions*. 2d ed. New York: Wiley.

Goldfried, M. R. 1959. "One-tailed Tests and 'Unexpected' Results." *Psychological Review* 66:79–80.

Kimmel, H. D. 1957. "Three Criteria for the Use of One-tailed Tests." *Psychological Bulletin* 54:351–353.

McMullen, L. 1939. "'Student' As a Man." *Biometrika* 30:205–210.

11. One-way Analysis of Variance

Reducing Prison Violence with the VCR

You have been Warden Crowley's assistant at Livingstone Prison for the past three years. In all that time, you've never seen him so agitated. When you walked into his office this morning, he was pacing up and down wringing his hands. You're afraid to ask him what the problem is, and you decide to wait until he talks to you first. Finally, he turns to you and says, "I received a call from the director of prisons in the state capital. He reminded me that Livingstone State Prison had the highest rate of inmate violence for the fifth straight year. We continue to lead the state in the number of inmate assaults such as fistfights and knife attacks. The director let me know that my days as warden at Livingstone are numbered unless I do something right away about the violence here. But the state doesn't want to spend a lot of money to correct the problem. What do you suggest?"

The question leaves you stunned. You have been thinking and reading about inmate violence. Until today, however, the warden has never asked you for a specific plan to alleviate the problem at Livingstone. Fortunately, you recall an advertisement in *Corrections Today* magazine for videotapes that describe treatments to relieve inmates' aggressive tendencies while they are incarcerated. You remember that four different companies offer such tapes. Each tape proposes different approaches for handling violence behind bars. The first tape features hypnosis, the second, relaxation techniques, the third, social learning techniques, and the fourth, dispute resolution training. You mention the tapes to the warden. He thinks they're worth looking at because, "I'll give anything a chance to save my job!" He tells you to give him more information about the tapes. The warden also says that he'll call the director with a plan for using the tapes and asks you to return to his office in two days.

When you return to see Warden Crowley, he seems much less troubled, but he still has a look of concern on his face. The warden states that the director liked the idea of using the tapes except that it would be impossible to pay for all the treatments out of the state's current prison budget. The warden tells you emphatically, "We have to pick the best program of the four. I have already sent away for the four demonstration video packages. Each program runs for eight weeks and they all claim success with violent inmates. We have to determine which treatment works best and invest the little money we have available on that one. It is up to you to figure out a way to do that. If we can reduce violence here at Livingstone, it may save inmates' lives and it will certainly save my job. I'll expect an answer from you in about three months. Get to work!"

You feel optimistic about meeting this challenge. After all, you took a course in research design and you have already planned a study. There are 25 inmates on the dangerous inmate tier.

Livingstone works with a psychologist who has an assessment tool to evaluate an inmate's tendency toward compliant, nonviolent behavior while incarcerated. Your plan is to randomly assign inmates to the four different treatment programs, approximately six inmates per group. At the end of the programs, you will ask the psychologist to administer the assessment tool and you will compare the four groups on their scores. After you have the scores, how will you determine whether the four groups are different from one another? How will you decide which group has the best results?

The four groups of inmates finish the programs and are scored by the psychologist on their tendency toward compliant, nonviolent behavior while they are at Livingstone. Given what you remember from a summer course in introductory statistics, your natural inclination is to compare the groups of scores with multiple Student's t tests. This means you have to compare the means of groups 1 and 2, groups 1 and 3, groups 1 and 4, groups 2 and 3, groups 2 and 4, and groups 3 and 4, totaling six t tests. Before you start, however, you wonder, "Is this the right statistical procedure to follow? Might there be a better way to make all these comparisons?"

One-way Analysis of Variance

When students learn about statistical tests, they often attribute a sense of authority to them. For example, if someone is able to reject a null hypothesis with a t test for independent samples, he or she might think, "If the test result is significant, the two groups must be different." Although common, this is a naive way of thinking about tests of significance.

Statistical tests, like people, are vulnerable to error. This is because a test of significance helps only with decisions about the real-world event under investigation—the test is not the event itself. At first, this may seem confusing, but we show how decisions based on statistical analyses are similar to decisions made by other means. No matter how we go about it, some of the decisions that we make are going to be correct and others are going to be in error.

Decisions About Real-world Events

Everyone is familiar with making a decision error. On a cloudy day, for example, many of us have lugged an umbrella to work or school, only to find that it did not rain. Likewise, we can probably remember preparing for an important appointment, only to find that we arrived on the wrong day.

When we make a decision about something, we are attempting to make a statement about a real-world event based on prevailing information. If enough information is present, we have the capability to make a correct decision. If information is lacking or is incorrect, however, we run the risk of making a decision error. This process is presented in Table 11.1, which shows the correct and incorrect decisions that can be made by a jury about a defendant who is accused of a crime.

Table 11.1 shows how the truth of a real-world event and the decision about that event are related. Given a criminal court case, logic dictates that a defendant did or did not commit the crime for which he or she is accused. The jury, however, does not know the truth. It is assumed that none of the jury members

Table 11.1　Correct and Incorrect Decisions That Can Be Made by a Jury About a Defendant Who Is Accused of a Crime

		Truth About Defendant	
		Committed Crime	**Did Not Commit Crime**
Jury Decision	**Guilty**	Correct decision	Decision error
Based on Evidence	**Not Guilty**	Decision error	Correct decision

observed the crime and that the jury members are unable to peer into the mind of a defendant, who is the only one who really knows whether he or she committed the crime.

In court, prosecution and defense attorneys present to a jury evidence that supports their arguments. At some point, the jury discusses all information and arrives at a decision. The defendant is then declared to be guilty or not guilty.

Table 11.1 shows that the jury members make a correct decision when they declare a defendant guilty when he or she has committed the crime. They also make a correct decision when they declare a defendant not guilty when he or she has not committed the crime.

There can be instances, however, in which a jury pronounces a defendant guilty when he or she has not committed the crime; thus they falsely convict an innocent person. There also can be instances in which a jury pronounces a defendant not guilty when he or she has committed the crime; thus they release a culpable person back into society. It would be admirable if juries made correct decisions all the time, but we know that sometimes they make errors.[1]

Decision Errors with Statistical Analyses

Discussion of decision error makes sense within the context of a criminal court case, but what does this have to do with statistical analysis? To answer this question, consider a situation in which we are looking at the test scores of detectives who work in a large city, such as Chicago or New York.[2] Let us assume that the test measures knowledge of department policy regarding evidence acquisition and other aspects of criminal investigation. Also assume that we have two populations of detectives: novice and experienced. The novice detectives have been employed about one year, and the experienced detectives have been in their job for at least five years.

Figure 11.1 shows the two populations of test scores. Each population has its own mean but the two standard deviations are equal. In addition, a sampling distribution of means is constructed from each population.[3] As expected, the sampling distribution for the experienced detectives tends to have higher sample means (which indicate better performance) and sits to the right of the sampling distribution for the novice detectives. One can see, however, that the two sampling distributions overlap. This shows that high sample means from the novice population and low sample means from the experienced population possess similar values.[4]

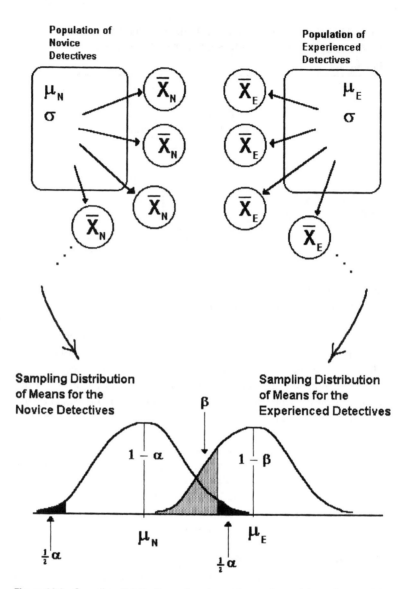

Figure 11.1   Sampling distributions of novice and experienced detectives and the probability of correct and incorrect rejection of the null hypothesis.

Hypothesis Testing When H_0 Is True

We can conduct tests of significance using samples from each of the populations. First consider the novice detectives. Let us take a sample of scores from this known population and test the null hypothesis that the performance of the sample is not different from the population of novice detectives whose mean is μ_N.

Given that we have staged this example, we know that H_0 is true (the performance of the sample is like that of the novice population because we have physically drawn the sample from that population). Therefore, the test of this hypothesis may seem odd. Because we know that the sample is drawn from the novice population, do we not automatically retain H_0?

The answer to this question would be "yes" if the hypothesis testing process were perfect and precisely reflected a real-world event. The fact, however, is that hypothesis testing is a procedure with conventions that lead us to make correct decisions *most* of the time, if the procedure is properly followed.[5]

To see how we can make a decision error, we test H_0. We do this with Equation 11.1 which allows us to compare a sample with a population.[6]

$$z = \frac{\overline{X}_N - \mu_N}{\frac{\sigma}{\sqrt{N}}}$$ Equation 11.1

In the hypothesis testing process, we choose an α level that gives a critical value for z. If, for example, $\alpha = .05$ and we conduct a two-tailed test, the critical z value is ± 1.96. Given that the sampling distribution of means for the novice detectives is normal in form, there is going to be a sample mean the value of which is high enough or low enough to make Equation 11.1 reach or exceed ± 1.96. When this happens, we wrongly decide to reject H_0. The decision is incorrect because the hypothesis testing procedure has led us to reject H_0 when we know that it should not be rejected.

The probability of rejecting H_0 when H_0 is true equals α level (the black area in the tails of the novice sampling distribution). If $\alpha = .05$, 5 percent of the sample means drawn from the novice population wrongly lead to rejection of H_0. Likewise, 95 percent $(1 - \alpha)$ of the sample means correctly lead us to retain H_0.

Hypothesis Testing When H₀ Is False

Consider the situation in which H_0 is false. To do this, we take a random sample of scores from the experienced detectives. We then test the same null hypothesis used before—that the performance of the sample is not different from that of the population of novice detectives whose mean is μ_N. This can be done with Equation 11.2.

$$z = \frac{\overline{X}_E - \mu_N}{\frac{\sigma}{\sqrt{N}}}$$ Equation 11.2

We know that H_0 is false. We have a sample of scores from the experienced detectives that we are comparing with scores from the population of novice detectives. Shouldn't a test of significance always give a z value of at least 1.96 and thus lead us to reject H_0?

The answer to this question would be "yes" if the hypothesis testing process were perfect and precisely reflected a real-world event. However, as Figure 11.1 shows, the sampling distributions of means for the novice and experienced detectives overlap. One can see that there are going to be some samples from the experienced population whose mean is so low that the z value from Equation 11.2 does not reach 1.96 (this is denoted by the shaded area under the tail of the sampling distribution for experienced detectives).

The probability of not rejecting H_0 when H_0 is false equals β (lower case Greek beta). The value of β depends on α, the difference in the population means, and the variation of sample means drawn from the respective populations. The probability for correct rejection of H_0 is $1 - \beta$.

Type I and Type II Error

Table 11.2 shows that decisions based on statistical analyses are similar to decisions made by other means. We conduct a statistical test with available information and are led to reject or not reject H_0. In reality, H_0 is either true or false. If

Table 11.2   Correct and Incorrect Decisions That Can Be Made by Means of a Statistical Test of Significance

		Null Hypothesis	
		True	**False**
Decision Based on Statistical Test	**Do Not Reject H₀**	Correct decision $(p = 1 - \alpha)$	Type II error $(p = \beta)$
	Reject H₀	Type I error $(p = \alpha)$	Correct decision $(p = 1 - \beta)$

we do not reject H_0 when it is true, we make a correct decision (declaring an innocent person not guilty). If we reject H_0 when it is false, we again make a correct decision (declaring the perpetrator of a crime guilty).

If statistical computations lead to rejection of H_0 when it is true, we make what is known as a Type I error (such as pronouncing an innocent person guilty). For example, we make a Type I error if the result of a *t* test leads us to believe that male and female police officers differ in perceived job satisfaction when in reality they do not.

When statistical computations lead us not to reject H_0 when it is false, we make what is known as a Type II error (such as proclaiming the perpetrator of a crime not guilty). For example, we make a Type II error if the result of a χ^2 test leads us to say that we do not find a difference in the frequency of court appearance for defendants who are and are not electronically monitored when there really is a difference.

Exercise 11–1   Type I and Type II Errors

For the following decisions, which are based on statistical findings, indicate whether a correct decision, Type I error, or Type II error has been made.

1. A medical researcher decides that a pill to reduce high blood pressure works when the pill actually has no effect on blood pressure.
2. An intensive supervision program for sex offenders on probation does reduce recidivism. The investigator studying the program does not reject the null hypothesis.
3. A special firearms training seminar for police officers does improve shooting accuracy. On the basis of target practice data, the training academy researcher decides that the course is effective.
4. An assertiveness training course for women detention officers gives them more confidence and helps them maintain better control over inmates. A study leads the captain of the officers to decide to discontinue the program.
5. After investigating a drug testing program for parolees, a researcher concludes that the program works as a deterrent. In reality, parolees who are not tested for drugs use them as much as parolees who are tested.

Type I Errors with Multiple Statistical Tests

Type I errors are of more concern than Type II errors. This is because Type I errors masquerade as important research findings.[7] Assume that in the previous example investigators were to find incorrectly that male and female police officers have different levels of job satisfaction. This result would probably concern the administrative staff (such as the police commissioner), who might then delegate time, resources, and personnel to work on a problem that does not exist. It is important to acknowledge the Type I error.

The probability of making a Type I error is equal to α level. One has a 5 percent chance of making a Type I error when $\alpha = .05$. What happens, however, if one conducts multiple statistical tests? In the opening vignette, you were faced with the possibility of conducting six Student's t tests to make all pairwise comparisons of four group means. What do you think would have been the probability of making at least one Type I error among those six tests? You probably guess that it is more than 5 percent.

Statisticians calculate the probability of making at least one Type I error as follows:

$$1 - (1 - \alpha)^t \qquad \text{Equation 11.3}$$

where t is the number of tests that are conducted.[8] For one test ($t = 1$) that uses a .05 α level, the probability of making a Type I error is $1 - (1 - .05) = 1 - (.95) = .05$, or 5 percent. For two tests, the probability is $1 - (1 - .05)^2 = 1 - (.95)^2 = 1 - (.903) = .098$, or 9.8 percent. Figure 11.2 shows how the probability of a Type I error increases as a function of the number of conducted tests. One line is for $\alpha = .05$ and the other is for $\alpha = .01$. The situation is worse for the former, but the graph demonstrates how the risk of a Type I error mounts as one

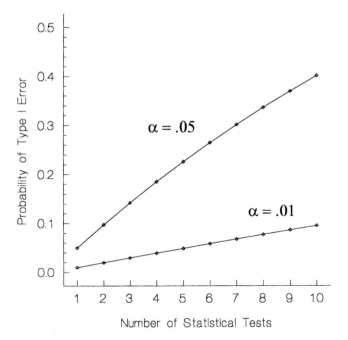

Figure 11.2 Probability of making a Type I error as a function of the number of statistical tests conducted.

conducts multiple statistical tests. The graph shows that if the staff member in the opening problem had used a .05 α level, his chance of making at least one Type I error among six t tests would be about 26 percent. If he had used a .01 α level, the probability would be about 6 percent.

Exercise 11–2   Probability of Type I Error

For the following situations, calculate the probability of making at least one Type I error when performing multiple t tests.

α Level	No. of t Tests
.05	5
.01	7
.001	3
.05	4

Analysis of Variance

The pioneering work of the noted statistician Sir Ronald Fisher produced a method that allows comparison of multiple group means without risking a high probability of making a Type I error. The analytic method is called the *analysis of variance* (ANOVA). The process of computing ANOVA is time consuming, but the concept is not difficult to comprehend.

To help understand ANOVA, consider the problem in the opening vignette. Twenty-five inmates have been randomly assigned to undergo treatment with one of four methods of handling violence behind bars. At the end of the programs, the inmates are rated by a psychologist with an assessment tool to evaluate inmates' propensities toward compliant, nonviolent behavior while incarcerated. A high score indicates a prisoner has a high likelihood of behaving. The main question is, Which method of handling violent behavior, if any, is best?

Figure 11.3 depicts the results of the study in which each of the therapeutic methods performs equally well. The dots indicate compliant behavior scores, and each group mean is identified. All group means are at the same level, indicating that prisoners scored the same for all four therapeutic methods.

In a study in which it is found that the methods have differential effects on inmates, we see results that look like Figure 11.4. The group means (and thus the average assessment of inmates) are different from one another. The figure shows that prisoners treated with hypnosis do not score well. The prisoners treated with relaxation techniques score slightly better, and those treated by means of a social learning approach have the worst evaluations. The prisoners treated with instruction in dispute resolution techniques have the best scores. The results show that differential effect of therapeutic methods is manifested in the variability of group means.

The goal of ANOVA is to conduct a test of significance that examines all groups at once. For this procedure, the variance of the total test scores (i.e., all scores taken as a whole) is broken down into two components. One component is called *error variance*. It reflects the natural variation in scores that is inherent in the variable under study. The term *error* does not mean that anything is wrong. It is a statistical term that refers to the variation of scores due to naturally occur-

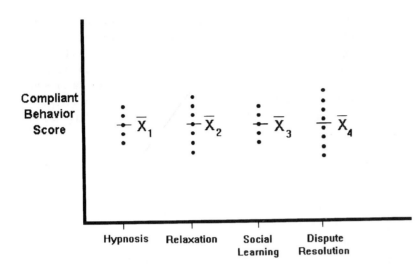

Therapeutic Methods

Figure 11.3 Schematic diagram shows how compliant behavior scores of inmates treated with four different therapeutic methods of violence control do not show a statistical difference.

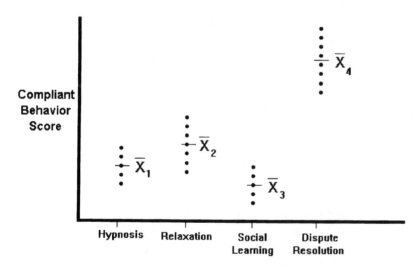

Therapeutic Methods

Figure 11.4 Schematic diagram shows how compliant behavior scores of inmates treated with four different therapeutic methods of violence control show a statistical difference.

ring individual differences and other random factors. One finds this variance by computing the variability of scores within a group around the group mean. The result is often referred to as *within-group variance*.

The second component is called *treatment variance*. It reflects the variation in the scores attributable to experimental manipulation. In the example, treatment variance is the variability of the compliant behavior scores produced by the different therapeutic methods. One finds this variance by computing the variability of group means around the grand mean (which is the mean of all the scores taken as a whole). The result is often referred to as *between-group variance*.

Figure 11.5 provides a visual display of how the total variance of a set of scores is allotted, or partitioned, into within-group and between-group components. To gain full appreciation of the figure, we must remember that one measures variance by finding the average squared deviation of scores around their mean. In of ANOVA, the starting point is the total variance[9] of the scores, which is measured as follows:

$$s^2 = \frac{\Sigma (X - \overline{\overline{X}})^2}{N - 1}$$

Equation 11.4

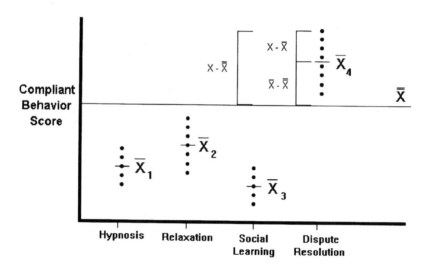

Therapeutic Methods

Figure 11.5 Schematic diagram shows how the total variance in a set of scores can be partitioned into within-group and between-group components.

The mean in this case is the *grand mean* (i.e., the mean of all the scores irrespective of group) and is denoted $\overline{\overline{X}}$ (read *X double bar*).

Figure 11.5 shows that the difference between a score and the grand mean is composed of the difference between the score and its group mean plus the difference between the group mean and the grand mean. The equation is as follows:

$$(X - \overline{\overline{X}}) = (X - \overline{X}) + (\overline{X} - \overline{\overline{X}})$$

Equation 11.5

Squaring the left-hand side of Equation 11.5 and summing the deviations for all scores results in the numerator of Equation 11.4. Doing the same to the right-hand side of Equation 11.5 preserves equality and results in the following:

$$\sum (X - \overline{\overline{X}})^2 = \sum [(X - \overline{X}) + (\overline{X} - \overline{\overline{X}})]^2$$

Equation 11.6

Completing the algebraic operations results in the following:

$$\sum (X - \overline{\overline{X}})^2 = \sum (X - \overline{X})^2 + \sum n(\overline{X} - \overline{\overline{X}})^2$$

Equation 11.7

where *n* is the number of people per group. Equation 11.7 shows that total variation of scores equals variation of scores around their means (within-group variation) plus variation of group means around the grand mean (between-group variation).

ANOVA Terminology

One needs to understand the special terminology of ANOVA to interpret the results, especially when reading computer printouts or journal articles. The terminology begins with re-examination of the generic variance equation

$$s^2 = \frac{S(X - \overline{X})^2}{N - 1}$$ Equation 11.8

Variance comprises two terms. In the numerator is the sum of the squared deviations of scores about the mean. In ANOVA terminology this is called the *sum of squares* (SS). The denominator contains a figure that reflects the number of scores that composes the sum of squares. This is referred to as *degrees of freedom* (*df*). Equation 11.8 is used to compute an average sum of squares, which is referred to as a *mean square* (MS). In ANOVA nomenclature, the expression *mean square* is the term for *variance*.

Rewriting Equation 11.8 with the new terminology gives the following:

$$MS = \frac{SS}{df}$$ Equation 11.9

which can be computed for within-group (wg) and between-group (bg) variance as follows:

$$MS_{wg} = \frac{SS_{wg}}{df_{wg}}$$ Equation 11.10

and

$$MS_{bg} = \frac{SS_{bg}}{df_{bg}}$$ Equation 11.11

Computation of MS_{total} gives the following result:

$$MS_{total} = \frac{SS_{total}}{df_{total}}$$ Equation 11.12

which is the total variance of the scores as a whole.

F Ratio and the Null Hypothesis

The variance of scores within a group and between groups is measured with MS_{wg} and MS_{bg}, respectively. MS_{wg} is a measure of error variation. It accounts for only variance in scores that is due to individual differences and other random influences. MS_{bg}, however, measures variance in scores that is due to treatment effects, if present.

What happens if the null hypothesis is true? In other words, what do MS_{wg} and MS_{bg} measure when no treatment effects are present? With respect to the example, what would we expect these two terms to reflect if the four therapeutic methods were equal in efficacy in controlling prison violence?

In the absence of treatment effects, MS_{wg} continues to assess error variance because this type of variation exists irrespective of anything else. Error variance is intrinsic to all data. Without treatment effects, however, MS_{bg} does not reflect treatment variance, because none is present. In such a case, MS_{bg} simply reflects the same thing as MS_{wg}, that is, error variance. This is because error variance coexists with treatment variance, and the former is present even when the latter is not.

We can create a statistical index that helps test for the presence of treatment effects in the hypothesis testing process. This is called the F ratio (named in honor of Sir Ronald Fisher) and is formed by dividing MS_{bg} by MS_{wg}, as follows:

$$F = \frac{MS_{bg}}{MS_{wg}} \qquad \text{Equation 11.13}$$

When H_0 is true, meaning that treatment effects are not present, MS_{bg} and MS_{wg} both measure error variance, and we expect the F ratio to equal 1.00.[10] When H_0 is false, meaning that treatment effects are present to some degree, MS_{bg} increases but MS_{wg} remains unaffected. Here, the F ratio is larger than 1.00 and at some point is large enough to allow rejection of the null hypothesis.

ANOVA Equations

Now that we have discussed the main concepts of ANOVA, we are ready to undertake the computational procedures. Table 11.3 shows the compliant behavior scores for the inmates who were exposed to the four therapeutic methods. The table also provides the means and standard deviations of the scores. The pattern of the means is similar to that shown in Figure 11.4.

Table 11.4 presents the equations for calculating the sum of squares and degrees of freedom for ANOVA. These are *computational* formulas and do not easily reveal the underlying concepts of between-group and within-group variation. These equations may seem formidable, but they are not difficult to work with once all the terms are understood.

One needs to appreciate the following expressions to compute the formulas in Table 11.4. The following term

$$\sum \left(\sum_j x_j^2 \right)$$

indicates that one computes the sum of the squared scores within a group. The sums are computed for each group and then added together. The j subscript indi-

Table 11.3   Compliant Behavior Scores from 25 Inmates Who Experienced One of Four Therapeutic Methods for Controlling Prison Violence

	Therapeutic Method			
	Hypnosis	*Relaxation*	*Social Learning*	*Dispute Resolution*
	21	22	20	27
	22	24	21	28
	24	25	19	30
	23	24	20	32
	20	22	20	30
		24		29
		25		31
				31
Mean	22.000	23.714	20.000	29.750
SD	1.581	1.254	0.707	1.669
N	5	7	5	8

SD, standard deviation.

Table 11.4   Equations Used to Compute the Sums of Squares and Degrees of Freedom for a One-way Analysis of Variance

Source of Variation	Sum of Squares (SS)	Degrees of Freedom (df)	Variation Measured with Term
Total	$\sum\left(\sum x_j^2\right) - \dfrac{T^2}{N}$	$N - 1$	Total
Between groups	$\sum\left(\dfrac{T_j^2}{N_j}\right) - \dfrac{T^2}{N}$	$K - 1$	Treatment and error
Within groups	$\sum\left(\sum x_j^2\right) - \sum\left(\dfrac{T_j^2}{N_j}\right)$	$N - K$	Error only

cates that an operation is conducted for a group—$j = 1$ for the first group, $j = 2$ for the second group, and so on until $j = K$, the total number of groups. The term T^2 stands for the total (i.e., sum) of all scores, quantity squared. N is the total number of scores. The following term:

$$\sum\left(\frac{T_j^2}{N_j}\right)$$

represents the total (i.e., sum) of scores within a group, quantity squared, which is divided by the number of scores in that group. The quotients are formed for each group and then added together.

Computing ANOVA

To use the ANOVA equations, information needs to be computed from each group of scores. Table 11.5 shows that one needs to obtain the following:

Table 11.5   Computing Terms for Analysis of Variance

	Therapeutic Method				
	Hypnosis	Relaxation	Social Learning	Dispute Resolution	Total
	21	22	20	27	
	22	24	21	28	
	24	25	19	30	
	23	24	20	32	
	20	22	20	30	
		24		29	
		25		31	
				31	
T_j	110	166	100	238	$614 \rightarrow T$
N_j	5	7	5	8	$25 \rightarrow N$
$\dfrac{T_j^2}{N_j}$	2,420.000	3,936.571	2,000	7,080.500	$15,437.071 \rightarrow \sum\left(\dfrac{T_j^2}{N_j}\right)$
$\sum X_j^2$	2,430	3,946	2,002	7,100	$15,478 \rightarrow \sum\left(\sum x_j^2\right)$

T_j, the sum of scores for each group

N_j, the number of scores for each group

$$\frac{T_j^2}{N_j}$$

ΣX_j^2, the sum of the squared scores for each group

Adding these quantities across all groups provides the terms needed to compute SS_{total}, SS_{bg}, and SS_{wg}. For SS_{total} the equation is as follows:

$$SS_{total} = \Sigma \left(\Sigma x_j^2 \right) - \frac{T^2}{N}$$

thus

$$SS_{total} = 15,478 - \frac{614^2}{25} = 398.160$$

For SS_{bg} the equation is as follows:

$$SS_{bg} = \Sigma \left(\frac{T_j^2}{N_j} \right) - \frac{T^2}{N}$$

therefore

$$SS_{bg} = 15,437.071 - \frac{614^2}{25} = 357.231$$

For SS_{wg} the equation is as follows:

$$SS_{wg} = \Sigma \left(\Sigma X_j^2 \right) - \Sigma \left(\frac{T_j^2}{N_j} \right)$$

thus

$$SS_{wg} = 15,478 - 15,437.071 = 40.929$$

The degrees of freedom are computed as follows:

$$df_{total} = N - 1 = 25 - 1 = 24$$
$$df_{bg} = K - 1 = 4 - 1 = 3$$
$$df_{wg} = N - K = 25 - 4 = 21$$

At this point, the reader should not overlook the fact that $SS_{total} = SS_{bg} + SS_{wg}$ and that $df_{total} = df_{bg} + df_{wg}$. This is consistent with the earlier description of how the total variability of scores in ANOVA is partitioned into between-group and within-group components. We now compute the between-group and within-group variances to arrive at an F ratio as follows:

$$MS_{bg} = \frac{SS_{bg}}{df_{bg}} = \frac{357.231}{3} = 119.077$$

$$MS_{wg} = \frac{SS_{wg}}{df_{wg}} = \frac{40.929}{21} = 1.949$$

Finally

$$F = \frac{MS_{bg}}{MS_{wg}} = \frac{119.077}{1.949} = 61.096$$

Table 11.6   ANOVA Summary Table

Source of Variation	SS	df	MS	F
Therapeutic method (between groups)	357.231	3	119.077	61.096
Error (within group)	40.929	21	1.949	
Total	398.160	24		

which renders a value far greater than 1.00.

All the computations can be outlined in an ANOVA summary table (Table 11.6). This type of summary is used in research journal articles, group presentations, and departmental reports, and it is often the basis for computer printouts.

ANOVA and the Steps of Hypothesis Testing

We have discussed the computation of an F ratio, but we have not shown how this fits the process of hypothesis testing. Even though the ANOVA computations are somewhat more cumbersome than those of other tests, the hypothesis testing process is the same as that presented in previous chapters.

Null and Rival Hypotheses

Like other statistical tests of significance, ANOVA involves a null and a rival hypothesis. In the example, the null hypothesis is that the four therapeutic methods do not differ in effectiveness in controlling prison violence. The rival hypothesis, however, must be inclusive because there are a number of possible outcomes. For example, dispute resolution may be better than all the methods, or it only may be better than the social learning method, and so on. Therefore, we specify the rival hypothesis simply as "not H_0" so that we do not overlook the many possible outcomes of the analysis. The two hypotheses are written in the following way:

H_0: The therapeutic methods do not differ in effectiveness in controlling prison violence, $\mu_1 = \mu_2 = \mu_3 = \mu_4$

H_1: Not H_0

Level of Significance

After choosing an α level, we need to find a critical F ratio that allows rejection of H_0. This ratio has to be greater than 1.00. Critical F ratios are contained in Table E of the Appendix.

To find a critical F value, df_{bg} and df_{wg} are needed. Table E is organized so that the degrees of freedom for the numerator (n_1) are along the top and degrees of freedom for the denominator (n_2) are along the left side. These represent df_{bg} and df_{wg}, respectively. In the example, the between-group df is 3 and the within-group df is 21. We locate *3* along the top of the table and *21* along the side. The number at the intersection of the column and row in the table headed $p = .05$ is the critical F ratio for $\alpha = .05$. If we choose the usual .05 α level, the critical F value is 3.07.

Decision Rule

By its nature, the F ratio in the context of ANOVA is a one-tailed test. This is because the numerator is expected to be equal to or larger than the denominator. We therefore write the decision rule in the following way:

If F < 3.07, do not reject H_0

If F > 3.07, reject H_0 in favor of H_1

Given that the observed F ratio is 61.096, we reject H_0 in favor of H_1 and conclude that the therapeutic methods have a differential effect in their ability to control violent prison behavior. At this point, however, it is not clear which method or methods are statistically better than others. This is explored later in this chapter.

Assumptions for Conducting ANOVA

Four basic assumptions or conditions must be met for a researcher to apply ANOVA properly to his or her data. These assumptions are essentially the same as those for Student's t test for independent samples.

First, all groups are formed by means of random selection from independent samples of individuals. Second, the groups are independent. This means that an individual is in only one group. Third, the population variances from which the groups are formed are homogeneous. In the prison violence example, this means that

$$\sigma_1^2 = \sigma_2^2 = \sigma_3^2 = \sigma_4^2$$

If this assumption is not met, computation of MS_{wg} does not provide an accurate estimate of the variability of scores within the respective groups.[11]

The fourth assumption is that the population distribution of the variable under study is normal in form. Although one cannot fashion a normal distribution with a finite sample of scores, a rough bell-shaped distribution should be visible if enough scores are present. The accuracy of the F ratio depends on this assumption's being met.

Exercise 11–3   Calculating ANOVA

Fifteen volunteers have been randomly assigned to one of three methods of training patrol officers on how to handle domestic violence. Officers are taught by way of (1) written case scenarios, (2) actual incidents of domestic violence captured on videotape, or (3) interaction with actors who stage incidents of domestic violence.

After the programs are completed, the officers are tested and scored on their skills. The data are as follows:

	Score with Written Scenarios	Score with Videotaped Incidents	Score with Actors
	7	3	12
	5	1	11
	3	2	10
	7	2	8
	8		9
			14
Mean	6.000	2.000	10.667
SD	2.000	0.816	2.160

SD, standard deviation.

Conduct an ANOVA that tests the null hypothesis that the three program formats do not differentially affect officers' skills in handling incidents of domestic violence. Use a .05 level of significance and place your results in an ANOVA summary table.

After ANOVA: Comparing Group Means

ANOVA with the compliant behavior test data leads to the conclusion that the therapeutic methods probably influence inmates differently.[12] We are, however, left with a nagging question. Which therapeutic method or methods are statistically better than others?

A significant F ratio is a statistical alerting device, it tells the data analyst that there is an effect worthy of further investigation. By itself, the F ratio does not provide enough information for one to see why H_0 was rejected. Group means must be compared in some way to assess that level of detail.

It may appear that comparison of individual group means brings us back to the problems we faced at the beginning of the chapter. Not really. ANOVA is used to compare all groups simultaneously and thus limits the probability of a Type I error at α, which is usually 5 percent. In addition, comparisons of group means in light of a significant ANOVA can be protected from the unrestrained accumulation of Type I error that plagues multiple t tests.

Over the years, statisticians have developed procedures that allow all pairwise comparisons of means if ANOVA has been conducted first. These procedures are called *post hoc* or *a posteriori* tests. As the names imply, these tests are intended to be used *after* ANOVA that has reached statistical significance. If an ANOVA result is not significant, a post hoc test is unnecessary and should not be performed. There are a number of post hoc tests (Diekhoff 1992; Hays 1994; Winer 1971), but we present one that has general utility. It is called the *Tukey honestly significant difference* (HSD) test and bears the name of its developer, John W. Tukey. The main advantage of this test is that it limits the probability of Type I error at α, no matter how many group means are compared.

The HSD test employs what is known as the *studentized range statistic*, commonly called q. A description of the q statistic is beyond the scope of this text, but suffice it to say that it provides information about the maximum difference (i.e., range) of a group of means drawn from a common population. It is a critical value similar to Student's t.

The first step in conducting the HSD test is to compute the absolute difference of all pairs of means. Table 11.7 displays a convenient format for this computation and shows the absolute differences for the means of the four groups in the example. The HSD is found with Equation 11.14.

$$HSD = q(\alpha, df_{wg}, k) \sqrt{\frac{MS_{wg}}{n}} \qquad \text{Equation 11.14}$$

To compute the HSD, one needs to find a q value. The equation shows that q is linked to three parameters: α level; the df_{wg} from the preceding ANOVA; and k, the number of groups being compared. Table F in the Appendix provides values of q.

To locate the q value, find df_{wg} in the column labeled *Error df*. The df_{wg} in the example is 21, but that number does not exist in the table. We therefore use the error df of 20 because it is the closest value in the table that is less than 21.[13] We then select the line of figures where $\alpha = .05$ (in this table x rather than α is used) because that is the α level for the ANOVA ($\alpha = .01$ is selected if we want to be

Table 11.7   All Pairwise Mean Differences for Compliance Behavior Scores of 25 Inmates Treated with One of Four Therapeutic Methods of Controlling Prison Violence

	Hypnosis	*Relaxation*	*Social Learning*	*Dispute Resolution*
Hypnosis	0.000			
Relaxation	1.714	0.000		
Social learning	2.000	3.714*	0.000	
Dispute resolution	7.750*	6.036*	9.750*	0.000

*Exceeds honestly significant difference (HSD).

more conservative). The required q value is in the column where $k = 4$ (in this table r rather than k is used) because four means are being compared. The q value is 3.96.

The HSD also requires n, the number of individuals per group. In the example, however, n must be an average because there are not an equal number of prisoners in each group. In such cases, statisticians often recommend that one compute the *harmonic mean of the group sizes* (Hays 1994).

Unlike the arithmetic mean, which has been used throughout this text, the harmonic mean ($\overline{X}_h$) is relatively insensitive to large differences in group sizes (this is not a problem with the current example). The harmonic mean is computed in the following way:

$$\overline{X}_h = \frac{N}{\dfrac{1}{X_1} + \dfrac{1}{X_2} + \dfrac{1}{X_3} + \cdots + \dfrac{1}{X_N}} \qquad \text{Equation 11.15}$$

For the example, n, the harmonic mean of group sizes, is

$$n = \overline{X}_h = \frac{4}{\dfrac{1}{5} + \dfrac{1}{7} + \dfrac{1}{5} + \dfrac{1}{8}} = 5.989$$

Importing the MS_{wg} from the ANOVA summary table, the HSD is found as follows:

$$HSD = 3.96\left(\sqrt{\frac{1.949}{5.989}}\right) = 2.259$$

which is the value that mean differences must reach or exceed to be considered statistically significant. Four of the six mean differences in Table 11.7 exceed the HSD and are marked with an asterisk. The compliant behavior scores of inmates treated with dispute resolution were statistically better than those of inmates treated with all the other methods. We also see a statistically significant difference in the scores of inmates treated with relaxation and social learning methods (the former did slightly better). The overall impression, however, is that conflict resolution seems to have an edge over the other methods for controlling violent prison behavior and probably will be the therapeutic method chosen for subsequent use.

If multiple t tests were conducted to make all pairwise comparisons of the means, we would find the same results except that the comparison between hypnosis and social learning also would be statistically significant. In light of the

HSD procedure, we can see that multiple t tests would render a false-positive finding. It is for this reason that post hoc procedures are used.

Exercise 11–4   Post Hoc Testing

Using the data in Exercise 11–3, conduct a Tukey HSD test to determine which pairs of group means differ from each other.

Computing the Amount of Explained Variance

So far we have seen that the overall ANOVA and some of the pairwise comparisons of group means reach statistical significance. We should not lose sight of the fact, however, that statistical significance is expressed as a *probability* of having made a Type I error. If, for example, the computed F ratio is 3.07 (which is the critical value), we reject H_0 and conclude that the results are significant at the .05 level. Because the computed F ratio is 61.096, we can say that the results are significant beyond the .05 level, meaning that the probability of having made a Type I error is less than .05.

Although important, statistical significance does not mean that the results are of practical use. We can, for example, encounter a situation in which the F ratio is statistically significant, but the mean compliant behavior scores of the four groups do not differ by more than one or two points. Despite the statistical significance, such results would give Warden Crowley essentially no option for choosing the best therapeutic method for controlling prison violence.

A simple index for evaluating the practical significance of one's results is called η^2 (lower case Greek eta squared). It is easily computed from information provided in the ANOVA summary table. Equation 11.16 shows that η^2 is a quotient of the between-group sum of squares and the total sum of squares.

$$\eta^2 = \frac{SS_{bg}}{SS_{total}}$$

Equation 11.16

The prison violence example shows the following:

$$\eta^2 = \frac{357.231}{398.160} = 0.897$$

which means that 89.7 percent of the variance in compliant behavior scores is attributable to the four therapeutic methods under evaluation.[14] In other words, there is a strong relationship between inmates' behavior scores and the therapeutic methods used in the study.

The square root of η^2 is η, which gives the correlation between compliant behavior scores and the therapeutic methods, as follows:

$$\sqrt{.897} = .947$$

This is a very high correlation and reflects the fact that inmates who were treated with conflict resolution techniques had substantially higher compliant behavior scores than inmates who were treated with the other therapeutic methods.

Exercise 11–5   Computing η^2

Using the ANOVA summary table that you constructed for Exercise 11–3, compute η^2. How much of the variance in officers' test scores is attributable to the program format?

Summary

Errors inevitably occur in the process of decision making, and statistical hypothesis testing is no exception. Even though one follows the rules of hypothesis testing perfectly, there are going to be times when H_0 is wrongly rejected or wrongly retained. When this happens, we make what are called *Type I* and *Type II errors*, respectively.

Even though both Type I and Type II errors are a matter of concern, investigators more often are concerned about the former. This is because Type I errors masquerade as important findings. The probability of making a Type I error on a single test of significance is α. However, the probability increases rapidly as a function of the number of tests one performs. As such, this becomes a serious problem when a researcher conducts a study in which multiple groups are compared.

Analysis of variance (ANOVA) is a method that allows statistical comparison of a number of groups in the context of a single test. The analysis achieves this by partitioning the *variance of scores* into within-group and between-group components. *Within-group* components reflect variability due to natural, individual differences and to other random factors. *Between-group* components reflect variability due to treatment effects, if present. If treatment effects are lacking, between-group variance is the same as within-group variance.

An *F ratio* is formed by dividing between-group variance by within-group variance. If no treatment effect exists, the ratio is expected to be 1.00. If a treatment effect is present, the ratio is expected to be greater than 1.00 and eventually reaches a value that allows rejection of H_0.

If ANOVA reaches statistical significance, a pairwise comparison of all means can be conducted with *post hoc tests*. Although there are a number of such procedures, the *Tukey HSD test* is commonly used. This is because the Tukey test holds the probability of a Type I error at α no matter how many comparisons are made.

The *practical significance* of statistical results can be assessed with η^2, which represents the percentage of variance in an outcome variable that is attributable to the groups in an ANOVA. The square root of η^2 is η and is a correlation coefficient. One should always evaluate η^2 because it adds information beyond the statistical significance of findings.

Answers to Exercises

Exercise Answer 11–1
1. Type I
2. Type II
3. Correct decision
4. Type II
5. Type I

Exercise Answer 11–2
1. $1 - (1 - .05)^5 = 1 - (.95)^5 = 1 - .774 = .226 = 22.6\%$
2. $1 - (1 - .01)^7 = 1 - (.99)^7 = 1 - .932 = .068 = 6.8\%$
3. $1 - (1 - .001)^3 = 1 - (.999)^3 = 1 - .997 = .003 = 0.3\%$
4. $1 - (1 - .05)^4 = 1 - (.95)^4 = 1 - .815 = .185 = 18.5\%$

Exercise Answer 11–3

$H_0: \mu_1 = \mu_2 = \mu_3$

$H_1:$ Not H_0

$\alpha = .05$

$df_{total} = N - 1 = 15 - 1 = 14$

$df_{bg} = K - 1 = 3 - 1 = 2$

$df_{wg} = N - K = 15 - 3 = 12$

Decision rule:

If $F < 3.88$, do not reject H_0

If $F \geq 3.88$, reject H_0 in favor of H_1

Conclusion: Reject H_0 in favor of H_1

	Program Format			
	Writtten Scenarios	Videotaped Incidents	Live Actors	Total
	7	3	12	
	5	1	11	
	3	2	10	
	7	2	8	
	8		9	
			14	
T_j	30	8	64	$102 \rightarrow T$
N_j	5	4	6	$15 \rightarrow N$
$\dfrac{T_j^2}{N_j}$	180	16	682.667	$878.667 \rightarrow \Sigma\left(\dfrac{T_j^2}{N_j}\right)$
ΣX_j^2	196	18	706	$920 \rightarrow \Sigma\left(\Sigma x_j^2\right)$

$$SS_{total} = 920 - \frac{102^2}{15} = 226.400$$

$$SS_{bg} = 878.667 - \frac{102^2}{15} = 185.067$$

$$SS_{wg} = 920 - 878.667 = 41.333$$

$$MS_{bg} = \frac{185.067}{2} = 92.534$$

$$MS_{wg} = \frac{41.333}{12} = 3.444$$

$$F = \frac{92.534}{3.444} = 26.868$$

ANOVA Summary Table

Source of Variation	SS	df	MS	F
Program format (between groups)	185.067	2	92.534	26.868
Error (within groups)	41.333	12	3.444	
Total	226.400	14		

Conclusion: Reject H_0 in favor of H_1

Exercise Answer 11–4

$\alpha = .05$

$df_{wg} = 12$

$K = 3$

From Table F in the Appendix, $q = 3.77$

$$n = \overline{X}_h = \frac{3}{\frac{1}{5} + \frac{1}{4} + \frac{1}{6}} = 4.865$$

$$HSD = 3.77 \sqrt{\frac{3.444}{4.865}} = 3.172$$

All Pairwise Mean Differences

	Written Scenarios	Videotaped Incidents	Live Actors
Written scenarios	0.000		
Videotaped incidents	4.000*	0.000	
Live actors	4.667*	8.667*	0.000

Exercise Answer 11–5

$$\eta^2 = \frac{185.067}{226.400} = 0.817$$

This means that 81.7 percent of the variance in officers' test scores is attributable to program format.

Computer Applications for Selected Exercises

Exercise Answer 11–3   *Calculating ANOVA*

Although the data appear to be in summary form, there is actually one unique data value per cell in the table. There are 15 numbers in the table, each representing one officer's score. To construct the data set, you need the following: a column for the officer number so you can keep track of the rows; a column for the score the officer received; and a column to indicate which training method the officer used. *SPSS for Windows* calculates the summary data displayed at the bottom of the exercise, so you do not have to enter these data.

The officers are assigned to groups randomly when they arrive for training. The data in Figure 11.6 are sorted by officer number, instead of by group, so the table looks messy. Data in the real world, outside of textbooks, often start out looking like this.

	officer#	method	skill	var
1	1	Live Actor	10	
2	2	Videotaped Incident	2	
3	3	Live Actor	12	
4	4	Written Scenario	7	
5	5	Live Actor	11	
6	6	Live Actor	9	
7	7	Written Scenario	8	
8	8	Written Scenario	7	
9	9	Videotaped Incident	1	
10	10	Written Scenario	5	
11	11	Videotaped Incident	2	
12	12	Written Scenario	3	
13	13	Live Actor	8	
14	14	Videotaped Incident	3	
15	15	Live Actor	14	

Newdata — 15:skill — 14

Figure 11.6

Because officer numbers are not given in the example, your data set may look different. However, your method and skill value pairs should still be identical to the ones in Figure 11.6.

Because there is only have one factor in this analysis (training method) you can use one-way ANOVA. This is found in Compare Means in the Statistics menu (Figure 11.7).

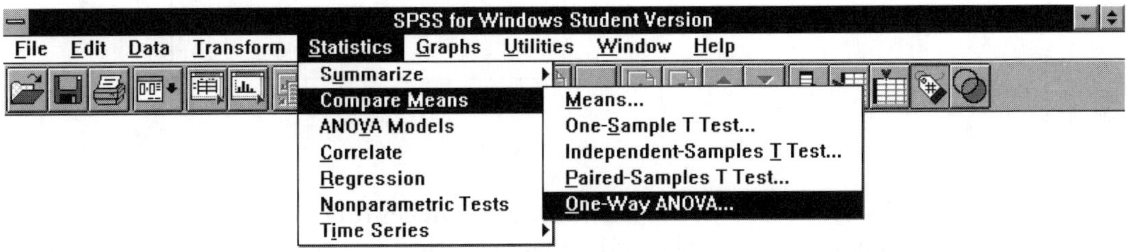

SPSS for Windows Student Version

File   Edit   Data   Transform   **Statistics**   Graphs   Utilities   Window   Help

Summarize
Compare Means   Means...
ANOVA Models   One-Sample T Test...
Correlate   Independent-Samples T Test...
Regression   Paired-Samples T Test...
Nonparametric Tests   One-Way ANOVA...
Time Series

Figure 11.7

The `Dependent List:` variable in this analysis is `skill` score. The `Factor` is training `method`. When you move the method variable into the Factor area of the dialog box, two question marks appear in parentheses after the variable name (Figure 11.8).

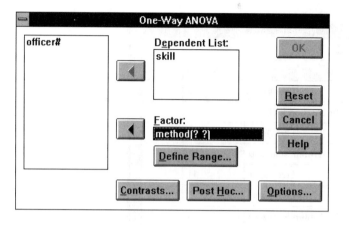

Figure 11.8

You have to specify which levels of the factor you want to analyze. There were three training methods, and they were coded *1*, *2*, and *3* in the Data Editor. You can verify that by right-clicking on the method variable. An information box appears below and to the right of the variable name (Figure 11.9). Click on the underscored arrow in this box. A menu of the defined values drops down (Figure 11.9). You can use this list to verify the upper and lower bounds of the defined factor range. In this case, the range limits are *1* and *3*.

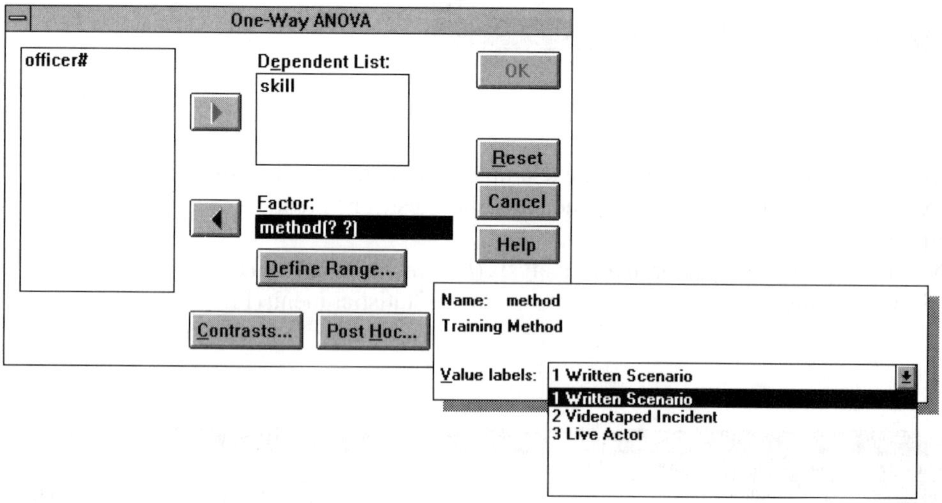

Figure 11.9

Choose `Define Range` and fill in these values (Figure 11.10).

Choose `Continue` and verify that the correct values appear after `method` (Figure 11.11).

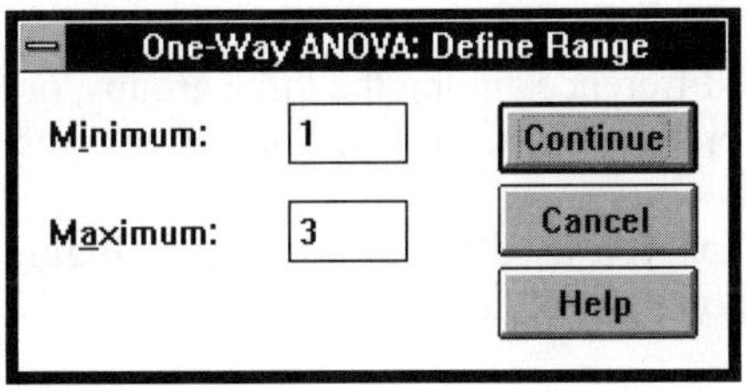

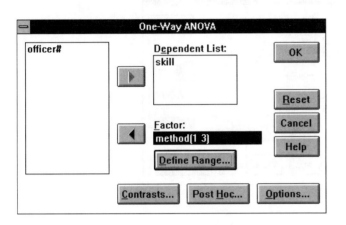

Figure 11.10

Figure 11.11

Choose OK to run the analysis.
The output is the ANOVA table (Figure 11.12).

```
- - - - - O N E W A Y - - - - -


      Variable  SKILL      Skill Score
   By Variable  METHOD     Training Method

                           Analysis of Variance


                              Sum of        Mean            F      F
          Source       D.F.  Squares       Squares       Ratio  Prob.

Between Groups          2    185.0667      92.5333      26.8645  .0000
Within Groups          12     41.3333       3.4444
Total                  14    226.4000
```

Figure 11.12

The F probability is .0000. This means that a difference this great among the three groups could have occurred by chance less often than 5 times in 10,000. There is a statistically significant difference between the three groups on skills in handling incidents of domestic violence.

Exercise Answer 11–4 Post Hoc Testing

In Exercise 11–3, you found a significant difference among the three groups, but you did not determine which groups differed from each other. You can use post hoc tests to investigate those differences.

Return to the One-Way ANOVA dialog box you used in Exercise 11–3 (Figure 11.13). You can use the dialog recall icon on the toolbar or go through the Statistics menu.

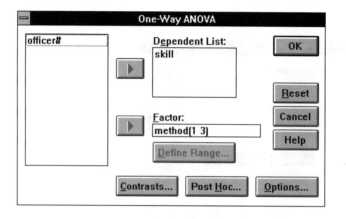

Figure 11.13

Choose Post Hoc . . . in the bottom center of the dialog box. Check the box next to the Tukey HSD Test (Figure 11.14).

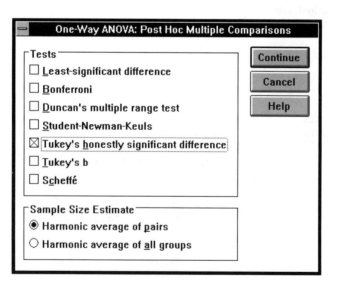

Figure 11.14

Choose Continue to return to the main one-way ANOVA dialog box.

To facilitate interpretation of the output, you need to change one more setting before you run the procedure. Choose Options in the lower right corner of the dialog box. Check the Display labels box in the middle of this dialog box (Figure 11.15).

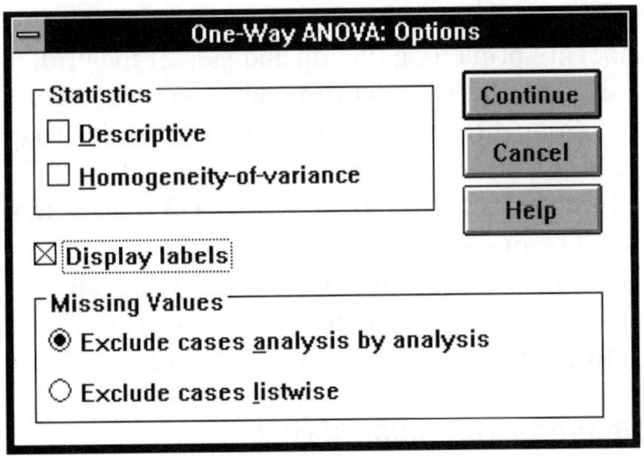

```
┌──────────────────────────────────────────────────┐
│ ▬        One-Way ANOVA: Options                    │
├──────────────────────────────────────────────────┤
│ ┌─Statistics──────────────────┐   ┌──────────┐    │
│ │ ☐ Descriptive               │   │ Continue │    │
│ │ ☐ Homogeneity-of-variance   │   └──────────┘    │
│ │                             │   ┌──────────┐    │
│ └─────────────────────────────┘   │  Cancel  │    │
│                                    └──────────┘    │
│ ☒ Display labels                   ┌──────────┐    │
│ ┌─Missing Values──────────────┐    │   Help   │    │
│ │ ⦿ Exclude cases analysis by analysis            │
│ │ ○ Exclude cases listwise    │                   │
│ └─────────────────────────────┘                   │
└──────────────────────────────────────────────────┘
```

Figure 11.15

Choose `Continue` and then `OK` in the main dialog box to run the analysis.

The output is fairly straightforward. It is divided into two parts. The top section documents the actual values used in the procedure to test for significant differences (Figure 11.16).

```
          - - - - -  O N E W A Y  - - - - -


        Variable  SKILL      Skill Score
     By Variable  METHOD     Training Method

Multiple Range Tests:  Tukey-HSD test with significance level .050

The difference between two means is significant if
   MEAN(J)-MEAN(I)  >= 1.3123 * RANGE * SQRT(1/N(I) + 1/N(J))
   with the following value(s) for RANGE: 3.77

   (*) Indicates significant differences which are shown in the lower triangle

                          V   L
                          i W i
                          d r v
                          e i e
                          o t
                          t t A
                          a e c
                          p n t
     Mean      METHOD

     2.0000    Videotap
     6.0000    Written     *
    10.6667    Live Act    *  *
```

Figure 11.16

The `Mean` list shows that videotape gave the lowest skill score with a mean of 2.0. Exposure to written scenarios gave a mean score of 6.0. Exposure to actors gave the best results with a mean skill score on the final test of 10.67.

The grid at the bottom of the output is where the main part of the interpretation is done. The rows of the grid are listed in descending mean order. Each asterisk

(*) in the grid shows where two groups differ at the .05 level or better. The first eight characters of each value label are printed on the top and side of the grid.

In the `Videotap` column, there is an asterisk next to both `Written` and `Live Act`. This means that the videotape group differed from the written scenario group and the exposure to actors group.

In the `Written` column, there is an asterisk next to `Live Act`. This means that the written scenarios group differed from the group exposed to actors.

There are no asterisks in the `Live Act` column. The analysis has already accounted for all possible combinations of the three categories. Thus, each method is significantly different from the other two.

Exercise Answer 11–5   Computing Eta Squared (η²)

SPSS calculates η and η² in the Means procedure. Go to the Statistics menu and choose `Compare Means`. The `Means . . .` procedure is the first choice (Figure 11.17).

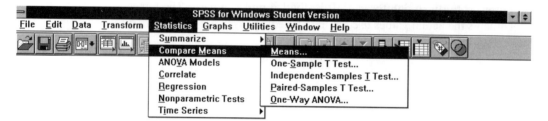

Figure 11.17

The dependent variable is `skill` score. The independent variable is training `method` (Figure 11.18).

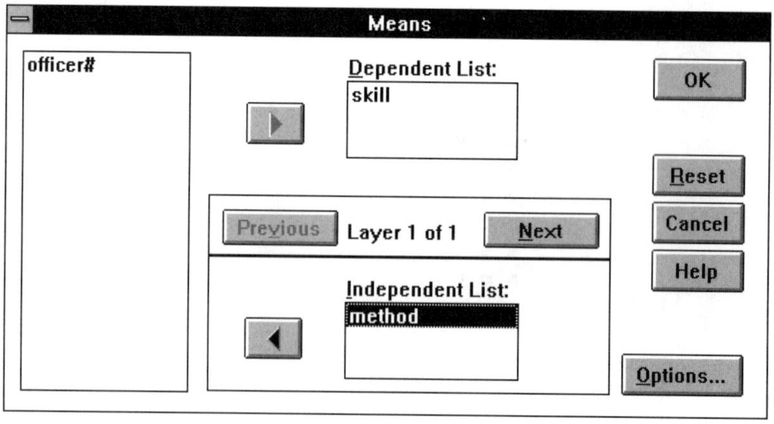

Figure 11.18

Choose `Options` in the lower right-hand corner of the dialog box to request the η² statistic. In the `Statistics for First Layer` section in the lower-right corner of the Options dialog box, check `ANOVA table and eta` (Figure 11.19).

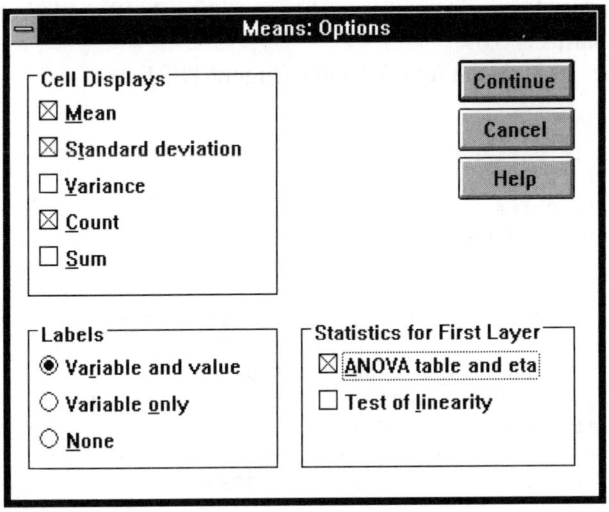

```
┌─────────────────────────────────────────────────────────┐
│ ─             Means: Options                 .            │
├─────────────────────────────────────────────────────────┤
│ ┌─Cell Displays──────────────┐    ┌──────────────┐       │
│ │ ☒ Mean                     │    │  Continue    │       │
│ │ ☒ Standard deviation       │    └──────────────┘       │
│ │ ☐ Variance                 │    ┌──────────────┐       │
│ │ ☒ Count                    │    │   Cancel     │       │
│ │ ☐ Sum                      │    └──────────────┘       │
│ │                            │    ┌──────────────┐       │
│ │                            │    │    Help      │       │
│ └────────────────────────────┘    └──────────────┘       │
│ ┌─Labels──────────────┐ ┌─Statistics for First Layer──┐  │
│ │ ● Variable and value│ │ ☒ ANOVA table and eta       │  │
│ │ ○ Variable only     │ │ ☐ Test of linearity         │  │
│ │ ○ None              │ │                             │  │
│ └─────────────────────┘ └─────────────────────────────┘  │
└─────────────────────────────────────────────────────────┘
```

Figure 11.19

You may leave the other choices in their default settings or you may uncheck them for this analysis. Choose Continue and then OK in the main Means dialog box to run the analysis.

The output is presented in two sections. The mean subpopulation analysis comes first (Figure 11.20).

```
              - - Description of Subpopulations - -

Summaries of      SKILL        Skill Score
By levels of      METHOD       Training Method


Variable      Value  Label                    Mean     Std Dev   Cases

For Entire Population                         6.8000    4.0214     15

METHOD            1   Written Scenario        6.0000    2.0000      5
METHOD            2   Videotaped Incident     2.0000     .8165      4
METHOD            3   Live Actor             10.6667    2.1602      6

   Total Cases = 15
```

Figure 11.20

This output shows the mean, standard deviation, and number of valid cases for all three groups as a whole (for the entire population). The mean skill score for the entire population is 6.8. What other *SPSS* procedures that you have used provide this information?

The dependent variable, skill score, is broken down into categories based on levels of the independent variable, training method. The group means and statistics are displayed in the numeric order of the codes used to represent the categories in the Data Editor. You used *1* for written scenario, so it is listed as the first training method in this table. The mean skill score for correctional officers being trained with written scenarios is 6.0.

The second part of the output is the ANOVA table (Figure 11.21).

```
              - - Analysis of Variance - -

Dependent Variable   SKILL      Skill Score
        By levels of   METHOD     Training Method


      Value  Label                    Mean    Std Dev  Sum of Sq   Cases

         1  Written Scenario         6.0000    2.0000    16.0000      5
         2  Videotaped Incident      2.0000     .8165     2.0000      4
         3  Live Actor              10.6667    2.1602    23.3333      6
                                    ---------------------------------------
Within Groups Total                  6.8000    1.8559    41.3333     15


                      Sum of                    Mean
Source                Squares       d.f.        Square         F        Sig.

Between Groups        185.0667        2         92.5333     26.8645    .0000

Within Groups          41.3333       12          3.4444

                Eta =   .9041      Eta Squared =   .8174
```

Figure 11.21

The means and standard deviations match those in the group analysis. This section also shows the sums of squares and valid cases used to obtain the between-group and within-group totals.

Eta squared (last line of the output) is the ratio of the between-group sum of squares to the total sum of squares. Sum of squares is the sum of between-group and within-group sums of squares. The η^2 formula is as follows:

Eta squared = (Between-group sum of squares) ÷ (Between-group sum of squares + Within-group sum of squares)

Eta squared is 0.8174 in this example. Variance in the independent variable accounts for the proportion of the total variance in the dependent variable. This means that roughly 82 percent of the variance in skill score is explained by training method.

Notes

1. Juries make decisions based on the evidence that is presented in a court of law. The judicial system recognizes that decision error can occur and prefers to set a guilty person free than to convict someone who is innocent. That is one of the reasons why a defendant is considered innocent until proved guilty beyond a reasonable doubt.

2. We could consider detectives from anywhere, but the size of cities like Chicago or New York gives numbers of detectives that make this hypothetical example plausible.

3. As discussed in chapter 10, a sampling distribution is constructed with summary statistics rather than individual scores. In the case of Figure 11.1, a very large number of

equally sized samples are drawn (with replacement) from each population and the sample means are computed. The frequency (normal) distributions at the bottom of the figure are produced with the sample means. Readers are encouraged to review the section on sampling distributions in chapter 10.

4. The degree of overlap in two sampling distributions is related to the variation (i.e., the standard error) of the sample means as well as the magnitude of the difference between population means. Given two populations, sampling distributions can have a great deal of overlap, whereas others can have only a little.

5. We must not only follow the conventions of hypothesis testing but also be sure that we meet the assumptions of the statistical tests we are using.

6. This example follows the same steps and uses the same equation as the example that is in Table 10.2.

7. This does not lessen concern about Type II errors. It certainly is not efficient to allocate time, money, and personnel to a research project that produces false-negative findings. From a philosophical point of view, however, scientists are more concerned about Type I errors.

8. With the use of Equation 11.3, it is assumed that all the statistical tests are independent. When pairwise comparisons are made among a set of group means, the tests are not all independent because a particular group mean is used in more than one test. In such cases, the probability of making a Type I error is actually higher than that computed with Equation 11.3.

9. We could compute the total standard deviation of the scores, but taking the square root is an unnecessary step. This is why we have analysis of variance rather than analysis of standard deviation.

10. Technically speaking, MS_{wg} and MS_{bg} are both estimates of error variance when H_0 is false. As such, the F ratio does not necessarily equal 1.00.

11. This assumption does not mean that the sample variances have to be equal, although they should be fairly close.

12. We say that the instructional methods *probably* influence trainees differently. The significance of the F ratio does not guarantee the falsehood of the null hypothesis. Even though it is not likely, a Type I error may have been made. It is for this reason that we do not use definitive terms.

13. When the exact error *df* is not contained in Table F, it is customary to use a value that is close to but less than the exact value. This is a conservative procedure. It renders an HSD that is slightly higher than that obtained if the error *df* in Table F was greater than that in the ANOVA.

14. Values of η^2 do not usually reach such a high level with real data. The statistical analyst has to determine the value of η^2 that is considered important or meaningful given the nature of the investigation.

References

Diekoff, G. 1992. *Statistics for the Social and Behavioral Sciences: Univariate, Bivariate, Multivariate*. Dubuque: Wm. C. Brown.

Hays, W. L. 1995. *Statistics*. 5th ed. Fort Worth: Harcourt, Brace College.

Winer, B. J. 1971. *Statistical Principles in Experimental Design*. 2d ed. New York: McGraw-Hill.

Appendices

TABLE A. PROPORTIONS OF AREA UNDER THE STANDARD NORMAL CURVE

z			z			z		
0.00	.0000	.5000	0.55	.2088	.2912	1.10	.3643	.1357
0.01	.0040	.4960	0.56	.2123	.2877	1.11	.3665	.1335
0.02	.0080	.4920	0.57	.2157	.2843	1.12	.3686	.1314
0.03	.0120	.4880	0.58	.2190	.2810	1.13	.3708	.1292
0.04	.0160	.4840	0.59	.2224	.2776	1.14	.3729	.1271
0.05	.0199	.4801	0.60	.2257	.2743	1.15	.3749	.1251
0.06	.0239	.4761	0.61	.2291	.2709	1.16	.3770	.1230
0.07	.0279	.4721	0.62	.2324	.2676	1.17	.3790	.1210
0.08	.0319	.4681	0.63	.2357	.2643	1.18	.3810	.1190
0.09	.0359	.4641	0.64	.2389	.2611	1.19	.3830	.1170
0.10	.0398	.4602	0.65	.2422	.2578	1.20	.3849	.1151
0.11	.0438	.4562	0.66	.2454	.2546	1.21	.3869	.1131
0.12	.0478	.4522	0.67	.2486	.2514	1.22	.3888	.1112
0.13	.0517	.4483	0.68	.2517	.2483	1.23	.3907	.1093
0.14	.0557	.4443	0.69	.2549	.2451	1.24	.3925	.1075
0.15	.0596	.4404	0.70	.2580	.2420	1.25	.3944	.1056
0.16	.0636	.4364	0.71	.2611	.2389	1.26	.3962	.1038
0.17	.0675	.4325	0.72	.2642	.2358	1.27	.3980	.1020
0.18	.0714	.4286	0.73	.2673	.2327	1.28	.3997	.1003
0.19	.0753	.4247	0.74	.2704	.2296	1.29	.4015	.0985
0.20	.0793	.4207	0.75	.2734	.2266	1.30	.4032	.0968
0.21	.0832	.4168	0.76	.2764	.2236	1.31	.4049	.0951
0.22	.0871	.4129	0.77	.2794	.2206	1.32	.4066	.0934
0.23	.0910	.4090	0.78	.2823	.2177	1.33	.4082	.0918
0.24	.0948	.4052	0.79	.2852	.2148	1.34	.4099	.0901
0.25	.0987	.4013	0.80	.2881	.2119	1.35	.4115	.0885
0.26	.1026	.3974	0.81	.2910	.2090	1.36	.4131	.0869
0.27	.1064	.3936	0.82	.2939	.2061	1.37	.4147	.0853
0.28	.1103	.3897	0.83	.2967	.2033	1.38	.4162	.0838
0.29	.1141	.3859	0.84	.2995	.2005	1.39	.4177	.0823
0.30	.1179	.3821	0.85	.3023	.1977	1.40	.4192	.0808
0.31	.1217	.3783	0.86	.3051	.1949	1.41	.4207	.0793
0.32	.1255	.3745	0.87	.3078	.1922	1.42	.4222	.0778
0.33	.1293	.3707	0.88	.3106	.1894	1.43	.4236	.0764
0.34	.1331	.3669	0.89	.3133	.1867	1.44	.4251	.0749
0.35	.1368	.3632	0.90	.3159	.1841	1.45	.4265	.0735
0.36	.1406	.3594	0.91	.3186	.1814	1.46	.4279	.0721
0.37	.1443	.3557	0.92	.3212	.1788	1.47	.4292	.0708
0.38	.1480	.3520	0.93	.3238	.1762	1.48	.4306	.0694
0.39	.1517	.3483	0.94	.3264	.1736	1.49	.4319	.0681
0.40	.1554	.3446	0.95	.3289	.1711	1.50	.4332	.0668
0.41	.1591	.3409	0.96	.3315	.1685	1.51	.4345	.0655
0.42	.1628	.3372	0.97	.3340	.1660	1.52	.4357	.0643
0.43	.1664	.3336	0.98	.3365	.1635	1.53	.4370	.0630
0.44	.1700	.3300	0.99	.3389	.1611	1.54	.4382	.0618
0.45	.1736	.3264	1.00	.3413	.1587	1.55	.4394	.0606
0.46	.1772	.3228	1.01	.3438	.1562	1.56	.4406	.0594
0.47	.1808	.3192	1.02	.3461	.1539	1.57	.4418	.0582
0.48	.1844	.3156	1.03	.3485	.1515	1.58	.4429	.0571
0.49	.1879	.3121	1.04	.3508	.1492	1.59	.4441	.0559
0.50	.1915	.3085	1.05	.3531	.1469	1.60	.4452	.0548
0.51	.1950	.3050	1.06	.3554	.1446	1.61	.4463	.0537
0.52	.1985	.3015	1.07	.3577	.1423	1.62	.4474	.0526
0.53	.2019	.2981	1.08	.3599	.1401	1.63	.4484	.0516
0.54	.2054	.2946	1.09	.3621	.1379	1.64	.4495	.0505

Source: P. Runyon and Audrey Haber, *Fundamentals of Behavioral Statistics*, 3rd ed., © 1976. Addison-Wesley, Reading, Massachusetts. Table A. Reprinted with permission.

TABLE A (continued)

z			z			z		
1.65	.4505	.0495	2.22	.4868	.0132	2.79	.4974	.0026
1.66	.4515	.0485	2.23	.4871	.0129	2.80	.4974	.0026
1.67	.4525	.0475	2.24	.4875	.0125	2.81	.4975	.0025
1.68	.4535	.0465	2.25	.4878	.0122	2.82	.4976	.0024
1.69	.4545	.0455	2.26	.4881	.0119	2.83	.4977	.0023
1.70	.4554	.0446	2.27	.4884	.0116	2.84	.4977	.0023
1.71	.4564	.0436	2.28	.4887	.0113	2.85	.4978	.0022
1.72	.4573	.0427	2.29	.4890	.0110	2.86	.4979	.0021
1.73	.4582	.0418	2.30	.4893	.0107	2.87	.4979	.0021
1.74	.4591	.0409	2.31	.4896	.0104	2.88	.4980	.0020
1.75	.4599	.0401	2.32	.4898	.0102	2.89	.4981	.0019
1.76	.4608	.0392	2.33	.4901	.0099	2.90	.4981	.0019
1.77	.4616	.0384	2.34	.4904	.0096	2.91	.4982	.0018
1.78	.4625	.0375	2.35	.4906	.0094	2.92	.4982	.0018
1.79	.4633	.0367	2.36	.4909	.0091	2.93	.4983	.0017
1.80	.4641	.0359	2.37	.4911	.0089	2.94	.4984	.0016
1.81	.4649	.0351	2.38	.4913	.0087	2.95	.4984	.0016
1.82	.4656	.0344	2.39	.4916	.0084	2.96	.4985	.0015
1.83	.4664	.0336	2.40	.4918	.0082	2.97	.4985	.0015
1.84	.4671	.0329	2.41	.4920	.0080	2.98	.4986	.0014
1.85	.4678	.0322	2.42	.4922	.0078	2.99	.4986	.0014
1.86	.4686	.0314	2.43	.4925	.0075	3.00	.4987	.0013
1.87	.4693	.0307	2.44	.4927	.0073	3.01	.4987	.0013
1.88	.4699	.0301	2.45	.4929	.0071	3.02	.4987	.0013
1.89	.4706	.0294	2.46	.4931	.0069	3.03	.4988	.0012
1.90	.4713	.0287	2.47	.4932	.0068	3.04	.4988	.0012
1.91	.4719	.0281	2.48	.4934	.0066	3.05	.4989	.0011
1.92	.4726	.0274	2.49	.4936	.0064	3.06	.4989	.0011
1.93	.4732	.0268	2.50	.4938	.0062	3.07	.4989	.0011
1.94	.4738	.0262	2.51	.4940	.0060	3.08	.4990	.0010
1.95	.4744	.0256	2.52	.4941	.0059	3.09	.4990	.0010
1.96	.4750	.0250	2.53	.4943	.0057	3.10	.4990	.0010
1.97	.4756	.0244	2.54	.4945	.0055	3.11	.4991	.0009
1.98	.4761	.0239	2.55	.4946	.0054	3.12	.4991	.0009
1.99	.4767	.0233	2.56	.4948	.0052	3.13	.4991	.0009
2.00	.4772	.0228	2.57	.4949	.0051	3.14	.4992	.0008
2.01	.4778	.0222	2.58	.4951	.0049	3.15	.4992	.0008
2.02	.4783	.0217	2.59	.4952	.0048	3.16	.4992	.0008
2.03	.4788	.0212	2.60	.4953	.0047	3.17	.4992	.0008
2.04	.4793	.0207	2.61	.4955	.0045	3.18	.4993	.0007
2.05	.4798	.0202	2.62	.4956	.0044	3.19	.4993	.0007
2.06	.4803	.0197	2.63	.4957	.0043	3.20	.4993	.0007
2.07	.4808	.0192	2.64	.4959	.0041	3.21	.4993	.0007
2.08	.4812	.0188	2.65	.4960	.0040	3.22	.4994	.0006
2.09	.4817	.0183	2.66	.4961	.0039	3.23	.4994	.0006
2.10	.4821	.0179	2.67	.4962	.0038	3.24	.4994	.0006
2.11	.4826	.0174	2.68	.4963	.0037	3.25	.4994	.0006
2.12	.4830	.0170	2.69	.4964	.0036	3.30	.4995	.0005
2.13	.4834	.0166	2.70	.4965	.0035	3.35	.4996	.0004
2.14	.4838	.0162	2.71	.4966	.0034	3.40	.4997	.0003
2.15	.4842	.0158	2.72	.4967	.0033	3.45	.4997	.0003
2.16	.4846	.0154	2.73	.4968	.0032	3.50	.4998	.0002
2.17	.4850	.0150	2.74	.4969	.0031	3.60	.4998	.0002
2.18	.4854	.0146	2.75	.4970	.0030	3.70	.4999	.0001
2.19	.4857	.0143	2.76	.4971	.0029	3.80	.4999	.0001
2.20	.4861	.0139	2.77	.4972	.0028	3.90	.49995	.00005
2.21	.4864	.0136	2.78	.4973	.0027	4.00	.49997	.00003

TABLE B   DISTRIBUTION OF CHI SQUARE (χ^2)

df							Probability							
	.99	.98	.95	.90	.80	.70	.50	.30	.20	.10	.05	.02	.01	.001
1	.0³157	.0³628	.00393	.0158	.0642	.148	.455	1.074	1.642	2.706	3.841	5.412	6.635	10.827
2	.0201	.0404	.103	.211	.446	.713	1.386	2.408	3.219	4.605	5.991	7.824	9.210	13.815
3	.115	.185	.352	.584	1.005	1.424	2.366	3.665	4.642	6.251	7.815	9.837	11.341	16.268
4	.297	.429	.711	1.064	1.649	2.195	3.357	4.878	5.989	7.779	9.488	11.668	13.277	18.465
5	.554	.752	1.145	1.610	2.343	3.000	4.351	6.064	7.289	9.236	11.070	13.388	15.086	20.517
6	.872	1.134	1.635	2.204	3.070	3.828	5.348	7.231	8.558	10.645	12.592	15.033	16.812	22.457
7	1.239	1.564	2.167	2.833	3.822	4.671	6.346	8.383	9.803	12.017	14.067	16.622	18.475	24.322
8	1.646	2.032	2.733	3.490	4.594	5.527	7.344	9.524	11.030	13.362	15.507	18.168	20.090	26.125
9	2.088	2.532	3.325	4.168	5.380	6.393	8.343	10.656	12.242	14.684	16.919	19.679	21.666	27.877
10	2.558	3.059	3.940	4.865	6.179	7.267	9.342	11.781	13.442	15.987	18.307	21.161	23.209	29.588
11	3.053	3.609	4.575	5.578	6.989	8.148	10.341	12.899	14.631	17.275	19.675	22.618	24.725	31.264
12	3.571	4.178	5.226	6.304	7.807	9.034	11.340	14.011	15.812	18.549	21.026	24.054	26.217	32.909
13	4.107	4.765	5.892	7.042	8.634	9.926	12.340	15.119	16.985	19.812	22.362	25.472	27.688	34.528
14	4.660	5.368	6.571	7.790	9.467	10.821	13.339	16.222	18.151	21.064	23.685	26.873	29.141	36.123
15	5.229	5.985	7.261	8.547	10.307	11.721	14.339	17.322	19.311	22.307	24.996	28.259	30.578	37.697
16	5.812	6.614	7.962	9.312	11.152	12.624	15.338	18.418	20.465	23.542	26.296	29.633	32.000	39.252
17	6.408	7.255	8.672	10.085	12.002	13.531	16.338	19.511	21.615	24.769	27.587	30.995	33.409	40.790
18	7.015	7.906	9.390	10.865	12.857	14.440	17.338	20.601	22.760	25.989	28.869	32.346	34.805	42.312
19	7.633	8.567	10.117	11.651	13.716	15.352	18.338	21.689	23.900	27.204	30.144	33.687	36.191	43.820
20	8.260	9.237	10.851	12.443	14.578	16.266	19.337	22.775	25.038	28.412	31.410	35.020	37.566	45.315
21	8.897	9.915	11.591	13.240	15.445	17.182	20.337	23.858	26.171	29.615	32.671	36.343	38.932	46.797
22	9.542	10.600	12.338	14.041	16.314	18.101	21.337	24.939	27.301	30.813	33.924	37.659	40.289	48.268
23	10.196	11.293	13.091	14.848	17.187	19.021	22.337	26.018	28.429	32.007	35.172	38.968	41.638	49.728
24	10.856	11.992	13.848	15.659	18.062	19.943	23.337	27.096	29.553	33.196	36.415	40.270	42.980	51.179
25	11.524	12.697	14.611	16.473	18.940	20.867	24.337	28.172	30.675	34.382	37.652	41.566	44.314	52.620
26	12.198	13.409	15.379	17.292	19.820	21.792	25.336	29.246	31.795	35.563	38.885	42.856	45.642	54.052
27	12.879	14.125	16.151	18.114	20.703	22.719	26.336	30.319	32.912	36.741	40.113	44.140	46.963	55.476
28	13.565	14.847	16.928	18.939	21.588	23.647	27.336	31.391	34.027	37.916	41.337	45.419	48.278	56.893
29	14.256	15.574	17.708	19.768	22.475	24.577	28.336	32.461	35.139	39.087	42.557	46.693	49.588	58.302
30	14.953	16.306	18.493	20.599	23.364	25.508	29.336	33.530	36.250	40.256	43.773	47.962	50.892	59.703

Source: Fisher & Yates; *Statistical Tables for Biological, Agricultural and Medical Research*. Published by Longman Group UK Ltd., 1974.

TABLE C   CRITICAL VALUES OF THE CORRELATION COEFFICIENT

	Level of significance for one-tailed test			
	.05	.025	.01	.005
	Level of significance for two-tailed test			
df	.10	.05	.02	.01
1	.988	.997	.9995	.9999
2	.900	.950	.980	.990
3	.805	.878	.934	.959
4	.729	.811	.882	.917
5	.669	.754	.833	.874
6	.622	.707	.789	.834
7	.582	.666	.750	.798
8	.549	.632	.716	.765
9	.521	.602	.685	.735
10	.497	.576	.658	.708
11	.476	.553	.634	.684
12	.458	.532	.612	.661
13	.441	.514	.592	.641
14	.426	.497	.574	.623
15	.412	.482	.558	.606
16	.400	.468	.542	.590
17	.389	.456	.528	.575
18	.378	.444	.516	.561
19	.369	.433	.503	.549
20	.360	.423	.492	.537
21	.352	.413	.482	.526
22	.344	.404	.472	.515
23	.337	.396	.462	.505
24	.330	.388	.453	.496
25	.323	.381	.445	.487
26	.317	.374	.437	.479
27	.311	.367	.430	.471
28	.306	.361	.423	.463
29	.301	.355	.416	.456
30	.296	.349	.409	.449
35	.275	.325	.381	.418
40	.257	.304	.358	.393
45	.243	.288	.338	.372
50	.231	.273	.322	.354
60	.211	.250	.295	.325
70	.195	.232	.274	.303
80	.183	.217	.256	.283
90	.173	.205	.242	.267
100	.164	.195	.230	.254

Source: Fisher & Yates; *Statistical Tables for Biological, Agricultural and Medical Research.* Published by Longman Group UK Ltd., 1974.

TABLE D   DISTRIBUTION OF t

	Level of significance for one-tailed test					
	.10	.05	.025	.01	.005	.0005
df	Level of significance for two-tailed test					
	.20	.10	.05	.02	.01	.001
1	3.078	6.314	12.706	31.821	63.657	636.619
2	1.886	2.920	4.303	6.965	9.925	31.598
3	1.638	2.353	3.182	4.541	5.841	12.941
4	1.533	2.132	2.776	3.747	4.604	8.610
5	1.476	2.015	2.571	3.365	4.032	6.859
6	1.440	1.943	2.447	3.143	3.707	5.959
7	1.415	1.895	2.365	2.998	3.499	5.405
8	1.397	1.860	2.306	2.896	3.355	5.041
9	1.383	1.833	2.262	2.821	3.250	4.781
10	1.372	1.812	2.228	2.764	3.169	4.587
11	1.363	1.796	2.201	2.718	3.106	4.437
12	1.356	1.782	2.179	2.681	3.055	4.318
13	1.350	1.771	2.160	2.650	3.012	4.221
14	1.345	1.761	2.145	2.624	2.977	4.140
15	1.341	1.753	2.131	2.602	2.947	4.073
16	1.337	1.746	2.120	2.583	2.921	4.015
17	1.333	1.740	2.110	2.567	2.898	3.965
18	1.330	1.734	2.101	2.552	2.878	3.922
19	1.328	1.729	2.093	2.539	2.861	3.883
20	1.325	1.725	2.086	2.528	2.845	3.850
21	1.323	1.721	2.080	2.518	2.831	3.819
22	1.321	1.717	2.074	2.508	2.819	3.792
23	1.319	1.714	2.069	2.500	2.807	3.767
24	1.318	1.711	2.064	2.492	2.797	3.745
25	1.316	1.708	2.060	2.485	2.787	3.725
26	1.315	1.706	2.056	2.479	2.779	3.707
27	1.314	1.703	2.052	2.473	2.771	3.690
28	1.313	1.701	2.048	2.467	2.763	3.674
29	1.311	1.699	2.045	2.462	2.756	3.659
30	1.310	1.697	2.042	2.457	2.750	3.646
40	1.303	1.684	2.021	2.423	2.704	3.551
60	1.296	1.671	2.000	2.390	2.660	3.460
120	1.289	1.658	1.980	2.358	2.617	3.373
∞	1.282	1.645	1.960	2.326	2.576	3.291

Source: Fisher & Yates; *Statistical Tables for Biological, Agricultural and Medical Research.*
Published by Longman Group UK Ltd., 1974.

TABLE E   DISTRIBUTION OF F

					$p = .05$					
n_2 \ n_1	1	2	3	4	5	6	8	12	24	∞
1	161.4	199.5	215.7	224.6	230.2	234.0	238.9	243.9	249.0	254.3
2	18.51	19.00	19.16	19.25	19.30	19.33	19.37	19.41	19.45	19.50
3	10.13	9.55	9.28	9.12	9.01	8.94	8.84	8.74	8.64	8.53
4	7.71	6.94	6.59	6.39	6.26	6.16	6.04	5.91	5.77	5.63
5	6.61	5.79	5.41	5.19	5.05	4.95	4.82	4.68	4.53	4.36
6	5.99	5.14	4.76	4.53	4.39	4.28	4.15	4.00	3.84	3.67
7	5.59	4.74	4.35	4.12	3.97	3.87	3.73	3.57	3.41	3.23
8	5.32	4.46	4.07	3.84	3.69	3.58	3.44	3.28	3.12	2.93
9	5.12	4.26	3.86	3.63	3.48	3.37	3.23	3.07	2.90	2.71
10	4.96	4.10	3.71	3.48	3.33	3.22	3.07	2.91	2.74	2.54
11	4.84	3.98	3.59	3.36	3.20	3.09	2.95	2.79	2.61	2.40
12	4.75	3.88	3.49	3.26	3.11	3.00	2.85	2.69	2.50	2.30
13	4.67	3.80	3.41	3.18	3.02	2.92	2.77	2.60	2.42	2.21
14	4.60	3.74	3.34	3.11	2.96	2.85	2.70	2.53	2.35	2.13
15	4.54	3.68	3.29	3.06	2.90	2.79	2.64	2.48	2.29	2.07
16	4.49	3.63	3.24	3.01	2.85	2.74	2.59	2.42	2.24	2.01
17	4.45	3.59	3.20	2.96	2.81	2.70	2.55	2.38	2.19	1.96
18	4.41	3.55	3.16	2.93	2.77	2.66	2.51	2.34	2.15	1.92
19	4.38	3.52	3.13	2.90	2.74	2.63	2.48	2.31	2.11	1.88
20	4.35	3.49	3.10	2.87	2.71	2.60	2.45	2.28	2.08	1.84
21	4.32	3.47	3.07	2.84	2.68	2.57	2.42	2.25	2.05	1.81
22	4.30	3.44	3.05	2.82	2.66	2.55	2.40	2.23	2.03	1.78
23	4.28	3.42	3.03	2.80	2.64	2.53	2.38	2.20	2.00	1.76
24	4.26	3.40	3.01	2.78	2.62	2.51	2.36	2.18	1.98	1.73
25	4.24	3.38	2.99	2.76	2.60	2.49	2.34	2.16	1.96	1.71
26	4.22	3.37	2.98	2.74	2.59	2.47	2.32	2.15	1.95	1.69
27	4.21	3.35	2.96	2.73	2.57	2.46	2.30	2.13	1.93	1.67
28	4.20	3.34	2.95	2.71	2.56	2.44	2.29	2.12	1.91	1.65
29	4.18	3.33	2.93	2.70	2.54	2.43	2.28	2.10	1.90	1.64
30	4.17	3.32	2.92	2.69	2.53	2.42	2.27	2.09	1.89	1.62
40	4.08	3.23	2.84	2.61	2.45	2.34	2.18	2.00	1.79	1.51
60	4.00	3.15	2.76	2.52	2.37	2.25	2.10	1.92	1.70	1.39
120	3.92	3.07	2.68	2.45	2.29	2.17	2.02	1.83	1.61	1.25
∞	3.84	2.99	2.60	2.37	2.21	2.09	1.94	1.75	1.52	1.00

TABLE E   DISTRIBUTION OF F (Continued)

	n_1									
n_2	1	2	3	4	5	6	8	12	24	∞
1	405284	500000	540379	562500	576405	585937	598144	610667	623497	636619
2	998.5	999.0	999.2	999.2	999.3	999.3	999.4	999.4	999.5	999.5
3	167.5	148.5	141.1	137.1	134.6	132.8	130.6	128.3	125.9	123.5
4	74.14	61.25	56.18	53.44	51.71	50.53	49.00	47.41	45.77	44.05
5	47.04	36.61	33.20	31.09	29.75	28.84	27.64	26.42	25.14	23.78
6	35.51	27.00	23.70	21.90	20.81	20.03	19.03	17.99	16.89	15.75
7	29.22	21.69	18.77	17.19	16.21	15.52	14.63	13.71	12.73	11.69
8	25.42	18.49	15.83	14.39	13.49	12.86	12.04	11.19	10.30	9.34
9	22.86	16.39	13.90	12.56	11.71	11.13	10.37	9.57	8.72	7.81
10	21.04	14.91	12.55	11.28	10.48	9.92	9.20	8.45	7.64	6.76
11	19.69	13.81	11.56	10.35	9.58	9.05	8.35	7.63	6.85	6.00
12	18.64	12.97	10.80	9.63	8.89	8.38	7.71	7.00	6.25	5.42
13	17.81	12.31	10.21	9.07	8.35	7.86	7.21	6.52	5.78	4.97
14	17.14	11.78	9.73	8.62	7.92	7.43	6.80	6.13	5.41	4.60
15	16.59	11.34	9.34	8.25	7.57	7.09	6.47	5.81	5.10	4.31
16	16.12	10.97	9.00	7.94	7.27	6.81	6.19	5.55	4.85	4.06
17	15.72	10.66	8.73	7.68	7.02	6.56	5.96	5.32	4.63	3.85
18	15.38	10.39	8.49	7.46	6.81	6.35	5.76	5.13	4.45	3.67
19	15.08	10.16	8.28	7.26	6.61	6.18	5.59	4.97	4.29	3.52
20	14.82	9.95	8.10	7.10	6.46	6.02	5.44	4.82	4.15	3.38
21	14.59	9.77	7.94	6.95	6.32	5.88	5.31	4.70	4.03	3.26
22	14.38	9.61	7.80	6.81	6.19	5.76	5.19	4.58	3.92	3.15
23	14.19	9.47	7.67	6.69	6.08	5.65	5.09	4.48	3.82	3.05
24	14.03	9.34	7.55	6.59	5.98	5.55	4.99	4.39	3.74	2.97
25	13.88	9.22	7.45	6.49	5.88	5.46	4.91	4.31	3.66	2.89
26	13.74	9.12	7.36	6.41	5.80	5.38	4.83	4.24	3.59	2.82
27	13.61	9.02	7.27	6.33	5.73	5.31	4.76	4.17	3.52	2.75
28	13.50	8.93	7.19	6.25	5.66	5.24	4.69	4.11	3.46	2.70
29	13.39	8.85	7.12	6.19	5.59	5.18	4.64	4.05	3.41	2.64
30	13.29	8.77	7.05	6.12	5.53	5.12	4.58	4.00	3.36	2.59
40	12.61	8.25	6.60	5.70	5.13	4.73	4.21	3.64	3.01	2.23
60	11.97	7.76	6.17	5.31	4.76	4.37	3.87	3.31	2.69	1.90
120	11.38	7.31	5.79	4.95	4.42	4.04	3.55	3.02	2.40	1.56
∞	10.83	6.91	5.42	4.62	4.10	3.74	3.27	2.74	2.13	1.00

$p = .001$

Source: Fisher & Yates; *Statistical Tables for Biological, Agricultural and Medical Research.* Published by Longman Group UK Ltd., 1974.

TABLE F PERCENTAGE POINTS OF THE STUDENTIZED RANGE (r IN THE TABLE IS THE SAME THING AS k IN THE HSD TEST)

Error df	x	r = number of means or number of steps between ordered means									
		2	3	4	5	6	7	8	9	10	11
5	.05	3.64	4.60	5.22	5.67	6.03	6.33	6.58	6.80	6.99	7.17
	.01	5.70	6.98	7.80	8.42	8.91	9.32	9.67	9.97	10.24	10.48
6	.05	3.46	4.34	4.90	5.30	5.63	5.90	6.12	6.32	6.49	6.65
	.01	5.24	6.33	7.03	7.56	7.97	8.32	8.61	8.87	9.10	9.30
7	.05	3.34	4.16	4.68	5.06	5.36	5.61	5.82	6.00	6.16	6.30
	.01	4.95	5.92	6.54	7.01	7.37	7.68	7.94	8.17	8.37	8.55
8	.05	3.26	4.04	4.53	4.89	5.17	5.40	5.60	5.77	5.92	6.05
	.01	4.75	5.64	6.20	6.62	6.96	7.24	7.47	7.68	7.86	8.03
9	.05	3.20	3.95	4.41	4.76	5.02	5.24	5.43	5.59	5.74	5.87
	.01	4.60	5.43	5.96	6.35	6.66	6.91	7.13	7.33	7.49	7.65
10	.05	3.15	3.88	4.33	4.65	4.91	5.12	5.30	5.46	5.60	5.72
	.01	4.48	5.27	5.77	6.14	6.43	6.67	6.87	7.05	7.21	7.36
11	.05	3.11	3.82	4.26	4.57	4.82	5.03	5.20	5.35	5.49	5.61
	.01	4.39	5.15	5.62	5.97	6.25	6.48	6.67	6.84	6.99	7.13
12	.05	3.08	3.77	4.20	4.51	4.75	4.95	5.12	5.27	5.39	5.51
	.01	4.32	5.05	5.50	5.84	6.10	6.32	6.51	6.67	6.81	6.94
13	.05	3.06	3.73	4.15	4.45	4.69	4.88	5.05	5.19	5.32	5.43
	.01	4.26	4.96	5.40	5.73	5.98	6.19	6.37	6.53	6.67	6.79
14	.05	3.03	3.70	4.11	4.41	4.64	4.83	4.99	5.13	5.25	5.36
	.01	4.21	4.89	5.32	5.63	5.88	6.08	6.26	6.41	6.54	6.66
15	.05	3.01	3.67	4.08	4.37	4.59	4.78	4.94	5.08	5.20	5.31
	.01	4.17	4.84	5.25	5.56	5.80	5.99	6.16	6.31	6.44	6.55
16	.05	3.00	3.65	4.05	4.33	4.56	4.74	4.90	5.03	5.15	5.26
	.01	4.13	4.79	5.19	5.49	5.72	5.92	6.08	6.22	6.35	6.46
17	.05	2.98	3.63	4.02	4.30	4.52	4.70	4.86	4.99	5.11	5.21
	.01	4.10	4.74	5.14	5.43	5.66	5.85	6.01	6.15	6.27	6.38
18	.05	2.97	3.61	4.00	4.28	4.49	4.67	4.82	4.96	5.07	5.17
	.01	4.07	4.70	5.09	5.38	5.60	5.79	5.94	6.08	6.20	6.31
19	.05	2.96	3.59	3.98	4.25	4.47	4.65	4.79	4.92	5.04	5.14
	.01	4.05	4.67	5.05	5.33	5.55	5.73	5.89	6.02	6.14	6.25
20	.05	2.95	3.58	3.96	4.23	4.45	4.62	4.77	4.90	5.01	5.11
	.01	4.02	4.64	5.02	5.29	5.51	5.69	5.84	5.97	6.09	6.19
24	.05	2.92	3.53	3.90	4.17	4.37	4.54	4.68	4.81	4.92	5.01
	.01	3.96	4.55	4.91	5.17	5.37	5.54	'5.69	5.81	5.92	6.02
30	.05	2.89	3.49	3.85	4.10	4.30	4.46	4.60	4.72	4.82	4.92
	.01	3.89	4.45	4.80	5.05	5.24	5.40	5.54	5.65	5.76	5.85
40	.05	2.86	3.44	3.79	4.04	4.23	4.39	4.52	4.63	4.73	4.82
	.01	3.82	4.37	4.70	4.93	5.11	5.26	5.39	5.50	5.60	5.69
60	.05	2.83	3.40	3.74	3.98	4.16	4.31	4.44	4.55	4.65	4.73
	.01	3.76	4.28	4.59	4.82	4.99	5.13	5.25	5.36	5.45	5.53
120	.05	2.80	3.36	3.68	3.92	4.10	4.24	4.36	4.47	4.56	4.64
	.01	3.70	4.20	4.50	4.71	4.87	5.01	5.12	5.21	5.30	5.37
∞	.05	2.77	3.31	3.63	3.86	4.03	4.17	4.29	4.39	4.47	4.55
	.01	3.64	4.12	4.40	4.60	4.76	4.88	4.99	5.08	5.16	5.23

Index